THE
RESET FACTOR
KITCHEN

ResetFactor.com/KitchenBonus

THE
RESET FACTOR
KITCHEN

101 Tasty Recipes to Eat Your Way to Wellness, Burn Belly Fat, and Maximize Your Energy

DR. MINDY PELZ & **BONNIE CARLSON**

Photographs by Elizabeth Vanderliet Patterson
Cover and Book design by Isabella Ferraz

First printing 2016
Printed in the United States of America
20 19 18 17 16   1 2 3 4 5

ISBN: 978-0692807712
Library of Congress Cataloging-in-Publication Data available upon request

Nutritional/Medical Disclaimer

All information in this book is for educational purposes only and is in no way intended to be used as a diagnostic, treatment, or cure for any condition, illness, or disease. We advise you to consult with your primary physician before starting any diet or exercise program. We are not trained nutritionists; nutritional information for our recipes is provided as a courtesy to our readers. We have calculated this information using a variety of online carbohydrate counting tools. We have done our best to be as accurate as possible, but you should independently calculate all nutritional information on your own, particularly for dosing any kind of insulin if you are diabetic. We expressly disclaim any and all liability of any kind with respect to any act or omission wholly or in part in reliance on anything contained in this cookbook.

This book is not intended to make any recommendations related to discontinuing any medication. All decisions relating to medication should be done in consultation with your doctor. The content of this book is intended to be used as an adjunct to consultation with your responsible healthcare professional.

Published by Reset Factor LLC
364 E. Main St., Suite 549
Middletown, DE 19709

CONTENTS

> **"What I needed was _A RESET._ A do-over."**
>
> – DR. MINDY PELZ

PREFACE

When your health goes south, it turns your whole life upside down. I know — I've been there.

If you've read my first book, *The Reset Factor,* you know about my journey back to health. Ultimately it was a multi-therapeutic natural approach to healing that got me my life back. A large part of that approach was a massive change in my diet.

I was a competitive tennis player who endured multiple injuries. Each injury led me to more and more medications, and ultimately to surgery. I came out of surgery in a completely fatigued state. Struggling to make it through the day, I bounced from medical doctor to medical doctor, looking for answers to my chronic fatigue. The solution was always the same: medication. At nineteen years old I had been on more medications than many people would be on in their lifetime. I felt discouraged and hopeless, unsure if I would ever feel good again. And I was not even twenty yet!

I now know that this is a reality many of you are experiencing with your health. Since *The Reset Factor* came out, I have heard from thousands of you, and I can relate to how frustrating it is when people you trust—like your medical doctor — don't have all the answers to your health problems. Where do you look? Whom do you turn to? These were questions I often asked myself after I was diagnosed with chronic fatigue syndrome. You can read my full story in *The Reset Factor,* but briefly, I came to realize that through my lifestyle, I had destroyed my body from the inside. Another medication wasn't going to be my answer—there wasn't a single chemical that was going to bring me back to normal again. And wasting a year of my life hoping a new "trial" medication or series of medications would solve my problem was not my definition of a plan.

What I needed was a reset. A do-over. I needed to repair the damage I had done to myself. I needed a doctor who could see the big picture—what systems were broken inside me. I needed a doctor who cared about finding the root *cause* of my health problems. I needed a doctor who believed in me and who could put me on a path to rebuilding my body back to its original design.

Through persistence and hard work, I ended up finding a team of doctors who did just that.

The first doctor I saw was a holistic MD who immediately taught me how to stop putting toxins into my body. He knew that 80 percent of the immune system lives in the gut and that if I wanted to heal, I would need to repair that system first. He put me on a healing diet and restricted me from eating any foods that would destroy my gut and suppress my immune system. He then prescribed a protocol of supplements to repair the damage that years of medications and poor diet had done to my body.

I next sought out the expertise of a "corrective" chiropractor to help open up the flow of information coming out of my brain and restore the function of my nervous system. This sped up my healing and had me sleeping and thinking better. Then I found an expert in stress management who taught me techniques for managing stress and showed me how to harness the power of my mind to visualize the body healing.

It was a powerful team approach to regaining my health—one that was focused on repairing the damage that my lifestyle, medications, and stress had done, giving my body back its power and giving it a fighting chance to heal itself. Much of what I teach my patients today came from what I was taught years ago by those doctors. Your body is a powerful healing tool; when you give it the right food and reduce its toxic load, you will be amazed at how well it will function and heal.

We have entered a new era of health care. The *New England Journal of Medicine* recently reported that medical errors are the third leading cause of death in America today. That sits right behind cancer and heart disease. What these statistics tell us is that the diseases that are killing people today are preventable. We need to start preventing them! The days of walking into the doctor's office for a prescription to answer all your health problems are over. Just as with my own healing experience

and the healing experiences of others who have gone through the reset process, if you want to get well, you're going to have to be an active participant in your own healing process.

I can't think of a better place to start than with what you're putting in your mouth. Food is so important because you eat so many times a day. If you're doing it wrong, you can destroy your body—quickly.

My hope is that you will find solutions to your and your family's health problems in the chapters and recipes that follow. Know that Bonnie and I have poured our heart and soul into the information that lies in front of you. We hope it transforms your life as much as it has ours.

As the protocols and recipes in this book help you reset your health, please share what you learn with others. Together, we can change the health of our country. Together, we can stop the growing number of diseases that are affecting those we love. Together, we can save lives.

Cheers to better health!

BONNIE'S STORY

In the fall of 2013, I went to Dr. Mindy for a simple adjustment before some major surgery—thinking that my recovery might be more relaxed, comfortable, and expedited if I were better aligned structurally. At the time, I wasn't aware of the scope of Dr. Mindy's practice—that it wasn't just about chiropractic care, but also about total wellness, with a lot of focus on nutrition to help fight and prevent disease. I attended an evening educational session—and went home overwhelmed.

The nutrition protocol Dr. Mindy recommended would require a lot of changes and big shifts—and I didn't have the energy to make them. Sure, I agreed that "sugar is poison"—but empty my cupboards and start over? I'm a working mom who's already stretched pretty thin. I went home, opened up my cupboards, and wanted to cry. I'd been to culinary school, and even I didn't know where to start with quinoa flour and coconut sugar! So I didn't.

Fast-forward six months to when one of my children was diagnosed with type 1 diabetes (T1D). Type 1 diabetes is an autoimmune disease in which your body cannot properly convert food to energy because your pancreas isn't producing insulin anymore. As many as three million Americans have type 1 diabetes, and there isn't a cure (yet). Type 1 diabetes is not caused by lack of exercise or poor eating habits—it just happens; the trigger that causes it is different for everyone. Unmanaged diabetes can lead to serious health complications, so it was important for me to do everything possible to understand this disease and help my child control it for the best health possible.

But doing the work of a pancreas is complicated; in fact, it's a 24/7/365 commitment. A diabetes patient's insulin dosage is based on the patient's carbohydrate intake and current blood sugar levels. Everything affects one's blood sugar: stress, exercise, hormones—you name it, it complicates the disease.

So it's not difficult to understand why I had a renewed interest in food and cooking. Cooking your own recipes at home requires time and math to determine the carbs per serving. Counting carbs is more complicated than it seems; not all apples are made the same. Because I'm a busy working mom, early into the diagnosis, I actually bought more packaged food than I had pre-diagnosis because the carb counts were on the package and it was just easier.

But in this case, easier was not better. Twelve months into living with T1D, we realized that the approach of "take your insulin and eat *anything* you want" was not effective. It was a roller coaster ride all day, every day. I thought to myself, *Sugar is poison! I see it at work and it's poison. I want to throw it all out!* That statement rang in my ears and kept me up at night.

Then I woke up one day and decided I was ready to throw out the processed sugar and wheat flour. But I needed help. I circled back to Dr. Mindy to discuss my daughter's diagnosis. I was a mother on a mission, and I told her that I was ready to empty my cupboards and start anew, with whole, more nutritious, and less processed ingredients. I was ready to jump—but I needed a parachute. She said she'd help!

The next step was to figure out what to do with all these amazing ingredients. Even with my culinary background, I had no idea how to implement Dr. Mindy's plan and get dinner on the table for my family with these new ingredients. I mentioned to her that there ought to be a manual or a cookbook to help people execute the Reset Factor plan. And that was the moment the notion of this cookbook was born.

This cookbook is as much a gift to myself as it is a gift to you. I have been on a mission to adapt, create, and curate recipes that are nutritious, that serve my family's health—AND that satisfy our taste buds. My journey on the Reset Factor program has been successful in resetting my taste buds; my mind can now easily make a choice that serves my health (not my taste buds) because I feel so much better when I eat this way. Most importantly, eating this way has helped my family grab the steering wheel of the T1D roller coaster, giving us more control over my child's blood sugar levels while contributing to the overall good health of our family. T1D had turned food, one of life's true pleasures, into a nightmare for my family. Because I had a sweet tooth, I knew that to be successful, I needed to change myself first and trust that eventually my family would come on this journey with me. This book reignited my passion for good food—and now *super foods*.

My wish for this cookbook is that it will help nourish you along your journey to find better health. Good health should be enjoyable and delicious! If you're the parent or caregiver of a T1D child, I encourage you to come on this journey with me; you and your family will benefit from resetting your palate and training your taste buds to crave health—not sugar. Take our hands—we'll help you along the way. Jump! This book can be your parachute.

Across the United States, up to thirty thousand kids are diagnosed with this disease annually. For those of you who are not familiar with type 1 diabetes, please take a few moments to identify the symptoms (http://jdrf.org/wp-content/uploads/2012/12/WarningSigns.pdf) because it might help you save a life. It was my mother who was able to connect the dots that led to my child's diagnosis. She is our real life superhero!

But even if diabetes is not part of your life, I welcome you to enjoy the tasty recipes in this book as a means of gaining and maintaining great health. Everyone deserves to eat in a way that nourishes their body and heart.

Bon appetit!

WELCOME TO
THE RESET FACTOR KITCHEN

The health of our communities is at a critical point. People are getting sicker. Diseases such as cancer, heart disease, diabetes, obesity, autoimmune conditions, thyroiditis, autism, dementia, and Alzheimer's are ALL on the rise.

Twenty years ago, when I first started my practice, we would give people a treatment plan and their body would heal. It didn't matter what it was—back pain, headaches, weight gain, insomnia, depression, or chronic fatigue. With the right treatment plan, the person would always get well, and quickly.

Then, about five years ago, I started to notice that my patients were not healing as fast as they used to. I would use the same protocols I always had, but their bodies were unresponsive. I also noticed that people were coming to me with a laundry list of complaints. A patient who had a headache also would complain of digestive symptoms. Someone with extreme low-back pain also had extreme fatigue and was gaining weight for no particular reason. Rarely would someone have just one symptom—multiple breakdowns were occurring.

The number of medications people were on was growing. In fact, I started noticing a trend: many of my patients were on three to five medications. Also, kids were coming to me with a growing list of medications and special health challenges—health challenges we rarely saw in kids decades ago—such as food allergies, chronic asthma, ADD, anxiety, type 1 diabetes, and cancer.

What had changed? Why were people so sick? And more importantly, what could I do to help these people?

I was reminded that science refers to the gut as our second brain, so I began to take a closer look there for the answers to my questions. Eighty percent of our immune system is controlled by the gut. Neurotransmitters that keep our brains working well are made there. B vitamins that give us energy are manufactured in the gut. The microbiome of the gut can impact weight gain and depression. And recently, we've learned that gut bacteria play a part in turning on genes that predispose us to obesity, autoimmune conditions, and cancer. Was it possible that the symptoms I was witnessing in my patients were due to a destruction of the gut?

I started to experiment with different protocols. The first step I took was to start pulling certain foods from my patients' diet, foods I knew were possible destroyers of the gut. Books like *Wheat Belly* and *Grain Brain* were linking wheat consumption with chronic inflammatory problems, so I started by having patients take wheat out of their diet for two weeks to see what would happen. For many of my patients, the results were instantaneous—years of chronic pain were gone after two weeks off wheat. People also dropped weight fast and noticed improvement in their mental clarity. Was it possible that all these mysterious symptoms were coming from wheat? And what was in wheat that was destroying people's guts and causing so many health problems?

As I learned more, I became aware of *glyphosate*, a chemical that is sprayed on wheat. Glyphosate is the active ingredient found in the herbicide Roundup*, and yes, America allows this to be sprayed on many of our foods, especially wheat. In our country, glyphosate is creating a major health epidemic called leaky gut syndrome (LGS). It is estimated that over 90 percent of people are affected by leaky gut, caused by glyphosate.

Leaky gut syndrome is a condition that happens when a person is exposed to genetically modified foods, wheat, and dairy. These foods create micro-holes in the gut that allow undigested food and toxins to leak into the bloodstream. Once these foreign materials are in the bloodstream, the brain recognizes them as foreign invaders and creates an inflammatory response to help rid the body of these harmful particles. Every time one of these foods is eaten, the inflammatory process is initiated. It's as if someone turned on an inflammation switch, causing bloating, constipation, fatigue, lack of mental clarity, and chronic pain.

So I asked myself whether most of my patients were suffering from a leaky gut, and if so, what strategies could I put in place to help them fix this condition? One of the major challenges we have in health care right now is that there is not enough research on how conditions involving the gut contribute to poor health. Up until now, most doctors have only looked to the gut if a patient had a digestive complaint. Despite the gut's global connection—to every part of the body—most doctors have never linked it to other problems the body may be experiencing. But luckily, more and more medical and natural doctors are starting to speak out about the success they're having with patients when they repair the gut.

So I made it my mission to address the gut with all my patients. Although patients thought I was crazy when I told them to take wheat out of their diet to help their back pain or depression, I began to prescribe wheat-free protocols to many of my more difficult cases, with great success. But the puzzle wasn't completely solved. I still had a group of patients who were not getting well, even when they removed wheat from their diet.

Then research began emerging about how fat deprived we are as a nation. Fat deprived? How could that be? Isn't fat bad for us? This intrigued me. I started researching more, and sure enough, I learned that we need "good" fat for a variety of reasons. There are two ways the human body produces energy: by burning sugar and by burning fat. Every disease known to man has been created in a sugar-burning body. You can switch how your body burns energy by pulling sugar out of your diet and adding in fat—good fat. So back to my difficult cases I went. What would happen if I had patients pull wheat and sugar out of their diet and add in good fat? What kind of changes would I see then?

This was a major turning point for me—and many of my patients. Patients who had been struggling with their weight started releasing pounds for the first time. My chronic fatigue patients regained their energy and mental clarity. And the hunger that many people were experiencing on a wheat-free diet went away completely.

The results were so profound that I started doing thirty-day challenges with all my patients. For thirty days I had patients pull all grains, all bad fats, and all sugar out of their diet. It was truly amazing to watch my patients' health return. It was not uncommon to see a person lose ten to twenty pounds in thirty days. The only challenge we had was that once the 30-day challenge was over, some of my patients would slowly gain weight back and see all their health problems return within a matter of months. And this happened even if they were still following some of the protocols from the thirty-day program.

It occurred to me that you can remove the source of irritation from the gut, but you still need to repair the damage from years of poor diet.

WHAT NEEDED REPAIR?

Enter the microbiome. Many doctors are starting to wake up to the fact that the microbiome of our gut—the home of both good and bad bacteria—plays a pivotal role in our health. Is it possible that eating improperly for years destroys all the good bacteria in our gut? The answer is yes! And we need that good bacteria to be permanently well.

You see, we have tens of thousands of bacteria living in our gut. When we eat the wrong foods for years, we damage the good bacteria and feed the bad. Once we remove harmful foods, the gut gets a break but we're still left with the damage that was created from the years prior.

This is how the Reset Factor's 15-day Detox was born. I wondered what would happen if I started with a massive repair of the gut and liver before implementing the thirty-day challenge. Would a person get a more lasting result? Again, the answer was a resounding yes!

In fact, this was where the magic really happened for many patients. So I called my program the 45-Day Reset and wrote about it in *The Reset Factor*. With the 45-Day Reset, I could take a patient who was in a severely worsening health crisis and turn his or her health around in a matter of weeks, sometimes even days. It was the perfect combination of the right foods with the right supplements.

To date, we have put thousands of people through the 45-Day Reset and the results are always the same: weight loss, improved mental clarity, reduced pain, better sleep, reduced depression, energy through the roof, and happiness at an all-time high. The 45-Day Reset is a miracle gift to an ailing body. Because it works by addressing the major breakdowns of the gut, helps an overstressed liver, and unblocks hormone receptor sites on the cell membrane, the body goes into a massive repair phase.

WHAT YOU'LL FIND IN THIS BOOK

Bonnie has a gift for making healthy food taste incredible. She has a degree from the California Culinary Academy in San Francisco and a passion for cooking. Perhaps the most important thing to know about Bonnie—which you learned from her story in the preface—is that her daughter has type 1 diabetes. When *The Reset Factor* came out, she decided to try the 45-Day Reset on herself. As she started to understand and apply the principles I taught in the book, a lightbulb turned on in her head: *What would happen if I applied these same principles to my daughter? Could I avoid the mood changes, reduce her insulin intake, and give her the tools to manage this disease in a healthier way?*

And that is exactly what happened. The more good fats she added in, the more chemicals she pulled out. The more probiotic-rich foods she served her child, the easier it became to manage her daughter's diabetes. What I have learned from watching Bonnie is that having a child with type 1 diabetes is an incredibly exhausting experience—an experience no one wants to go through. But Bonnie discovered in cooking with the principles of the Reset Factor program that she could begin to gain some control over this devastating disease.

Bonnie and I began working closely together with various recipes. The result was a greater understanding of just what the 45-Day Reset does to your blood sugar. Bonnie's daughter tested almost every recipe in this book, enabling us to see which ingredients spiked her blood sugar levels and which ingredients didn't. This is crucial information for everyone—not just a diabetic. If you want to lose weight, reduce inflammation, improve your energy, have more mental clarity, and get your health back, you need to learn how to eat like a diabetic does. This book will give you a roadmap to doing that.

We also found that "resetters" following the 45-day plan needed more of an understanding of ingredients, knowledge of how to read labels, protocols to speed up the healing of specific health conditions, information on how to eat out while on the 45-Day Reset, shopping guides, menu ideas, and a better understanding of which new ingredients they should be cooking with. That's how this book was born. Consider it a follow-up to *The Reset Factor*. I strongly feel that when you put these two books together, you can start to become your own health advocate. You will have enough of an understanding of your own health that you can get control of it back. You will have the tools to live in the body that you deserve to live in. You will get your life back.

If you haven't yet read *The Reset Factor* but are eager to learn the basics, Part 1 of this book reviews the 45-Day Reset (Chapter 1), the 15-Day Detox (Chapter 2), and the 30-Day Habit Reset (Chapter 3). We will also teach you important skills, such as how to navigate a nutrition label (Chapter 4), ingredients that will destroy your health (Chapter 5), and ingredients that will help you build your health (Chapter 6). I will show you how to accelerate your results (Chapter 7) and how to choose and use supplements to support and maintain your health (Chapter 8). And I'll teach you how to eat out successfully, without blowing all your efforts at taking care of your health through nutrition (Chapter 9)! You'll notice that I repeat a number of principles throughout Part 1. This is because I want to present information I feel is critical to your health in different contexts so that you'll have the big picture no matter where you start.

Part 2 contains an all-important shopping guide (Chapter 10), followed by the best recipes you'll ever find for tasty, healthful meals and snacks for your family (Chapters 11 through 21). And at the end of the book, in Chapter 22, you'll find a detailed 45-Day Menu Plan.

You will hear me say over and over that your body is a miracle. Treat it like one and you will be blown away by how amazing you can feel regardless of your age, your diagnosis, your genetics, or your circumstances. If you take the Reset Factor principles and apply them diligently, you WILL reset your health.

We are cheering you on! We are excited to share with you a journey that has worked not only for our families, but for thousands of people who have gone through the 45-Day Reset. You can find us on social media. Reach out if you need any help.

RESETTING YOUR HEALTH

CHAPTER 1

WHAT IS THE 45-DAY RESET?

The 45-Day Reset is an easy-to-follow nutrition plan that is the quickest path to health I have seen in my twenty years of practice. It starts with a 15-Day Detox and is followed by a 30-Day Habit Reset (described in detail in the next two chapters).

The 45-Day Reset incorporates four healing principles: balancing your blood sugar, getting nutrients to your liver, repairing your gut, and turning off your inflammation switch. Let's look at each of these principles in detail to see why health breaks down and what we can do about it.

HEALING PRINCIPLE #1: BALANCING YOUR BLOOD SUGAR

One of the biggest reasons people are gaining weight today is that their blood sugar is out of balance. When you eat too much sugar, you cause your pancreas to work overtime. The more insulin the pancreas pushes into the bloodstream, the more resistant your cells become to the insulin. I equate this to the results you get from yelling at your kids. Do you become more effective or less effective when you tell your kids to change a behavior? In the beginning, you might get them to respond to requests. But when you yell at them over and over again, they stop hearing you. You have to find new ways to get your point across to them. Once you discover a new way of communicating your message to them, your effectiveness goes up.

The same thing happens with your cells. The more food you eat that is filled with sugar, the more insulin that gets secreted. At first, this insulin is effective. But as you eat more sugar and secrete more insulin, your cells stop "hearing" the insulin. This causes extra insulin to be floating around in your bloodstream. Extra insulin turns into fat. If you want to balance this blood sugar out and lose weight, you need to get your cells hearing insulin again.

This is one of the main reasons even the most famous weight-loss programs don't offer a lasting solution. They may temporarily reduce your calorie intake, but if you continue to eat low-calorie sugar-filled foods, you will never balance your blood sugar. With cells that are resistant to insulin, your body will always be prone to accumulating weight.

If you're like most people, a typical day looks something like this: You start the morning with very low blood sugar and energy. You reach for oatmeal, cereal, or—worse yet—a donut and coffee with creamer. This quickly spikes your blood sugar, giving you energy. Around ten o'clock, your blood sugar starts coming down. This is when you reach for another cup of coffee or a Snickers bar, which immediately brings your blood sugar back up. A few hours later your blood sugar starts crashing again. If you eat a high-carbohydrate lunch, the same up-and-down cycle happens again, and around 3:00 p.m., you start feeling sleepy. By this point in the day, your blood sugar has gone up and down multiple times, putting a significant load on your pancreas to keep up with your body's sugar demands. The harder the pancreas works, the less effective it becomes. The more your blood sugar spikes up and drops down in a day, the more unresponsive your cells become to insulin.

It's at this point that your health begins to break down. When your cells are not able to access insulin, two conditions will arise in your body: weight gain and fatigue. Since your body is low in energy, your adrenals will start to kick into high gear to keep your energy up. By the time you reach your dinner plate, your blood sugar will be so off that you'll crave starchy foods to bring back some balance to your system. Your body is brilliantly designed: When your blood sugar drops too low or too quickly, a signal gets sent to your brain to eat sugar and starches.

Most people go to bed after a starchy dinner followed by a sugary dessert. This is the worst nutrition mistake you can make. A high-sugar meal means high levels of insulin surging through your body while you sleep. This insulin will turn to fat. It will also make it really hard to get out of bed in the morning. The more exhausted you are in the morning, the more you will crave stimulants and sugary food, starting the cycle all over again.

Balancing this blood sugar cycle is crucial to feeling well again. In the 15-Day Detox, that is exactly what will happen. You will pull out of your diet anything that will spike your blood sugar. This includes grains, sugar, and high-sugar fruits. It may seem impossible at first, but I promise you will quickly notice your energy going through the roof and your cravings and hunger disappearing.

HEALING PRINCIPLE #2: GETTING NUTRIENTS TO THE LIVER

As I mentioned in *The Reset Factor*, the liver is the hardest-working organ—especially in today's world, where we're exposed to an abundance of toxins. Luckily, our body secretes a natural detoxifier called *glutathione*. Produced by the liver, glutathione acts like sticky fly paper to attach to toxins for removal from your body. This key nutrient is depleted in many people because the toxic load most bodies are carrying forces the liver to work so hard.

Supporting the liver with key nutrients like milk thistle, alpha lipoic acid, and N-acetylcysteine will allow your liver to produce more glutathione. Ultimately, this will make your body a more efficient detoxifier. In the 45-Day Reset, you'll add these key nutrients into your diet to give some much needed support to your liver.

WHAT DESTROYS YOUR GLUTATHIONE LEVELS?

The following stressors destroy glutathione levels:

- Genetically modified foods
- Artificial sweeteners
- Infections
- Chronic stress
- Injuries
- Environmental toxins
- Overuse of antibiotics

WHAT FOODS INCREASE GLUTATHIONE PRODUCTION?

Several categories of foods increase the production of glutathione. These include the following:

Cruciferous Foods
- Garlic
- Onions
- Broccoli
- Cauliflower
- Arugula
- Bok choy
- Brussels sprouts
- Cabbage
- Collard greens
- Kale
- Mustard greens
- Radishes
- Turnips
- Watercress

Folate-Rich Foods
- Avocados
- Garbanzo beans
- Pinto beans
- Lentils
- Spinach
- Asparagus
- Beets
- Black-eyed peas

Dairy

- Eggs
- Raw milk
- Whey protein from grass-fed sources

Selenium-Rich Foods
- Grass-fed beef and organ meats
- Brazil nuts
- Yellowfin tuna
- Halibut
- Sardines
- Turkey
- Chicken

Vitamin C-Rich Foods
- Oranges
- Red peppers
- Strawberries
- Grapefruit
- Guavas
- Kiwis
- Green peppers

Vitamin E-Rich Foods
- Almonds
- Spinach
- Sweet potatoes
- Avocados
- Wheat germ
- Sunflower seeds
- Butternut squash
- Trout

When you eat these foods on a regular basis, they will give your body a nice boost of glutathione. Remember, you always want your fruits and vegetables to be organic and raw if possible. When you cook your vegetables, you destroy 30 to 60 percent of the glutathione that would otherwise be of benefit to your body.

Because the 45-Day Reset requires you to remove many toxins from your daily routine, you'll be giving your liver a much needed break. You also will be building up your glutathione reserves. It's not uncommon for patients to tell me that they're not as vulnerable to colds and flus after they've completed the 45-Day Reset. This is because the immune system is greatly enhanced by the removal of toxins and the addition of extra glutathione.

HEALING PRINCIPLE #3: REPAIRING YOUR GUT

You can dramatically change your health by repairing your gut. Not only does the bacteria in your gut control 80 percent of your immune system, but it also produces key nutrients like B vitamins, neurotransmitters, and vitamins C and E.

Following are three main conditions occurring in the gut that can throw off your health:

1. Small Intestinal Bacterial Overgrowth (SIBO)

SIBO is a condition in the microbiome of your gut in which you have more bad bacteria than good bacteria. The classic signs of SIBO include:

- Brain fog
- Chronic fatigue
- Bloated belly
- Constipation
- Trouble losing weight
- Acne
- Depression, anxiety, and mood disorders

Often, people with SIBO start off with one or two of these symptoms, and if the bad bacteria is not dealt with, more symptoms appear.

What causes SIBO?

Causes of SIBO include the following:

- Antibiotic use
- Birth by C-section
- Genetically modified foods
- High-sugar foods
- Pasteurized dairy

What's the best way to get rid of SIBO?

The best way to get rid of SIBO is to add good bacteria to your diet. Foods that are high in good bacteria include the following:

- Sauerkraut
- Sauerkraut juice (Gut Shot by Farmhouse Cultures)
- Kimchi
- Fermented vegetables
- Raw kefir
- Kombucha
- Bone broth (one of those rare foods that doesn't add good bacteria but does an excellent job of killing bad bacteria)

2. Candida

Candida is a condition of too much yeast in the gut. Yeast is a fungus that will take over your small and large intestine and make it incredibly difficult for any good bacteria to live. It's like a wild weed in your garden that is killing your beautiful, healthy plants. Of all the conditions I see in the gut, this is the most devastating and the hardest to treat. But it is also the most rewarding to finally cure in the body.

What are the signs of candida?

Classic signs of candida include the following:

- Chronic fatigue
- Memory loss
- Trouble focusing
- Skin rashes
- Chronic pain
- Yeast infections
- Uncontrollable sugar and bread cravings
- Trouble losing weight
- Bad breath

- Chronic allergies
- Loss of sex drive
- Hormonal imbalances

What causes candida?

Causes of candida include the following:

- Eating foods or drinking beverages that are high in yeast, such as bread, beer, and wine
- Consuming sugar daily
- Eating high-sugar fruits such as mangoes, papayas, and pineapple
- Taking antibiotics
- Taking birth control pills

What's the best way to get rid of candida?

One of the best ways to kill candida is to starve it. The 45-Day Reset does this well. For forty-five days you pull everything out of your diet that would feed the candida fungus living in your gut. There are also foods you can eat and herbs you can add to kill candida. The following are my top recommendations for killing this fungus:

Remove these foods from your diet:

- Gluten and processed grains
- Sugar (including coconut sugar, honey, and turbinado)
- All sources of alcohol
- All caffeine
- All cold drinks with ice
- All fruit juice
- All dried fruits and high-sugar fruits, such as mangos, papayas, and pineapple
- If candida is severe, pull out all fruits

Add these foods to your diet:

- Bitter foods, such as chicory, chard, endive, artichokes, broccoli, thistles, cabbage, Brussels sprouts, asparagus, rocket lettuce, chayote, dandelion, tomatoes, cucumbers, pumpkins, and lemons
- Warm fall vegetables (in small amounts to support the spleen in clearing out candida), such as sweet potatoes, yams, peas, mung beans, lentils, kidney beans, adzuki beans, carrots, beets, corn, butternut squash, spaghetti squash, acorn squash, zucchini, yellow squash, rutabaga, and pumpkin. These are best consumed earlier in the day.

- Fermented vegetables, such as sauerkraut and kimchi
- Organic meats, like grass-fed beef, lamb, venison, chicken, duck, turkey, wild game, chicken, and liver
- Bone broth
- Warm soups made in a slow cooker with non-starchy vegetables, such as broccoli, kale, cabbage, and chard
- Ground flaxseeds, chia seeds, and pumpkin seeds
- Coconut oil for cooking and olive oil for salad dressings (both have antifungal and antimicrobial qualities that will kill candida)
- Herbal teas like pau d'arco, chai (without sugar added), and licorice

3. Leaky Gut Syndrome (LGS)

It's estimated that leaky gut syndrome affects over 90 percent of the population. LGS is a condition in which micro holes form in the gut, allowing undigested food and toxins to enter into the bloodstream. Once these foreign particles are in your blood, your brain registers them as harmful and orchestrates an inflammatory response. If these micro holes remain there, the inflammatory response will never stop—leading to a host of health problems.

What conditions are caused by LGS?

Conditions caused by LGS include the following:

- Chronic pain
- Pain in multiple joints
- Chronic fatigue syndrome
- Stomach pain
- Autoimmune conditions, including Hashimoto's
- Hormone imbalance
- Poorly functioning thyroid
- Trouble losing weight
- Alzheimer's
- Crohn's disease
- Fibromyalgia
- Autism
- Irritable bowel syndrome (IBS)
- Lupus
- Migraine headaches
- Multiple sclerosis
- Parkinson's

- Polycystic ovary syndrome (PCOS)
- Restless leg syndrome
- Rheumatoid arthritis
- Skin conditions, such as eczema, psoriasis, rosacea, dermatitis, and acne
- Type 1 diabetes
- Type 2 diabetes
- Ulcerative colitis
- Various allergies and food sensitivities

What causes LGS?

The main causes of LGS include the following:

- Genetically modified foods
- Heavy metals
- Chronic stress
- Overuse of medications, including NSAIDs and pain killers
- Antibiotic use
- Grains, including wheat
- Pasteurized dairy
- Pesticides found in nonorganic food
- Food additives and preservatives

Foods to avoid for LGS

To heal (or prevent) LGS, avoid the following foods:

- All grains (even organic grains), especially wheat
- All sugars
- All genetically modified foods
- All dairy

Foods to add to your diet for LGS

The foods listed below combat LGS:

- Consuming bone broth is an excellent way to heal and seal those holes. It also adds magnesium and calcium for healing.
- Fermented foods such as sauerkraut and kimchi have trillions of good bacteria that help kill the bad bacteria that contribute to LGS.
- Coconut products are high in lauric acid, which kills bad bacteria.
- Kefir—raw fermented dairy kefir is best. Or make your own yogurt from raw milk with a probiotic starter.

- Cooked vegetables. Although nutrients get lost in the cooking process, it's easier on the gut to eat cooked vegetables when trying to heal LGS.
- Organic meats, such as wild-caught fish and grass-fed beef. Both these meats are high in Omega-3 fatty acids, which reduces the inflammation caused by LGS.

HEALING PRINCIPLE #4: TURN OFF YOUR INFLAMMATION SWITCH

Most doctors would agree that inflammation is the cause of most diseases. If you could figure out how to turn off your inflammation switch, your metabolism would speed up, your pain would go away, your immune system would improve, your energy would skyrocket, and your focus would be laser sharp. Sound too good to be true? It's not. Just ask anyone who has followed the 45-Day Reset.

Whenever patients come to me with chronic pain, I ask myself what systems in their body have broken down to turn their inflammation switch on. Usually, it's one of four systems: the brain and nervous system, the gut, the liver, or the hormones. If I can evaluate those systems and figure out the best path to repair them, then I can turn the switch off and my patients will feel better.

How would you know whether your inflammation switch had been turned on?

The following symptoms indicate that your inflammation switch is on:

Chronic pain. If you're taking NSAIDs or painkillers to manage pain, your switch is definitely turned on. Unfortunately, the vicious cycle that begins with taking pain medications contributes to the conditions that caused your switch to get turned on in the first place. This is why I will continue to say that pain relief from taking medication is a short-term gain traded for long-term consequences.

Chronic fatigue. If you're often exhausted, your body is most likely worn down from your inflammation switch being turned on for too long. The 45-Day Reset does an amazing job of turning your inflammation switch off, which is why most people notice a resurgence of their energy after forty-five days.

Chronic disease. If you have been diagnosed with an autoimmune disease, cancer, heart disease, or diabetes, your inflammation switch has most likely been turned on for years. All these diseases have been linked to chronic inflammation. In order for your body to heal from these conditions, you are going to have to turn that switch off.

Chronic stress. If you feel that your stress keeps piling up and is causing you to be depressed or anxious, or if stress is turning you into an insomniac, then no doubt your switch is on. The brain can swell from the inflammation switch being on for too long. This will lead to mood disorders, insomnia, negative thoughts, and trouble sleeping.

Chronic weight issues. I have great news for you: Weight loss is not an issue of willpower. It is a by-product of your inflammation switch being turned on. A bloated belly, swollen ankles and knees, and a sluggish thyroid all can be caused by your inflammation switch being on.

Chronic digestive problems. Many digestive issues either cause your switch to turn on or are exacerbated by your switch being on. Once you begin to experience a digestive condition, such as constipation, cramping, or diarrhea, your body will keep causing inflammation in the corresponding areas to repair it. Getting your switch to turn off becomes an essential part of healing your digestive issues.

What causes your switch to turn on?

Many things turn on your inflammation switch, but the main culprits include the following:

- Anything white: white flour, sugar, rice, and potatoes
- Bad oils, such as sunflower, safflower, vegetable, and canola
- Artificial ingredients, such as artificial flavors, preservatives, high-fructose corn syrup, and partially hydrogenated oils
- Toxins: everything from toxins in your beauty products, to amalgam fillings in your teeth, to lead in the water, to glyphosate sprayed on your GMO food

What can you do to turn your inflammation switch off?

The 45-Day Reset is a great starting point. But specifically, you want to pull out all of the above offending foods and add in foods such as the following:

- Good oils: avocado, coconut, sesame, and grapeseed
- Good fats: avocados, raw nuts, and raw organic grass-fed butter
- Omega-3 foods: wild salmon, grass-fed beef, and grass-fed whey protein powder

I know this is a lot to take in.

If this is the first time you're hearing this information, it can be overwhelming. I recommend you read *The Reset Factor*, as I explain in detail in that book why your body got out of balance in the first place. It also will give you a great idea of how your body works and why the 45-Day Reset will put your health back on track.

It took me years of studying and trial and error to get the 45-Day Reset to a place where it was in line with the above four principles. Other than fasting (which I recommend to many of my chronically ill patients), it is the quickest way to bring the body back to health.

CHAPTER 2

THE 15-DAY DETOX

The 45-Day Reset I refer to throughout this book contains two parts: a 15-Day Detox, followed by a 30-Day Habit Reset. This book is meant to be a roadmap and recipe book for the 45-Day Reset; if you need more information about why I recommend the following protocol and what it does for your body, I highly recommend you go back and reference *The Reset Factor*.

This chapter gives you the basic nuts and bolts of the first part, the 15-Day Detox.

GENERAL PRINCIPLES OF THE 15-DAY DETOX

- Upon rising in the morning, you'll have a glass of Morning Detox water (see Chapter 11: Reset Factor Kitchen Pantry).
- Replace two of your meals with detox smoothies. Make your first smoothie of the day for breakfast. Your second smoothie of the day can be for either lunch or dinner—it's your choice.
- Enjoy one meal per day with a clean protein, together with steamed vegetables or a fresh green salad.
- Avoid all grains, including pasta, bread, cereal, rice, and corn.
- Avoid all alcohol of any kind.
- Avoid all coffee and caffeine.
- Avoid all processed foods.
- Only use real organic butter, raw nut butter, olive oil, avocado oil, and coconut oil. Avoid all other oils and butters.
- Avoid dairy of any kind, including cheese, milk, yogurt, and sour cream.
- Enjoy five cups of raw vegetables a day; snacking on them throughout the day is encouraged.
- Limit fruit to berries and green apples.
- Anytime you're feeling hungry during the day, you can eat all the green apples, berries, and vegetables you want.
- Take all supplements as directed on the protocol list for maximum results (see "Supplements" section below).

WHAT YOU'LL NEED

Here's what you'll need to prepare for your 15-Day Detox program:

A blender. My favorite is the Vitamix. You can get one easily at Costco, but any blender will do.

Plenty of fresh organic fruits and organic vegetables. My favorites ones to munch on during the day are carrots, celery, red bell peppers, and green apples. My favorite ones to put into a smoothie are wild blueberries, cherries, and spinach. Keep in mind that you can always use frozen organic fruits if fresh ones are not available.

A high-quality protein powder. See the supplement list below for my recommendations.

Organic lemons for your daily lemon water.

Clean proteins, like organic poultry, grass-fed beef, eggs from pasture-raised hens, hormone- and nitrite-free deli meats, and wild fish.

Healthy and satisfying fats, like avocados, coconut oil, raw cashews, and almond butters.

Approved snacks, such as raw nuts, red cabbage, hummus, kale chips, organic hard-boiled eggs, green apples with nut butter, or avocados with sauerkraut.

Plenty of organic salad mixes and organic greens, such as parsley, kale, romaine lettuce, and spinach.

Supplements — those found on the list below.

A GREAT attitude! You should be excited! You are about to experience what it's like to live in a body that is full of energy and that functions at a higher level than many people have ever experienced before.

Your Detox Supplements

- Probiotic (50 billion CFU)
- Vitamin D3 (5,000 IU)
- Turmeric (225 mg)
- N-Acetyl-L-Cysteine (100 mg)
- L-Glutamine (powder form) (5 g)
- Glutathione (250 mg)
- Milk thistle (425 mg)
- Alpha lipoic acid (ALA) (50mg)
- High-quality thyroid support that includes iodine (150 mg)
- Plant-based or grass-fed whey protein powder (1 scoop)
- Greens superfood supplement with chlorophyll (1 scoop)
- Omega-3 fish oils (5 g)

Your Meal Replacement Smoothie

Your two smoothies a day will help to reset your metabolism and give your gut and liver a break. In your smoothies, you want to use low-glycemic fruits such as berries to minimize sugar intake during the 15-Day Detox. Coconut milk or almond milk are both great liquid sources for the smoothies. Adding in healthy fats—such as a tablespoon of coconut oil, half an avocado, or a tablespoon of raw almond or cashew butter—is an excellent way to make sure your smoothie is satisfying. Then add in your protein powder, greens, and supplements.

Here's an example of a great detox smoothie:

- 1 scoop protein powder
- 1 scoop green superfood supplement
- 1 scoop L-Glutamine
- 1 cup frozen organic berries
- 1 cup organic kale or spinach
- 1 tablespoon coconut oil
- 1 cup coconut milk or almond milk (organic, non-flavored, and no added sugar)
- 1/2 avocado
- 1 cup water

Avoid using the following in your smoothies:

– Fruit juice

– Yogurt

– Honey

– Coconut sugar

– Ice cream or frozen yogurt

– High-glycemic fruits like mango, papaya, pineapple, or banana

Approved Meal Ingredients

You'll enjoy one meal a day while on the 15-Day Detox. We have included lots of delicious, easy-to-prepare, flavor-packed recipes in this book, so experiment. You will be surprised how many new flavors Bonnie has created that your taste buds will love. Here's an overview of what you can eat:

Clean proteins, like organic poultry, grass-fed beef, pasture-raised eggs, hormone- and nitrite-free deli meats, and wild fish.

Plenty of fresh organic fruits and organic vegetables. My favorite ones to munch on during the day are carrots, celery, red bell peppers, and green apples. My favorite ones to put into a smoothie are wild blueberries, blackberries, and spinach.

Healthy and satisfying fats, like avocados, coconut oil, raw cashews, and almond butters.

Plenty of organic salad mixes and organic greens, such as parsley, kale, romaine lettuce, and spinach.

Probiotic-rich foods and drinks, such as kimchi, sauerkraut, tempeh, pickles, pickled fruits and vegetables, and raw kefir (only allowed raw with no added sugar).

Bone broth, which helps to heal and seal the gut (see Chapter 11: Reset Factor Kitchen Pantry)

Approved Drinks

- At least six to eight glasses of water every day
- Fresh-squeezed juice made with veggies and fruits from the "approved" list above
- Kombucha tea
- Mineral water or club soda (without sugar)
- Herbal organic tea (Green tea is a great detoxifier and the only caffeinated drink approved.)
- Bone broth

YOUR DAILY ROUTINE

Upon waking in the morning
- Drink 1 glass of lemon water at room temperature.
- Take 1 probiotic (50 billion CFU).
- Take glutathione (250 mg).
- Take milk thistle (425 mg).

Breakfast
Drink one delicious and nutritious smoothie, which includes 1 scoop protein powder, 1 scoop greens, and 1 scoop L-glutamine (5 g).

After morning smoothie
- Take Acetyl-L-Cysteine 100 mg (2 tablets).
- Take turmeric 225 mg (2 tablets).
- Take vitamin D3 (5,000 IU).
- Take Omega-3 fish oils (3 g).

Lunch
Drink one delicious and nutritious smoothie, which includes 1 scoop protein powder, 1 scoop greens, and 1 scoop L-glutamine (5 g).

Dinner
Eat one delicious and nutritious meal with clean protein, organic vegetables, or a fresh salad.

Snacks
Raw nuts, red cabbage, hummus, kale chips, organic hard-boiled eggs, green apples, and almond butter

You can eat snacks anytime throughout the day.

Before bed:
Take 1 probiotic (50 billion CFU), preferably two hours after dinner.

A WORD ABOUT SUPPLEMENTS

A common question we got after *The Reset Factor* came out was, which supplements do I use? I cannot emphasize enough the importance of using quality, food-based supplements. Many supplements are synthetic and filled with harmful chemicals. Many people get fooled by buying cheaper supplements. I think this is a waste of money. If you buy a high-quality supplement, it will be more effective and you won't have to take it for as long.

The supplements I recommend in the 15-Day Detox are therapeutic, or target, supplements. What that means is you take them for a short period of time to correct a problem in your body. Once that problem is corrected, you should be able to use high-quality organic food to keep your health on track. A good example of this is probiotics. I strongly recommend you take a high-quality probiotic during your detox. For many of you, that will replenish your microbiome and repair your gut enough that once the bottle is empty, you can focus on eating probiotic rich foods, such as sauerkraut, kimchi, kombucha, and raw kefir.

One of the biggest mistakes I see people make with supplements is taking the same supplements over and over again. If you've been taking the same supplement for years and are not sure if it's working, it probably isn't. You should feel a difference when you take a supplement, and you should keep switching your supplements around.

For information on supplements and why I use the ones above for the 15-Day Detox, check out Chapter 8: The Healing Power of Supplements. You can also find links to the products I use with my patients on my office's webpage at www.familylifechiropractic.com.

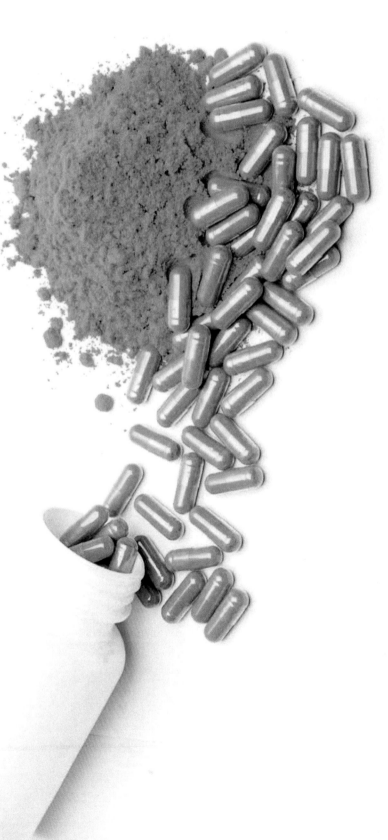

CHAPTER 3

THE 30-DAY HABIT RESET

The 30-Day Habit Reset is the second part of the 45-Day Reset, immediately following the 15-Day Detox described in the previous chapter. It is designed to help you create lasting good health habits that you can easily stick to for life.

This chapter tells you what you need to know about the 30-Day Habit Reset—and why it's important to avoid sugar, alcohol, grains, and dairy.

WHAT TO DO DURING YOUR 30-DAY HABIT RESET

- Avoid all grains, pastas, and white potatoes.
- Avoid all alcohol.
- Avoid all sugars.
- Avoid bad fats and processed foods.
- Eat as many raw organic vegetables as you can throughout the day.
- Eat as many meals as you want.
- Eat only raw, organic cow dairy, goat dairy, or sheep dairy. Avoid all pasteurized dairy.
- You may eat ALL organic fruits.
- Take the following supplements: high-quality food-based multivitamin (1 tablet daily), raw organic turmeric supplement (350 mg daily), vitamin D3 (5,000 IU daily), and omega-3s (5 grams daily).

RULES FOR THE 30-DAY HABIT RESET

Remember, the 30-day Habit Reset is designed to help you change your health habits *as a lifestyle*. Here's an important overview of the effects of sugar, alcohol, grains, dairy, etc.—and how to create new and positive habits around these substances.

Reset Rules of Sugar

You may feel nervous about avoiding sugar during the 30-day Habit Reset, but let me tell you, there are great alternatives to refined white sugar. Just be open-minded and a bit adventurous. Over the next thirty days, you can have as much stevia and xylitol as you desire. You may also have coconut sugar, but do so in moderation. You'll notice the recipes in Part 2 include these sugars.

My experience has been that not everyone likes stevia; many people prefer coconut sugar. If you're looking at a new recipe and it calls for sugar, coconut sugar has a 1:1 ratio to refined sugar. If the recipe calls for a cup of sugar, replace it with a cup of coconut sugar.

A question I'm asked frequently is, what about organic refined sugar? Unfortunately, even organic refined sugar will cause your pancreas to work too hard and keep your insulin receptor sites blocked.

You will find that Bonnie has been very creative in finding wonderful ways to make a food taste sweet, satisfying your taste buds but not spiking your blood sugar. Remember that you have trained your taste buds to like sweet foods. As you try new forms of sugar, like stevia and coconut sugar, you will begin to see that the level of sweetness you liked before will taste too sweet now. I have witnessed people with lifelong sugar addictions lose their sweet tooth following the 45-Day Reset. Be patient with yourself.

Reset Rules of Oil

The United States is one of the most fat-deprived nations. You absolutely need fat to keep your body healthy. So for the next thirty days, you're going to substitute good, health-promoting fats for all bad, harmful, inflammatory fats!

Eliminate inflammatory fats such as these:

- Canola oil
- Safflower oil
- Sunflower oil
- Vegetable oil
- Crisco
- Margarine

Replace bad fats with these health-promoting fats:

- Avocado oil
- Olive oil (don't heat above 100 degrees)
- Coconut oil
- Sesame oil
- Grapeseed oil
- Organic butter (from pasture-raised cow's milk)

Reset Rules of Dairy

The pasteurization process causes dairy to have a higher sugar content, so when you buy dairy, always look for raw dairy. This is usually pretty easy when you're searching for cheese but a lot more difficult when you're looking for milk.

Many people are sensitive to dairy, so make sure to eat only raw organic dairy and notice if you have any kind of reaction after eating it. A reaction to dairy might be bloating, skin rash, or overall feelings of sluggishness. If you notice a reaction like this, I highly recommend you take dairy out of your diet completely.

Research has found that a glass of milk can contain a cocktail of as many as twenty painkillers, antibiotics, and growth hormones. It also contains estrogen-mimicking hormones that can lead to breast cancer and other hormonal imbalances. The other challenge with cow's milk is that it's molecules are significantly bigger than those of human breast milk. Our bodies were designed to break down human breast milk molecules, not the larger cow's milk molecules. Goat's milk is a great alternative, as it consists of smaller molecules that are easier for our digestive system to handle.

Reset Rules of Eggs

You can eat as many eggs as you want during your 30-Day Habit Reset. When buying eggs, make sure you get organic, cage-free eggs. These have the most nutrients with the lowest number of harmful chemicals. Pasture-raised organic eggs are the absolute best, and you'll notice that their yolk's color is a deep orange/yellow. They are filled with more helpful nutrients, and fewer harmful alterations are made to the chickens that lay them.

Reset Rules of Grains

Grains turn to sugar once they enter the bloodstream. A piece of bread is said to have as high a glycemic index as a candy bar.[1] Like consuming sugar, consuming grains is one of the fastest paths to gaining weight. This is one of the reasons I have you continue to remove grains from your diet during the 30-Day Habit Reset. Although I like gluten-free flours, which are better for your gut than wheat and white bread, for the whole thirty days, I want you to pull out ALL grains. This is the fastest path to weight loss and health. However, that doesn't mean you'll never be able to have your muffins, pancakes, and breads again; there are great alternatives to wheat and white flour.

Here's a list of foods containing grains that you should avoid during your 30-Day Habit Reset program:

- White bread (use Paleo Bread instead)
- All pastas (use zucchini noodles and sweet potato noodles instead)
- White and red potatoes (use sweet potatoes instead)
- Rye bread
- Whole-wheat bread
- Muffins (substitute almond and coconut flour in recipes)
- English muffins
- Baked goods and pastries
- Crackers
- Potato chips
- Pie crust
- Cookies
- Brown and white rice (use wild rice and quinoa instead)
- Corn and corn chips
- Popcorn
- Corn and flour tortillas (use Paleo Wraps instead—check out Thrive Market online)

---

1. Harvard Health Publications, "Glycemic Index and Glycemic Load for 100+ Foods," February 3, 2015, http://www.health.harvard.edu/healthy-eating/glycemic_index_and_glycemic_load_for_100_foods/

Avoid these flours if you see them listed on a label, as they're high in sugar:

- White flour
- Whole-wheat flour
- Sourdough flour
- Rye flour
- Barley flour
- Graham flour
- Matzo flour
- Malt flour
- Durum flour
- Couscous flour
- Bulgur flour
- Semolina flour
- Brown-rice flour

- Spelt flour
- Kamut flour
- Amaranth flour
- Arrowroot flour
- Buckwheat flour
- Corn flour
- Corn meal
- Millet flour
- Oat flour
- Potato flour
- Sorghum flour
- Tapioca flour
- White-rice flour

Other starches to avoid:

- White rice
- Brown rice
- White potatoes
- Oats

Flour substitutes with low sugar include the following (you can have these on the 30-Day Habit Reset):

- Almond flour
- Coconut flour
- Hemp flour
- Lupin flour
- Chickpea flour
- Chia flour

Reset Rules of Fruits and Vegetables

First, eat only organic fruits and vegetables. Second, keep vegetables raw since raw vegetables are more beneficial to your body than cooked vegetables. When you cook vegetables, you destroy many of their nutrients. Make a point of having raw vegetables at every meal. The only exception to this is if you feel bloated after you eat. People who have too much bad bacteria, as with SIBO, can feel extremely bloated after eating raw vegetables. If this is your experience, cut back on the raw vegetables and give your gut more time to repair itself. Keep trying to add raw vegetables back in every few

days. If you're taking a high-powered probiotic, with enough time the bloated feeling will go away and you'll be able to eat more raw vegetables.

The other thing to think about with fruits and vegetables is their sugar content. Many people are surprised to hear that the following healthy foods have a high sugar content, but they can as easily raise your blood sugar as organic refined sugar can.

Highest-sugar vegetables — eat only in moderation:

- Carrots
- Beets
- Potatoes

Medium-sugar vegetables — eat as much as you want:

- Red, yellow, and orange peppers
- Red cabbage
- Tomatoes

Lowest-sugar vegetables — eat as much as you want:

- Green lettuces
- Parsley
- Celery
- Avocados
- Cucumber
- Kale
- Green cabbage
- Cauliflower

Highest-sugar fruits — avoid during your entire 30-Day Habit Reset:

- Tropical fruits, such as pineapple, papaya, mango, banana, and grapes

Medium-sugar fruits — eat in moderation during your 30-Day Habit Reset:

- Citrus fruits
- Melons
- Nectarines
- Peaches
- Pears
- Apples (except green)
- Kiwi

Lowest-sugar fruits — eat as much as you want throughout your entire 30-Day Habit Reset:

- Any kind of berries—including strawberries, raspberries, blueberries, blackberries, boysenberries, and huckleberries
- Green apples

When it comes to deciding whether to buy organic fruits and vegetables, I recommend that you try to buy as many organics as possible. If money is a consideration, we've talked about the Environmental Working Group's (EWG) Dirty Dozen and Clean Fifteen lists. The Dirty Dozen are those fruits and vegetables most heavily sprayed with pesticides. You want to buy these organic. The Clean Fifteen, on the other hand, are not as heavily sprayed with pesticides; it's safer to eat conventional versions of these, if you have to. Here are the lists for easy reference:

THE CLEAN FIFTEEN (OK TO BUY NONORGANIC)

- Onions
- Avocados
- Pineapple
- Mangoes
- Sweet peas
- Eggplant
- Cauliflower
- Asparagus
- Kiwi
- Cabbage
- Watermelon
- Grapefruit
- Sweet potatoes
- Honeydew melon

You may have noticed that this list contains only fourteen fruits and vegetables. I removed sweet corn from the list because corn is one of the most genetically modified crops and should *only* be bought organic.

THE DIRTY DOZEN (ALWAYS BUY ORGANIC)

- Apples
- Celery
- Tomatoes
- Cucumber
- Grapes
- Nectarines
- Peaches
- Potatoes
- Spinach
- Strawberries
- Blueberries
- Sweet bell peppers

Some experts suggest that you add kale and green beans to this list, as these have been more heavily sprayed in recent years. I also would add corn to this list due to the fact that it is genetically modified.

Reset Rules of Meat and Fish

Unfortunately, if you're eating grain fed conventional beef, you're getting a large dose of antibiotic- and hormone-injected meat. Every chemical that's put into the animal, including the chemical-laden food that the animal is fed, is still in the meat as it sits on your dinner plate. These chemicals slow down your digestion, making you bloated or constipated, and they raise your estrogen levels. Grain-fed meat also typically has more fat than other meats. Toxins live in the fat of an animal. When you eat that fat, you're getting all the toxins the animal's liver tried to excrete and ended up storing in the fat.

According to Dr. Sara Gottfried in her book *The Hormone Reset Diet*, we are hardwired by our DNA and the microbes in our gut to eat mostly vegetables, nuts, seeds, occasional fruit, and clean protein. Eating this way will keep you lean and your hormones balanced.

During your 30-Day Habit Reset, you can have organic meat and fish in moderation. Since meat carries the highest amount of toxins, it's imperative that you go organic. If money is a concern, I would rather you bought your meats organic and your fruits and vegetables nonorganic. Just be sure to follow the guidelines set out by the EWG when buying foods from the Dirty Dozen and Clean Fifteen lists.

Here's what else you need to know about various meats:

Beef: Avoid all grain-fed beef. A great alternative to grain-fed beef is grass-fed beef. Unlike grain-fed beef, grass-fed beef is incredibly good for your body. Beef from cows that are allowed to graze on grass and roam in large fields is high in omega-3 oils that are crucial for improving brain function, lowering inflammation, and keeping your metabolism working efficiently. Include grass-fed beef in your meals at least twice a week.

Chicken: Organic chicken of all types (drumsticks, wings, breasts, skin-on) is OK. Nonorganic chicken is packed with antibiotics and hormones that have been injected into the animals. Avoid nonorganic chicken at all costs.

Fish: Farm-raised fish is an absolute no-no, as it lacks key nutrients like omega-3 oils. Frozen or fresh fish is fine, but all fish should be wild, not farm raised. Sometimes you have to ask your butcher or waiter at a restaurant if the fish is wild.

Here's the Food & Water Watch's Dirty Dozen list of seafood. Avoid these during your 30-Day Habit Reset:

- King crab
- Caviar
- Atlantic Bluefin tuna
- Orange roughy
- Atlantic flatfish
- American eel
- American cod
- Imported catfish
- Chilean seabass
- Shark
- Atlantic and farmed salmon
- Imported shrimp
- Tilapia

Deli Meats: These meats carry the highest possibility of toxic overload, so you absolutely want these meats organic and nitrite-free. Several studies have been done on the increase in the incidence of leukemia in kids who eat processed deli meats. Sausages, salamis, and sliced turkey are all great choices when they're organic and free from nitrites.

Pork: This is the one meat you want to eat in moderation or cut out completely. The pig is the only animal that does not have sweat glands and thus holds on to all of its toxins. Since the 30-Day Habit Reset is about detoxifying your body, I highly recommend you eat pork rarely or not at all. If you do choose to eat pork, be sure that it's organic and has no caramel coloring or sodium nitrites in it.

Reset Rules of Alcohol

Pulling alcohol out of your diet will have a significant effect on your overall health. During your 30-Day Habit Reset, you are to pull ALL alcohol out of your diet. If you're trying to reset your health, drinking alcohol will hold you back from living in the body you deserve to live in.

What happens when you drink alcohol? Several detrimental chemical processes occur. First, you destroy your gut. Beer and wine have the highest amount of yeast in them. One of the major breakdowns of the gastrointestinal system is candida. Drinks like beer and wine feed candida, causing you to crave more beer and wine. A great way to stop the cravings is to stop feeding your body yeast. It can be difficult at first, but as the candida dies over time, so will your cravings.

Second, alcohol increases estrogen in your body. Now remember that estrogen is what makes a female body curvy. The more estrogen you have in your system, the more your body will convert that to fat. Even one glass of alcohol per day can make you put on extra pounds. While it may be hard for some of you to eliminate alcohol from your diet completely, I promise if you hang in there and give it enough time, you'll see the benefits quickly as the fat around your abdomen starts to disappear.

Third, as long as your liver is metabolizing alcohol, it can't burn fat. Many studies have shown how alcohol causes the body to stop the burning of fat for energy. For some of you, this is going to be the hardest part of your reset experience. But the whole idea of the 30-Day Habit Reset is to bring your body back to its original state, the way it was designed to be. You can't fully reset without giving up alcohol. Give your liver a break and watch your body flourish!

Although you won't be drinking alcohol during your 30-Day Habit Reset, once your reset is over, drinking alcohol in moderation (one to two drinks a week) is not harmful. But you do need to know a few key things about alcohol and how it's processed in the body.

Beer: This is probably the worst alcoholic beverage you can drink because of its high gluten and yeast content. Hopefully, if you've made it this far in the book, you know by now that the key to living with lifelong health starts by taking good care of your gut. Beer will quickly destroy the good bacteria in your gut and increase your estrogen levels, leaving you bloated and hanging on to extra fat. Sound appealing? I would avoid beer at all costs.

Wine: Although many scientific papers show that the high antioxidant content of wine is beneficial to the body, the sulfites and high sugar content in wine are both destructive to the gut and stressful to the pancreas. Many people suffer from candida. Candida is caused by too much yeast—and most wines are packed with yeast. Bottom line: wine has too much sugar in it, and whenever you're trying to keep your weight down, avoiding wine is a good practice.

Mixed Drinks: The biggest challenge with mixed drinks is what you mix the alcohol with. Since we're trying to minimize your sugar content, mixing your gin with tonic gives you a burst of sugar that could easily put you back into insulin resistance. Hard liquor has less sugar than many nonalcoholic drinks, and if it's mixed with something mellow, such as a club soda, it's your best choice of alcoholic beverage.

Reset Rules of Nonalcoholic Drinks

The bottom line here is that you want to drink water—and lots of it! If you're fine for the next thirty days drinking *only* water, that is the quickest path to success. Other great choices for nonalcoholic drinks are herbal teas, kombucha, club soda, Zevia, or green juices with limited fruit.

There is only one way I recommend to drink coffee: buttered and organic. The challenge with coffee is that it is heavily sprayed with pesticides. When drinking coffee, make sure it's organic. A great way to drink coffee is with butter. Dave Aspery, who wrote *The Bulletproof Diet,* made this style of coffee popular after he watched people of the Tibetan culture put butter into their tea and coffee. What I love about drinking buttered coffee is that it is a great way to get your good fats in. You can find the recipe in this book for the way we recommend making it. The good fat helps nourish your brain and speed up your metabolism. Organic herbal teas can also be buttered. Green tea and yerba mate tea will give you an energy lift without draining your adrenal glands.

The best way to wean yourself off coffee is to have a little less each day. If you serve yourself a quarter of a cup less every day, over a few days to a week you'll be completely off it without any headaches or extreme exhaustion. The other thing about coffee that destroys people's health is what they put in their coffee. Added sugar, nonorganic dairy, artificial sweeteners, creamers, syrups, and whipped cream are all destroyers of your health.

Reset Rules of How Often and How Much to Eat

The 30-Day Habit Reset is not a food deprivation plan. You can eat as much as you want of the approved foods at whatever time you want to eat. The only time of day I highly recommend limiting your food intake is before bed. The reason for this is that going to bed with a full stomach often causes food to ferment in your gut, which can destroy good bacteria and increase your chances of candida. Also, your body cannot properly digest and metabolize food that you eat right before bed. In fact, one of the strategies sumo wrestlers use to fatten up is to always take a nap after their largest meal. Going to sleep on a full stomach forces the body to store most of the calories as fat, as it doesn't have the ability to metabolize large amounts of food while sleeping.

Studies used to show that you needed three meals a day and that you needed to eat first thing in the morning. This is an outdated theory—eat when you want to eat. As your body resets and comes back to its original design, it will tell you when it's hungry. Honor that. A well-functioning body knows best. If you're trying to lose weight, I highly recommend following the principles of intermittent fasting. You can find them under the weight-loss section in Chapter 7: Accelerating Your Results.

CHAPTER 4

HOW TO NAVIGATE A NUTRITION LABEL

So many people in our country are truly suffering from poor health. It's not because they don't have access to health care; it's due to the fact that we have a serious lack of understanding about the foods we eat and what they do to our body when we eat them.

One of my favorite quotes comes from Ann Wigmore, founder of the Hippocrates Health Institute: "The food you eat can be either the safest and most powerful form of medicine or the slowest form of poison." You could avoid so many health problems if at every meal you ate, every time you put something into your mouth, and with every trip you made to the grocery store, you asked yourself, Is this food growing me a healthy body or poisoning me?

The problem is that the food industry cares more about its profits than your health. So every time you walk into the grocery store, you have to realize that just because a food is on the shelf, it doesn't mean that it's safe.

I dedicated *The Reset Factor* to my friend Lani, who was diagnosed with metastatic breast cancer at the age of forty. When I started working with her, I remember one of the first things we talked about was ingredients and whether she knew how to read an nutrition label. She looked surprised, as if to ask why she would need to know how to read a label. "It's just food; don't I just pick the food that my family likes?" she asked. As I started to walk her through the strategies below, she changed from surprised to angry. I will never forget the day she said to me, "Are you telling me that just because the food is in Safeway, it doesn't mean it's safe?"

Yes, that is what I'm telling you. If you want to be healthy, if you want to live in a body that you love, and if you want to prevent diseases like cancer, you are going to have to learn to read a nutrition label.

Have I got your attention? Great. Let's get to it. Here are my strategies for reading labels.

STOP LOOKING AT THE CALORIES

Everyone goes straight to the calories. The calories tell you nothing. Your body is more complex than that. In fact, weight gain has more to do with your gut microbiome, your toxic load, and your blood sugar than calories. Free yourself from this calorie nonsense. It is not serving you.

The 45-Day Reset has helped thousands of people lose weight—and none of them ever counted calories. If you want to lose weight, you need to focus on building health in your body, not minimizing calories.

FAT DOESN'T MAKE YOU FAT

Once you're done counting calories, stop looking at the fat content as well. Stop and think about it for a moment. We have access to more fat-free foods than ever before, yet we have a larger obesity problem than ever before. If cutting out fat made us skinny, then we should be the skinniest country in the world. Yet in case you haven't noticed, obesity is a major problem in America. In fact, I always say if you want the results that most Americans are getting with their health, keep eating like them. If you want different results, you're going to have to eat differently. Start with the fats you're eating—or NOT eating.

From this point forward, whenever you think of fat, remind yourself there are good fats and bad fats. When you look at the fat content on a nutrition label, it only shows you the total fat content. Here are some of the more common bad and good fats you'll see on labels:

Bad Fats

- Canola oil
- Vegetable oil
- Sunflower oil
- Safflower oil
- Partially hydrogenated oils
- Peanut oil
- Corn oil
- Cottonseed oil

Good Fats

- Avocado oil
- Olive oil (when not heated)
- Coconut oil

SUGAR IS POISON

There are only three places I want you to look on a nutrition label: sugar content, carbohydrate count, and ingredients list (see next section). Sugar is one of the major destroyers of your health. It promotes inflammation. It causes you to gain weight. It suppresses your immune system. It feeds cancer cells. It puts you on a fast track to type 2 diabetes. I am not joking about this. You need to minimize your sugar intake.

I believe that a great guideline to follow for sugar is the recommendation from the American Heart Association. They recommend that men have no more than 36 grams of sugar per day, women no more 20 grams per day, and children no more than 12 grams per day. So when you look at a label, go straight to the sugar content. How many grams does it say the food has per serving? Don't forget there is also something called a serving size. For example, on a bottle of Coke, it may say 20 grams, so you think it's OK, thinking, *This will be my sugar for the day*. But if you look at the serving size, it will say five servings. If you do the math, you'll see that one bottle of coke actually has 100 grams of sugar—five times the recommended amount for women. No wonder type 2 diabetes, heart disease, and cancer are on the rise!

CARBOHYDRATE COUNT MATTERS

Ask anyone who has diabetes or a diabetic child and he or she will tell you that the carb count is the first thing they look at on a label. You will usually find the carb count right above the sugar count. The carb count will tell you how high your blood sugar will rise when you eat the food. Remember how I said one of the healing principles of the 45-Day Reset was to balance blood sugar? Well, the only way you're going to do that is by understanding what foods spike your blood sugar. We can learn so much from the diabetic world.

What I love about this recipe book is that it was born out of necessity. When *The Reset Factor* book came out, it sparked thousands of people to move into action with their health. We have a private Facebook group of Resetters from all over

the world who are following the 45-Day Reset. In that group, we learned what questions people had and what they needed to succeed at the 45-Day Reset. As we've noted, most of the recipes in this book were created by my co-author, Bonnie. Not only does she have a background in culinary arts, but as you read earlier, she has a child with type 1 diabetes. Bonnie spends a significant amount of her day counting carbs for her daughter; she taught me the power of carbohydrates.

Most of the recipes here have been tested on Bonnie's daughter. As a result, Bonnie was able to see which recipes caused her daughter's blood sugar to rise the quickest and which ones gave her the most sustained energy. (This is all reflected in the carb count next to each recipe in this book). The same is true when you look at a label at your grocery store. If the carbohydrate count is high, meaning in the twenties or thirties, you'll want to avoid that food. Remember that the higher the blood sugar goes, the more insulin the body has to secrete. The more insulin secreted, the more strain on the pancreas and the more quickly you will become insulin resistant.

Carbohydrate count is massively important for those of you trying to lose weight. In Chapter 7: Accelerating Your Results, I introduce you to a nutritional concept called the ketogenic diet. If you're trying to lose weight, I recommend you read that chapter, as I explain how to get into a state known as *ketosis*. When I'm working with a patient who is weight-loss resistant or who's trying to reverse a serious health condition, I often teach him or her how to get into ketosis. When your body is in ketosis, it burns energy from fat. This helps you release weight and boosts your immune system. In order to get into ketosis, you have to restrict your carbohydrate intake to less than 50 grams per day.

To learn more about ketosis, go to Chapter 7: Accelerating Your Results. It's really important to note that there's a major difference between ketosis and ketoacidosis, especially if you're a diabetic. The difference is explained below.

Nutritional Ketosis

When I refer to ketosis throughout this book, understand that I am referencing *nutritional ketosis*. This is a controlled, insulin-regulated process that results in a mild release of fatty acids and ketone production in response to either a fast or a reduction in carbohydrate intake. Inducing nutritional ketosis is a fabulous way to speed up the healing process. It will pull you out of insulin resistance, reduce cellular inflammation, and unblock clogged receptor sites.

Ketoacidosis

Ketoacidosis is a state of distress for the body. It is driven by a lack of insulin in the body. Without insulin, blood sugar will quickly rise and fat will be stored. As fat gets stored, ketones will rise in abnormally high quantities. A combination of high ketone levels and high blood sugar will begin to upset the normal acid/base balance in the blood. This is a dangerous place to be and *not* what the Reset program is designed to do. In order to reach a state of ketoacidosis, insulin levels must be so low that the regulation of blood sugar and fatty acid flow is impaired.

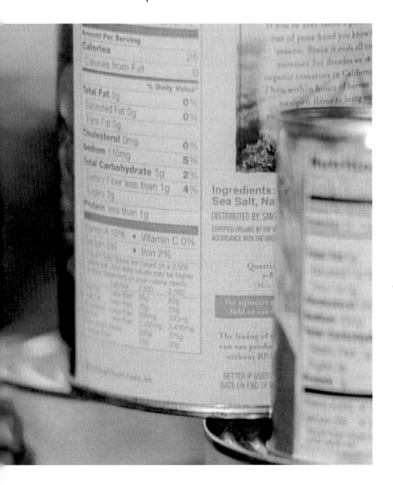

INGREDIENTS TRUMP EVERYTHING

The ingredients list is undoubtedly the most important part of the whole label. This is where you can tell if you're going to be eating a food that will build health or create disease. I recommend that my patients follow three steps when looking at the ingredients list.

The first thing is to check the *order* of ingredients. Ingredients are listed in order of the amount of that ingredient contained in the product. This means that the ingredient contained most in that food is listed first. The last ingredient listed is the least contained ingredient in that food.

The second step is to notice *how many* ingredients are listed. The more ingredients in a food, the less likely it is to be chemical free. Think about it. When you make chocolate chip cookies at home, there are usually four or five ingredients in the recipe, right? Next time you're in a store, pick up a package of Chips Ahoy chocolate chip cookies. How many ingredients are listed? Over twenty-five ingredients are listed for this processed version of a chocolate chip cookie!

The third step is to read the ingredients out loud. I love to have kids do this because they understand what is harmful for them right away. If you cannot pronounce an ingredient, it is most likely a chemical. If you want to have amazing health, you're going to have to stop eating chemicals. I know this is a complicated subject—that's why we've dedicated two whole chapters to ingredients in this book. My hope is for those chapters to demystify ingredients and help you understand which ones to use and which ones to avoid.

Once you understand a nutrition label, your whole relationship with food will change. You'll stop looking at food as just a treat for your taste buds and brain; you'll understand that food can be the greatest path to amazing health.

CHAPTER 5

INGREDIENTS THAT WILL DESTROY YOUR HEALTH

If you want to live in a healthy body, you need to understand ingredients. Unfortunately, the food industry hasn't made it easy for you, the consumer. So this chapter presents general guidelines to help you choose your foods and ingredients well, as well as lists you can refer back to as you become more skilled at reading labels.

The list of foods presented in this chapter was inspired by two great advocates for removal of dangerous chemicals from our foods: the Environmental Working Group (www.ewg.org) and the Food Babe (foodbabe.com). If you haven't checked out their websites, I highly recommend you do. They have been working tirelessly to get corporations to pull out of our foods the ingredients that are harming us. The foods/ingredients listed in this chapter are based on the research of these two groups; they're the ones that will destroy your health the fastest.

1. HIGH-FRUCTOSE CORN SYRUP

You will read this over and over throughout this book: Sugar is poison. All types. Sugar feeds cancer cells, makes you weight-loss resistant, burns your adrenals out, causes inflammation in your body, and puts you on a fast path to type 2 diabetes. During the 45-Day Reset, you will pull all forms of sugar out of your diet. There are a few exceptions, which we mentioned in the 30-Day Habit Reset chapter; you can also find them listed below.

I want to bring your attention to the worst sugar of them all: high-fructose corn syrup (HFCS). Remember glyphosate and genetically modified foods? Well, corn is one of the most heavily sprayed and modified foods available. And HFCS is made from corn—genetically modified corn.

The *International Journal of Obesity* stated that the rise in obesity in the past thirty-five years has paralleled the rise in the use of HFCS. Remember those hormone receptors I keep referencing? Well, HFCS blocks the receptors for two of the most important hormones for losing weight: leptin and insulin. When you ingest HFCS, your insulin skyrockets, promoting fat storage and suppressing your response to *leptin*, the hormone that tells your brain to burn fat.

Reset Factor Recommendation: Read labels to know if the food or drink you are consuming has HCFS in it. I would avoid this ingredient at all costs. The approved sugars that you will see throughout this recipe book include the following:

- Stevia
- Xylitol
- Erythritol
- Coconut sugar (not on 15-Day Detox)
- Honey (not on 15-Day Detox)
- Grade B maple syrup (not on 15-Day Detox)
- Dates (not on 15-Day Detox)
- Shredded whole fruits
- Coconut nectar

These sugars are approved not only for their natural qualities, but also because they won't spike your blood sugar levels as high as traditional sugar will.

2. ARTIFICIAL SWEETENERS

If I can't have sugar, then I should have sugar-free "diet" foods, right? Wrong! Nothing could be further from the truth. The 45-Day Reset is about regaining your health by eating in a way that builds health. Sugar-free and diet foods don't build health, they build disease. In fact, artificial sweeteners are linked to the following four main health conditions:

Weight Gain

The San Antonio Heart Study documented weight change in men and women over a seven- to eight-year period. It was discovered that weight gain and obesity were significantly greater in those drinking diet beverages compared with those who did not drink them.

Metabolic Syndrome

Metabolic syndrome is the combination of increased blood pressure, high blood sugar levels, excess body fat around the waist, and abnormal cholesterol levels. When these symptoms all occur together, it greatly increases your risk of stroke and heart disease. Recent studies suggest that people who drink artificially sweetened beverages may have double the risk of metabolic syndrome compared with those who don't.

Type 2 Diabetes

In a European study, the risk for developing type 2 diabetes more than doubled for participants who drank diet beverages. Data from the Nurse's Health Study also indicated that risk for developing type 2 diabetes was amplified in those consuming at least one diet drink a day.

Hypertension and Cardiovascular Disease

Multiple studies have shown that the risk for coronary heart disease was significantly elevated in women who consumed more than two artificially sweetened beverages per day.

One hypothesis as to why artificial sweeteners have such a negative effect on your health is that consuming sweet-tasting, reduced-calorie food and beverages interferes with your natural ability to adjust to glucose and energy. They do the opposite of what you're hoping for. They don't cause you to lose weight or stabilize your blood sugar; in fact, they mess with your metabolism and make it harder for you to lose weight. Studies in mice and rats have even proved that consumption of noncaloric sweeteners dampens the physiological response to the sweet taste and causes the animals to overindulge in calorie-rich, sweet-tasting food, ultimately causing them to pack on more pounds.

Reset Factor Recommendation: I recommend you avoid the following artificial sweeteners:

- Splenda
- Aspartame
- NutraSweet
- Sucralose
- Saccharin

If you currently use them regularly, I recommend you go cold turkey in getting off them. Every day that you ingest them, you are harming your health. Try substituting stevia in their place. Stevia has a taste very much like NutraSweet. Many of my patients who start out addicted to diet drinks find sodas made with stevia (like the Zevia my kids love) very helpful to substitute.

3. REFINED AND ENRICHED FLOUR

Here's a great food rule to follow: If something is "refined," that is code for "We took something important out." Usually, it's the nutrients. Food product manufacturers often strip the nutrients from flours to make them softer and more palatable to your mouth. The sad thing is that refining a food makes it basically a dead food that adds no nutritional value to your body. "Enriched" means they put synthetic nutrients back into the product. When you see the word *enriched*, think "chemicals." Many flours are bleached with chlorine or peroxide to make them look white! If you want to destroy the cells of your body, eat some chlorine.

Refined and enriched flours are also loaded with added sugar. This is done to enhance the taste. As I've mentioned before, sugar is poison. It will make you weight-loss resistant, lead to type 2 diabetes, make you depressed, and destroy your gut.

Reset Factor Recommendation: Although I have you take grains completely out of your diet during the 45-Day Reset, many of you will begin to add these grains back in after the forty-five-day period is over. Go back and look at *The Reset Factor* for more details about the 80/20 rule I recommend you follow once your reset is done. This means twenty percent of the time you can eat whatever you want. However, I recommend that you never eat refined or enriched foods.

The best flours to eat are sprouted flours—the exact opposite of refined flours. In sprouted flours, all the nutrients and fiber have been left in. A great example of a food that uses sprouted flours is Ezekiel bread. You'll see other flours that may be new to you in the recipes in this book as well. Here are some of our favorite flours to cook with:

- Coconut flour
- Almond flour
- Tiger nut flour
- Garbanzo bean flour
- Teff flour
- Quinoa flour
- Sesame flour

4. NONORGANIC MEAT AND DAIRY

All nonorganic meats and dairy are filled with growth hormone. The United States is one of the only industrialized countries that allows its animals to be injected with growth hormone. Growth hormone will fatten an animal with estrogen-based hormones. This makes more money for the food industry but fills our bodies with excess estrogen. The Breast Cancer Fund is one of the best organizations around for teaching people how to minimize their risk of breast cancer. Breast cancer is an estrogen-loving cancer. The more estrogen you are exposed to, the more you increase your chances of getting this disease.

You also can find growth hormones in your glass of milk. Cows injected with growth hormone will produce more milk—again, making more money for the food industry.

A nutrition and cancer study done in 2011 reported that cow's milk stimulated the growth of prostate cancer cells.[2] Ironically, almond milk suppressed the growth of these cells.

Reset Factor Recommendation: Buy all your meats organic and hormone-free. Just ask your butcher before you buy meat or read the label on packaged meat, which will tell you if it's hormone-free. Look for tricky words like *natural.* "Natural" means nothing. It's there to fool you to think the food is hormone-free. But you need to see the words *hormone-free* to authenticate that the food is really free of growth hormone.

Further recommendations include the following:

Grass-Fed versus Grain-Fed Beef

During the 45-Day Reset, I strongly encourage you to eat as many good fats as possible. This will help lower inflammation, repair the membrane of your cells, and nourish your brain. One of the fats I want you to get a lot of is omega-3. Grain-fed beef is low in omega-3 fats and high in omega-6 fats—a combination that will promote inflammation in your body. Grass-fed beef is the opposite—very high in omega-3 fats and low in omega-6 fats. During the 45-day Reset, you are to eat only grass-fed beef.

What Type of Milk Is Best?

When it comes to milk, the best kind to get is raw organic milk. The challenge is that raw milk is hard to find; often, it can be found only at your local farmer's market. Unpasteurized raw milk has important enzymes in it to help you break down the lactose proteins found in dairy. It also has healthy probiotics in it to feed your microbiome with good bacteria, and it's high in omega-3 fatty acids to lower inflammation. This is the milk we primarily drink in our house. I have two athletic teens, and getting probiotics and omega-3s into them is top priority. I love that I can make a smoothie with raw kefir or that they can drink a glass of raw whole milk and get the necessary nutrients that will keep them healthy.

What About Nut Milks?

I love nut milks! I recommend almond and cashew milk. But you need to read the ingredients list. Once nut milks became popular, many companies started putting fillers in them. One of those ingredients is carrageenan (read about this in the list below). The best nut milks are the one with the fewest ingredients. My favorite brand has three ingredients: almonds, water, and sea salt. You will only find this type of almond or cashew milk in the refrigerated section of your natural foods market. We also included a recipe for nut milk in the Recipes chapter that's easy to make.

What About Pasteurized Organic Milk?

What you need to know about pasteurized milk is that it has no nutritional value. The pasteurization process kills all the helpful enzymes and good bacteria. The milk industry has done an amazing job of brainwashing us into thinking we need milk to get calcium. But did you know that pasteurized milk actually pulls calcium from your body, rather than adding it in? If you buy organic pasteurized milk, it won't be harmful to your body, but it won't be helpful either.

What About Goat's Milk?

I like goat's milk and cheese for several reasons. They have a protein molecule called beta-A2 casein. The human body can digest beta-A2 casein better than beta-A1, which is in most cow's milk, even raw. Goat's milk is easier for your gut to digest. The only challenge with goat's milk is that it's hard to find raw. In fact, I have never found it raw! Again, if it's pasteurized, all beneficial enzymes, probiotics, and fatty acids in it have been destroyed.

---

2. Patricia L. Tate, Robert Bibb, and Lyndon L. Larcom, "Milk Stimulates Growth of Prostate Cancer Cells in Culture," *Nutrition and Cancer* 63, no. 8 (2011), 1361–66.

Same rules apply as with nut milks: You have to look out for harmful fillers and make sure they're organic. If you have a nut allergy or don't like the taste of nut milks or goat's milk, then coconut and hemp milks are perfect for you. Since the 45-Day Reset has you drinking lots of smoothies, it's good to vary your milks so that your tastebuds don't get bored. I often use organic coconut or hemp milk in my smoothie. It adds a little extra sweetness without adding more carbs to your diet.

5. ANTIBIOTICS

The fastest way to destroy the microbiome of your gut is by ingesting antibiotics. Antibiotics destroy all the bacteria in your gut, good and bad. And there is growing evidence that the use of antibiotics leads to weight gain. A study published in the *International Journal of Obesity*[3] tracked 164,000 children in Pennsylvania and concluded that healthy youngsters at age fifteen who had been prescribed antibiotics seven or more times in their childhood weighed three pounds more than those who didn't take these medications. "Antibiotics at any age contribute to weight gain," according to Dr. Brian S. Schwartz, a physician and epidemiologist at the Johns Hopkins Bloomberg School of Public Health and lead author of the study.

Where do you find antibiotics in your food? Everywhere! Antibiotics are hard to escape. An estimated 80 percent of antibiotics used in this country are used on livestock. Farmers are putting antibiotics in the feed of animals to promote growth. Not only is this a significant reason so many people have gut conditions, but it has created a whole species of dangerous microbes called superbugs. Between the antibiotics in food and the overprescription of antibiotics to humans, we have a massive health crisis that many doctors are concerned about. In fact, the CDC is so concerned about these resistant bugs that it has refused to make any more new antibiotics and is encouraging parents to stop giving antibiotics to their children for colds and flus.

The CDC estimates that in the United States each year, at least two million people become infected with bacteria that are resistant to antibiotics and at least twenty-three thousand people die as a direct result of these infections.[4]

Reset Factor Recommendation: Another great reason to read your labels: Always buy antibiotic-free meats and dairy. If you are unsure, ask your butcher. When you eat out, avoid meat and dairy. This includes the cow's milk in your coffee at Starbuck's (they offer coconut milk).

6. PESTICIDES

For many years, I've had patients tell me that they can't afford organic food. My response to that is, "You can't afford not to buy organic!" I kid you not: Pesticides, fungicides, and herbicides that are sprayed on fruits and vegetables will destroy your health. Here's why:

They block hormone receptor sites in the cells of your body. Receptors for hormones such as insulin, leptin, and thyroid hormones can all get clogged with pesticide chemicals. Once a hormone receptor site gets clogged, you'll become weight-loss resistant, your thyroid will malfunction, and you'll put yourself on a fast path to cancers such as breast cancer.

They create microholes in your gut, which leads to leaky gut syndrome. Go back and read *The Reset Factor*; leaky gut is a major health problem, leading to many of the symptoms you're experiencing. The major pesticide creating these microholes is glyphosate, which I mentioned in the introduction and which I'll continue to reference many times throughout this book. When you eat nonorganic foods that are sprayed with glyphosate, these holes are created, allowing more toxins to enter your bloodstream. Your brain registers these toxins as foreign invaders and creates an inflammatory response. If you continue to ingest glyphosate, the inflammatory response will never turn off and will lead to a whole host of problems.

A senior scientist at MIT, Stephanie Seneff, PhD, has been researching the effects of glyphosate on the human body. According to Dr. Seneff, glyphosate engages "gut bacteria" through a process known as the *shikimate pathway*. This enables the chemical to interfere with the biochemistry of bacteria in our gut, resulting in the depletion of essential amino acids that

3. B. S. Schwartz et al., "Antibiotic Use and Childhood Body Mass Index Trajectory," *International Journal of Obesity* 40 (2016): 615–21, doi:10.1038/ijo.2015.218

4. Centers for Disease Control and Prevention, "Antibiotic/Antimicrobial Resistance," http://www.cdc.gov/drugresistance/

are crucial for brain function. Not only does Dr. Seneff feel that glyphosate is a large contributor to the growing Alzheimer's and dementia epidemics, but she has also declared that we are facing an epidemic of autism that may affect half of all children within ten years. Glyphosate is a serious problem.[5]

Reset Factor Recommendation: Purchase only organic produce. If cost is a serious concern, your next best strategy is to follow the EWG's guidelines for the Dirty Dozen and Clean Fifteen. Because of the effectiveness of the 15-Day Detox, I have had several patients who do the detox a couple of times a year. One patient noticed that when she made sure every fruit and vegetable was organic while on her detox, she got the best results. This one change to your food can make all the difference.

My other recommendation is to make sure you stay away from the common genetically engineered foods like corn, soy, wheat, alfalfa, canola, sugar beets, cottonseed, papaya, zucchini, and squash. Buy these foods organic only; otherwise, you can be assured of getting a dose of glyphosate.

7. BISPHENOL (BPA)

Is BPA an ingredient? No, but it is a harmful chemical that many of your foods are packaged in, which is why I want to bring it to your attention. BPA is the toxic chemical found in plastics and the lining of food cans. Here's what you need to know about it:

BPA is an endocrine disruptor, meaning it blocks hormone receptor sites. This is catastrophic for hormones such as insulin, leptin, and thyroid hormones. With key receptor sites blocked, you become weight-loss resistant, have hormonal imbalances, and increase your chances of hormonal cancers such as breast cancer.

It turns you into an Agouti mouse. *What? BPA turns me into a mouse?* No, not really. But now that I have your attention, the agouti mouse is something you want to become really familiar with. In 2000, a study was done at Duke University proving that our lifestyle had more of an effect on obesity than our genetics. Researchers studied twin mice who were genetically predisposed to obesity. They fed both mice the same food and gave them the same amount of exercise, but they exposed one mouse to BPA. What happened to that mouse will forever change the way we look at obesity. The mouse who was exposed to BPA became obese, and its hair turned yellow and began to fall out. The mouse that wasn't exposed to BPA stayed thin. Researchers concluded that chemicals, especially BPA, can trigger genes in your body that will cause you to gain weight. The great news is that once they stopped feeding the obese mouse BPA, it lost weight and returned back to the size and color of its twin. If you want to lose weight, you're going to have to take this chemical out of your diet.

Reset Factor Recommendation: Look for BPA-free cans. Or even better yet, look for boxes or glass jars. Stop using plastics. Throw out your plastic containers, water bottles, or cans. Switch everything over to glass. There are many great glass containers available. If you have a Costco near you, they have a line called Snapware that we store all our food in. You can also order it online.

8. PRESERVATIVES

Remember those words on labels that I pointed out you can't usually pronounce? Many of them are preservatives. These chemicals are put in food to extend its shelf life. Remember, if it extends a food's shelf life, it will likely shorten yours.

Preservatives have been linked to many conditions, such as multiple cancers, Alzheimer's, decreased sperm count, kidney damage, and many neurological disorders. The good news is that according to a publication out of Oregon, there is evidence that "marked" DNA can become "unmarked" with diet modification.[6]

There are NO health benefits to chemicals, and you need to avoid them at all costs. Here are the preservatives to avoid:

- Sodium nitrites
- Sodium nitrates
- BHA and BHT
- Propylene glycol

Reset Factor Recommendation: Try to buy fresh food whenever possible, and be sure to read your labels so that if you see any of these harmful chemicals, you can avoid them.

5. Janet Phelan, "MIT States That Half of All Children May Be Autistic by 2025 Due to Monsanto," *New Eastern Outlook*, January 26, 2015, http://journal-neo.org/2015/01/26/mit-states-that-half-of-all-children-may-be-autistic-by-2025/

6. Kent L. Thornburg, et al., "*In Utero* Life and Epigenetic Predisposition for Disease," *Advances in Genetics* 71 (2010): 57–78. doi: 10.1016/B978-0-12-380864-6.00003-1

9. TRANS FATS

The best way to describe trans fats is that they are bad fats. Very bad fats. They are used to extend shelf life. Trans fats turn on inflammation in your body, block receptor sites, and have even been shown to cause cancer. You will often find these fats in deep-fried fast foods, cookies, and crackers.

Numerous studies show that trans fats increase LDL (bad) cholesterol levels while decreasing HDL (good) cholesterol levels. This leaves your body wide open to heart attacks, strokes, and diabetes. Some of the most harmful trans fats are partially hydrogenated oils. These oils are so harmful that the FDA has officially announced that they are unfit for human consumption and will be banned from all foods by 2018.

Harmful fats you want to avoid include the following:

- Partially hydrogenated oils
- Margarine
- Canola oil
- Vegetable oil
- Safflower oil
- Sunflower oil
- Soybean oil

Reset Factor Recommendation: Read labels. I know I sound like a broken record, but you will see these oils right away in your food. These oils are abundant in fried foods, cookies, crackers, and most packaged food. Avoid at all costs.

Oils that are good for you include the following:

- Coconut oil
- Avocado oil
- Sesame oil
- Red palm oil
- Organic grass-fed butter

10. ARTIFICIAL AND NATURAL FLAVORS

The next time you pick up a food or drink that's neon green, ask yourself, Does this color exist in nature? If the answer is no, then put it down.

Many people choose food and drinks for taste first. They don't stop and think of the harmful chemicals that may be lurking in such food or drinks. Artificial and natural flavors are put in a food to do one thing: make you addicted to it.

Yep, these harmful flavors are *excitotoxins*, like glutamate, which tricks your brain into wanting more. The food industry purposely puts them in food to keep you addicted. When you grab a bag of gummy bears that are packed with artificial flavors and you notice that you can't put the bag down because they taste so good, the artificial colors are working their magic on you.

Flavoring is cheap and effective. It can be made from any toxic ingredient, like petroleum or even animal parts. Anyone who has watched Jamie Oliver's television show *Food Revolution* can tell you about the episode where he shows kids what cheap ice cream and candy are made from. Jelly beans, for example, contain an artificial flavoring that comes from beaver anal glands. I kid you not! It's called *castoreum* and is often put in vanilla ice cream, strawberry oatmeal, and raspberry-flavored products.

What about natural flavors? Those must be healthy, right? Nope. There is no regulation of the words *natural flavors* on labels. Anything can be lumped into that category, including the neurotoxin monosodium glutamate (MSG).

Reset Factor Recommendation: Run away as fast as you can from any food that is a neon color. These colors indicate harmful chemicals that will put you on the fast path to many health problems. Read labels even when you go into places like Jamba Juice or Baskin-Robbins. Look for the words *artificial* or *natural flavors*. Become a food detective. Investigate what's going into your mouth. It's worth taking the time—and your life depends on it.

11. FOOD DYES

Who doesn't love a maraschino cherry? Well, your body doesn't love it. Food dyes are in many candy products. Very similar to artificial flavors, food dyes are designed to trick your brain—to make you desire the food even more.

Studies show that artificial colorings, which are found in sodas, fruit juices, and salad dressings, may contribute to behavioral problems in children and lead to a significant reduction in IQ. Studies have also linked these harmful chemicals to cancer.

Following are some of the findings on food dyes:

Blue #1 and Blue #2

These food dyes are banned in Norway, Finland, and France. They may cause chromosomal damage. They are found in candy, cereal, soft drinks, sports drinks, and pet foods.

Red Dye #3 and Red Dye #40

Banned in 1990 from use in many foods and cosmetics after eight years of debate, these dyes have been proven to cause thyroid cancer and chromosomal damage in laboratory animals. They may also interfere with brain-nerve transmission. They're found in fruit cocktail, maraschino cherries, cherry pie mix, ice cream, candy, and bakery products.

Yellow #6 and Yellow Tartrazine

Banned in Norway and Sweden, these dyes increase the number of kidney and adrenal gland tumors in laboratory animals. They may cause chromosomal damage. They're found in American cheese, macaroni and cheese, candy, carbonated beverages, and lemonade.

Caramel Coloring

This is very commonly found in sodas, even "healthy" sodas like Zevia. Although the research on caramel coloring is highly controversial, *Consumer Reports*[7] cautions users against consuming this carcinogenic substance. In 2007, a federal government study concluded that a chemical in caramel color caused cancer in mice.[8]

....

Reset Factor Recommendation: Read labels, read labels, read labels. Is the print too small on the label? Get a magnifying app on your phone so you can read it. It's that important! These dyes are nasty and destroy not only your health, but also the health of generations to come.

7. Consumer Reports, "Caramel Color: The Health Risk That May Be in Your Soda," February 10, 2014, http://www.consumerreports.org/cro/news/2014/01/caramel-color-the-health-risk-that-may-be-in-your-soda/index.htm

8. Michael F. Jacobson, "**Carcinogenicity and Regulation of Caramel Colorings,**" *International Journal of Occupational and Environmental Health* 18, **no.** 3 (2012): 254–59.

12. DOUGH CONDITIONERS

Hopefully by now, you've heard about yoga mats being put in your bread from Subway. If not, let me bring you up-to-date. Yes, some food companies used to put a chemical in their breads that softened it and made it chewy—*azodicarbonamide,* a chemical also found in yoga mats. Luckily, awareness of this chemical became so high that companies were forced to take it out.

But they were not forced to take out other harmful chemicals used as dough conditioners. Why would your bread need conditioning? So that food companies can pass off bread as freshly baked, making the bread appear to be perfect every time.

One of the dough conditioners used is an amino acid called L-cysteine. Sounds harmless, right? Well, this amino acid comes from human hair or duck feathers. Makes you want to run out and get a dozen soft hamburger buns, doesn't it? Next time you're downing a muffin or biscuit and it appears to be the perfect chewiness, stop and remind yourself where that chewiness came from.

If that doesn't gross you out, know that several of the dough conditioners below have been linked to asthma, allergies, and cancer. Ingredients to look for include the following:

- Potassium bromate
- Diglyceride
- DATEM
- Azodicarbonamide
- "Dough conditioner"

13. CARRAGEENAN

Ah, good old carrageenan. How I hate you so! Why do I have such disdain for this ingredient? Because you often find it in many "health" foods, especially nut milks and gluten-free items.

Animal studies have repeatedly shown that food-grade carrageenan causes gastrointestinal inflammation and intestinal lesions, ulcerations, and even malignant tumors. According to Dr. Stephen Hanauer, MD, chief gastroenterologist at the University of Chicago School of Medicine, "The rising incidence and prevalence of ulcerative colitis across the globe is correlated with the increased consumption of processed foods, including products containing carrageenan." And Dr.

Andrew Weil, MD, says that all forms of carrageenan cause inflammation and that chronic inflammation is a root cause of many serious diseases, including heart disease, Alzheimer's, Parkinson's, and cancer.

Reset Factor Recommendation: Read labels, especially on dairy and alternative milks. Because it can be hard to find a nut milk that doesn't have this harmful substance in it, Bonnie has included a yummy, easy-to-make RFK Almond Milk recipe in Chapter 11.

14. MONOSODIUM GLUTAMATE (MSG)

MSG is the ultimate flavor enhancer. Most people think of Chinese food when they think of MSG, but unfortunately, this harmful chemical is in many other foods as well.

MSG is a neurotoxin. That means it's toxic to your nervous system, including your brain. This is why side effects of ingesting MSG can be headaches, heart arrhythmias, depression, skin rashes, itching, nausea, vomiting, and even seizures.

It is also linked to obesity. A 2008 study at the University of North Carolina looked at the diets of 752 men and women in China. Eighty percent of them added MSG to their cooking. They found that those who used MSG were three times more likely to be overweight than those who didn't add the neurotoxin to their meal.

So how do you avoid this toxin? Should you stop eating Chinese food? Well, it's not that simple. MSG has many hidden names. The list below (from *The Food Babe Way*) are some of the common names food companies use to hide MSG:

- Glutamic acid
- Glutamate
- Monopotassium glutamate
- Calcium glutamate
- Magnesium glutamate
- Natrium glutamate
- Anything "hydrolyzed"
- Any "hydrolyzed protein"
- Calcium caseinate
- Sodium caseinate
- Yeast extract
- Yeast food
- Yeast nutrient
- Autolyzed yeast
- Gelatin
- Textured protein
- Whey protein
- Whey protein concentrate
- Whey protein isolate
- Soy protein
- Soy protein isolate
- Soy protein concentrate

Reset Factor Recommendation: Well, you probably looked at the list above and thought, *I see those words on every label I read.* Unfortunately, that is often the case—which is why we felt the need to get you all a recipe book. Making your own food, with fresh organic ingredients, is the healthiest way to go.

15. HEAVY METALS AND NEUROTOXINS

One of the greatest insights I had after *The Reset Factor* was released had to do with just how many toxins people had been accumulating over the years. Many of those toxins are heavy metals. There is a direct correlation between how much weight you will release on the 45-Day Reset and how toxic you are. If you find that you only lose a few pounds in the forty-five-day period, you're going to have to look at heavy metal toxicity as a major source of your weight-loss resistance.

What are heavy metals and where do you get them from? The primary heavy metals affecting your health are mercury, aluminum, and lead. These harmful toxins are especially toxic to your pituitary and the hypothalamus in your brain, leading to hormonal imbalances, depression, insomnia, and anxiety. Heavy metals are linked to some of the fastest growing diseases, such as Alzheimer's and dementia. They are also linked to childhood conditions such as autism, ADD, ADHD, and learning difficulties.

Mercury

There are many reasons to minimize your exposure to this heavy metal. According to the World Health Organization (WHO), exposure to mercury can cause serious health effects, including damage to the digestive, nervous, and renal systems. It is a threat to a child and a baby in utero. And it's listed as one of the WHO's top ten most toxic and dangerous chemicals.

There are three areas you get mercury from: your amalgam fillings, fish, and vaccines like the flu shot. To give you some perspective on this harmful toxin, it's recommended that you avoid fish such as tuna because of the large amount of mercury it contains: 210 ppb of mercury, which is definitely one of the highest concentrations in all fish. It is a great idea to minimize your consumption of this fish.

But there is something that has an ever greater concentration of mercury in it: the flu vaccine, which contains 51,000 ppb of mercury in every shot—not to mention aluminum, which has been linked to Alzheimer's. Dr. Hugh Fudenberg, the world's leading immunologist and the thirteenth most quoted biologist of our time (with nearly 850 papers in peer-reviewed journals), says, "If an individual has had five consecutive flu shots between 1970–1980 (the years of the study), his/her chance of developing Alzheimer's disease is ten times greater than if they had one, two, or no vaccinations."

Mercury amounts have not changed since that time, and flu shots are highly encouraged for pregnant women and the elderly. No wonder Alzheimer's and dementia are the fastest growing diseases, now affecting 5.4 million Americans over the age of sixty-five. And it's not just Alzheimer's that is increasing dramatically. As noted earlier in this chapter, autism is predicted to affect one out of two children in the United States within a decade. The controversial link between autism and mercury has been well researched and documented for some time now. Something is damaging the brains of our children and our seniors. A great place to look for a cause is the increase of exposure to these heavy metals.

But this is a book about food, so I want you to know what food sources you need to limit in order to limit your exposure to mercury. The lists below are presented in terms of the amounts of mercury found in different types of fish (high, moderate, and low).

HIGH LEVELS OF MERCURY	MODERATE LEVELS OF MERCURY	LOWEST LEVELS OF MERCURY
Chilean seabass	Bass	Arctic cod
Shark	Carp	Anchovies
Tuna	Cod	Catfish
Orange roughy	Halibut	Clam
Farm-raised salmon	Lobster	Flounder
Blue-claw crab	Mahi mahi	Haddock
Grouper	Snapper	Wild salmon
Marlin	Sea trout	Scallops
Mackerel		Whitefish
		Oysters
		Butterfish

Aluminum

The Agency for Toxic Substances and Disease Registry recognizes aluminum as one of several metals known to affect the neurological system. Research shows that aluminum can produce toxic oxidative stress in the brain. A brain autopsy study done on elderly people found them to have aluminum levels twenty times higher than a middle-aged group.

So where are you getting aluminum? Some sources include the following:

Foods: baking soda, self-rising flour, salt, baby formula, coffee creamers, processed foods, coloring, and caking agents

Cosmetics and personal care products: deodorants, lotions, and shampoos

Drugs: antacids, analgesics, and antidiarrheals

Vaccines: Hepatitis A and B, Hib, DTaP (diphtheria, tetanus, pertussis), pneumococcal vaccine, Gardasil (HPV), and others. Go to the CDC's webpage and search for additives or excipients added to vaccines. You will find the list of toxins added to each vaccine well documented there.

Lead

Did you know that lead gets passed down from your mother and grandmother? In fact, research has shown that lead is passed down through four generations. That means many of you can have lead in your body that you had no control over getting.

The FDA states that exposure to lead, whether from food or any other source, can affect numerous body systems, including the central nervous system, the kidneys, and the immune system. According to the FDA, even at low levels, lead exposure is associated with impaired cognitive function (such as reduced IQ) and behavior difficulties. And as with many other heavy metals, bioaccumulation of lead can lead to learning difficulties, anxiety, depression, insomnia, brain fog, irritability, muscle fatigue, mood disorders, memory loss, and reduction in sperm count.

Where do you and your family get exposed to metals? Any of the following are possible sources:

Your mother. As mentioned above, lead gets passed down through four generations.

Your water supply. Almost everyone has heard about the tragedy in Flint, Michigan, but did you know that there could be dangerous levels of lead in your water as well? California, for example, has some of the highest levels in the country. I typed in my county on the EWG's webpage and found that my water source has been documented to have unsafe levels of lead.

Your food supply. In 2010, the FDA tested thirteen different foods they believed might contain higher-than-normal amounts of lead. These foods were of concern because of the frequency with which children were eating them. The foods they tested contained small levels of lead. Those foods were:

- Candy
- Fruit juice
- Peach slices
- Mixed fruit
- Fruit cocktail

Glyphosate

Here we are back at this harmful chemical. Is glyphosate a heavy metal? No, but many scientists feel that when glyphosate is mixed with heavy metals, it accelerates the damage these metals can do to your brain. In fact, statistics reveal that the number of cases of dementia, ADHD, and autism has grown at the same rate as the increase in the spraying of glyphosate on our foods. Dr. Daniel Pompa, author of the *Cellular Healing Diet* and founder of True Cellular Detox, strongly believes that the usage of glyphosate has magnified the damage heavy metals can do to the human brain.

Reset Factor Recommendation: The subject of heavy metals is complicated and scary to think about. But there are some easy first steps you can take. Avoid foods that are high in these heavy metals. Take steps to improve your immune system naturally so that you don't have to rely on flu shots containing dangerous amounts of mercury. Look for products like aluminum-free baking soda. And once again, the greatest danger for chemical-laden food lies in prepackaged, nonorganic foods. Hopefully, you will be inspired by the recipes in this book and will begin to fall in love with healthy cooking and healthy eating.

If you think you have symptoms from too many heavy metals—such as anxiety, depression, insomnia, chronic fatigue, thyroiditis, or inability to lose weight no matter what you try—you really should get tested. The challenge is that there is only one test that is accurate in determining these levels: a provoked 6-hour urine test by Doctor's Data. (Hair analysis is not an accurate way to test for these metals.) This test should be done under the guidance of a doctor who specializes in heavy metal detox.

Once you have identified the presence of heavy metals in your body, you need to be very careful about how you get them out of your body. An effective heavy metal detox will have a prep phase, a body phase, and a brain phase. And please don't rush out and have your mercury fillings taken out, as there is a safe protocol for doing that as well. I have watched many patients have their regular dentist take mercury fillings out of their mouth, only to have the mercury get reabsorbed in their brain and make their symptoms worse. Reach out to my office and my staff can walk you through how we detox heavy metals. We can also give you a referral to a dentist that is doing this procedure properly.

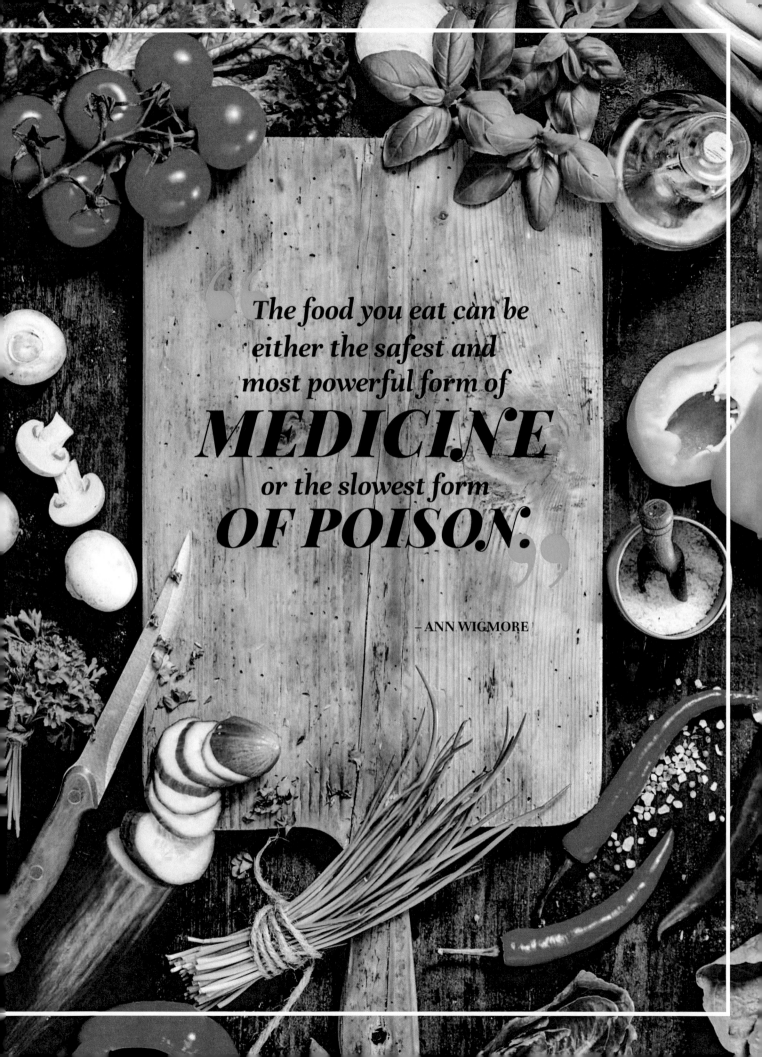

The food you eat can be either the safest and most powerful form of **MEDICINE** *or the slowest form* **OF POISON.**

– ANN WIGMORE

CHAPTER 6

INGREDIENTS THAT WILL BUILD YOUR HEALTH

Now that you know what ingredients to look for that are harming your health, I want to introduce you to some ingredients you may have not heard of yet that will build your health. You'll see that Bonnie has used many of these in her recipes. You'll also soon be reading labels on every food you buy, and you'll begin to see these ingredients as you go shopping for your 45-Day Reset.

In this chapter, I'm going to talk about flours, sweeteners, oils, dairy, and fermented foods—the ones that are good for you!

FLOURS

The 45-Day Reset is a grain-free experience. When *The Reset Factor* came out, the number-one question I got from Resetters was, what flours can I eat? If you're not used to cooking with or eating alternative flours, you'll notice a different texture and taste from the white or whole wheat flours you're used to. Bonnie has done an amazing job putting these flours into recipes that will not only help you succeed with your 45-Day Reset, but will also taste fantastic.

The following flours are the ones we recommend because they're easy to bake with, low on the glycemic index, and easy to find. There are a lot of other grain-free flours out there, but some of them are high in sugar. Remember that the 45-Day Reset is about bringing down your blood sugar levels and pulling you out of weight-loss resistance. These are the best flours to do that.

You'll notice that the glycemic index is listed below each flour. One of the many reasons wheat flour is not a good source of fuel is that it's high on the glycemic index (71).

Almond Flour

Almond flour is highly nutritious, easy to use, and available everywhere. It's also high in protein while low in carbohydrates and sugars. It's great for people with diabetes and those of you looking to lose weight.

Unlike some other wheat-alternative flours, almond flour is moist and delicious. Here are some tips to succeeding at cooking with almond flour:

1. *The finer the grind, the better your baked goods will turn out.*

2. *Nut flours burn easily.* Cook at a lower temperature for a longer period of time.

3. *Buy in bulk.* There are many online stores where you can find these flours.

4. *Buy organic.* Nuts can be sprayed with harmful pesticides.

5. *Almond meal is different from almond flour.* Almond meal has the skins left on and will be denser, with a different consistency from almond flour.

> **Glycemic Index:** 1
> **Carbohydrates:** 19 grams (1 cup)
> **Protein:** 21 grams (1 cup)

Quinoa Flour

Quinoa has recently become popular in the United States as a nutritional powerhouse. When compared to other grains, quinoa has more protein, antioxidants, minerals, and fiber. It is also gluten-free, which makes it a great alternative flour for people who are gluten intolerant.

This flour is an excellent choice for those looking for a more healthful twist on standard baked goods and pan-fried favorites such as breads, pancakes, and waffles. You can substitute this flour for half of the all-purpose flours in many recipes or completely replace wheat flour with it in cakes and cookies.

Most grains don't have all the amino acids needed to make a protein, but quinoa has enough to be considered a complete protein. The dietary fiber found in quinoa is also higher than that found in many other grains. This means that quinoa can be particularly beneficial for people with diabetes.

One study, published in the *Journal of Medicinal Food,* showed that a diet of Peruvian Andean grains, including quinoa, can help manage type 2 diabetes and the high blood pressure often associated with it.[9]

Glycemic Index: 40
Carbohydrate: 23 grams (1/4 cup)
Protein: 4 grams (1/4 cup)

Coconut Flour

This is one of my favorite flours. Not only does it taste great, but it's also low on the glycemic index, which makes it a perfect flour for the 45-Day Reset. Here's what you need to know about coconut flour:

1. *Aids in metabolism.* Coconut flour is high in healthy saturated fats. Remember all those healthy fats I talked about adding to your diet during your 45-Day Reset? Fats are a superior source of energy for your body—and coconut flour has those good fats in it. It will also help you balance your blood sugar, which is great for diabetes.

2. *High in fiber.* The coconut meat itself supplies 61 percent of your daily fiber. The more fiber a food source has, the fewer the calories and carbohydrates will be absorbed from it.

3. *Helps maintain a healthy blood sugar.* Coconut flour is one of the lowest on the glycemic index. This means that when you eat this yummy flour, it won't raise your blood

sugar. This is why coconut flour is such a great fuel source for diabetics. It's also great for people who want to kick themselves out of weight-loss resistance.

4. *Helps heart health.* Because of its high nutrient density, coconut flour has been known to help heart health. Studies have shown that coconut flour has the ability to help lower "bad" LDL cholesterol levels and serum triglycerides.

Glycemic Index: 3
Carbohydrate: 16 grams (1/4 cup)
Protein: 4 grams (1/4 cup)

Garbanzo Bean Flour

Garbanzo beans are also known as chickpeas. Mediterranean diets have been using garbanzo beans for years as a main source of protein. Garbanzo bean flour is a ground-up version of the raw garbanzo bean. This flour is not only gluten-free, but it's also high in protein, iron, and fiber. And it's packed with vitamins and minerals, including calcium, magnesium, B6, and selenium.

I love to recommend this flour to people who are trying to lose weight. Not only is it high in protein, which will help stabilize your blood sugar, but it's packed with the antioxidant selenium. The thyroid needs selenium to help it function normally. If you are deficient in selenium, it can cause your thyroid to become hypoactive.

Other health benefits that garbanzo bean flour may have include the following:

1. *Improves heart health* (lowers cholesterol naturally)

2. *Prevents type 2 diabetes* (stabilizes blood sugar)

3. *Aids in weight loss* (contains high fiber, fills you up faster because of low sugar, and provides key nutrients to the thyroid)

4. *Lowers inflammation* (lowers the body's pH level)

9. Lena Galvez Ranilla et al., "Evaluation of Indigenous Grains from the Peruvian Andean Region for Antidiabetes and Antihypertension Potential Using In Vitro Methods," *Journal of Medicinal Food* 12, no 4 (2009): 704–13. doi:10.1089/jmf.2008.0122

5. *Aids in digestion* (free from gluten and other flours that cause leaky gut and kill healthy gut bacteria)

> **Glycemic Index:** 10
> **Protein:** 6 grams (1/4 cup)
> **Carbohydrates:** 18 grams (1/4 cup)

Sesame Flour

Made from sesame seeds, sesame flour is another great gluten-free flour that won't spike your blood sugar but has a sweet taste to it. Sesame flour has an oily consistency and can help bind flours together. It's especially good for crackers and granola recipes. Sesame seeds themselves have a tremendous amount of nutritional value and have been shown to help by doing the following:

1. *Prevent type 2 diabetes* (high in magnesium and other nutrients)

2. *Lower blood pressure* (high magnesium amounts)

3. *Lower cholesterol* (contain phytosterols that block cholesterol production)

4. *Create healthy skin* (high zinc content helps produce collagen, giving skin more elasticity and repairing damaged body tissues)

5. *Prevent cancer* (contain anticancer compounds, including phytic acid, magnesium, and phytosterols; have the highest phytosterol content of all seeds and nuts)

6. *Help lessen anxiety* (contain stress-relieving minerals such as magnesium and calcium; also contain the calming vitamins thiamin and tryptophan, which help produce serotonin, which reduces pain, assists mood, and helps you get into a deep sleep)

> **Glycemic Index:** 3
> **Protein:** 9 grams (2 tablespoons)
> **Carbohydrates:** 7 grams (2 tablespoons)

Teff

Teff is a flour commonly used in Ethiopia because of its high nutritional content. Bonnie's husband is Ethiopian, so she has been cooking with teff flour for years. She loves to use it as a gluten-free flour for chicken nuggets for her kids because it's packed with so many nutrients. She also finds that when cooking with flours such as almond flour, the consistency can be quite dense, so she adds teff to lighten up the recipe.

There are many health reasons for adding Teff flour into your baking. Here are some of its amazing benefits:

1. *Reduces PMS symptoms* (has the highest calcium content of all the grains, which helps with PMS symptoms)

2. *Improves weight loss results* (One grain of teff is 40 percent resistant starch, which can help you lose weight if you swap out other starches, such as potato starch, for teff.)

3. *Regulate bowel movements* (Teff is packed with fiber and can keep your bowels moving.)

> **Glycemic Index:** 35
> **Protein:** 5 grams (1/4 cup)
> **Carbohydrates:** 29 grams (1/4 cup)

Tiger Nut Flour

The first thing to know about tiger nut is that it's not a nut—it's actually a root vegetable. It also has a very pleasing taste, a little on the sweet side. The greatest thing about tiger nut flour is its prebiotic qualities. This wonderful flour will help colonize the good bacteria in your gut. It's also high in monounsaturated fats. Other health benefits of the tiger nut include the following:

1. *Protects against cancer and cultures a healthy heart* (high in vitamin E)

2. *Helps control diabetes* (high in nonsoluble fiber; helps regulate blood sugar)

3. *Helps control blood pressure* (high in arginine, which helps maintain blood vessel dilation and normal blood flow)

4. *Helps with muscle fatigue, depression, and hormone imbalance* (high source of magnesium)

> **Protein:** 2 grams (1/4 cup)
> **Carbohydrate:** 19 grams (1/4 cup)

SWEETENERS

Another common question we got after *The Reset Factor* came out was, if I have to take sugar out of my diet for forty-five days, what can I replace it with?

Realize that most people's tastebuds change dramatically while on the 45-Day Reset. Many people tell me at the beginning of their Reset journey that they have a sweet tooth, have always had one, and are not sure how they'll handle their sugar cravings. So let's talk about sugar cravings for a moment. You were not born with an addiction to sugar; somewhere along the way in your life, you acquired it. This is great news because if you trained your taste buds to like sweet things, you can start to untrain them.

The other thing to know about your sugar craving is that it's often due to an imbalance in your gut—especially if you have a lot of yeast. One of the ways I know that a patient may have candida is that they tell me they have an uncontrollable craving for sugar. Yeast needs sugar to stay alive. If this is you, know that the reason for these cravings may be due to the yeast in your gut sending a signal to your brain to eat more sugar so it can stay alive and multiply. Once you start your 45-Day Reset, you'll begin to starve the yeast out. Once the yeast amounts have diminished, your cravings will be less.

Stevia

Stevia is derived from a plant. It has no calories and is two hundred times sweeter than sugar. Low-carb diets and the Paleo world caught on to this amazing sugar substitute because it has no effect on your blood sugar at all. This is great news for diabetics and people who are weight-loss resistant. Since stevia is naturally derived, it also doesn't have the dangerous health concerns that artificial sweeteners have.

One fact many people are not aware of is that artificial sweeteners have been known to increase a person's appetite. Yet there is evidence that stevia does nothing to change your appetite or hurt your metabolism. A 2010 study in the journal *Appetite* tested stevia against several artificial sweeteners and sugar itself. They found that people did not overeat after consuming a meal made with stevia as compared to sugar and artificial sweeteners and that their blood sugar and insulin levels were lower after a meal made with stevia.[10]

The downside of stevia is that it is super sweet. Many people struggle to enjoy the taste. The trick to cooking with stevia or buying products with stevia in them is to use very little.

> **Glycemic Index: 0**

Xylitol

Xylitol is another fabulous sweetener made from a plant. It tastes like sugar, but like stevia, it has very little effect on your blood sugar—so it's an excellent alternative to sugar. In fact, its glycemic index is only 7, compared to sugar, which has a glycemic index of 71.

This makes it ideal for people with diabetes, pre-diabetes, obesity, or other metabolic problems.

Although xylitol is yet to be studied in humans, studies on rats have shown it to improve symptoms of diabetes, reduce belly fat, and even prevent weight gain.

Xylitol is not as sweet tasting as stevia, and many people find it better to bake with than stevia. Dentists have been using xylitol for years in chewing gums because it can kill bad bacteria in your mouth and prevent tooth decay.

> **Glycemic Index: 7**

Erythritol

This is an up-and-coming sweetener. More products are starting to use this sweetener because it's not as sweet as stevia but rates very low on the glycemic index.

Erythritol is a natural sweetener, about 60 to 80 percent as sweet as traditional sugar. It is often used in chewing gum, baked goods, chocolates, and beverages. One treat that my kids like is the natural soda Zevia, which I've mentioned in earlier chapters. You can find these sodas everywhere now, and they're sweetened with stevia and erythritol. One of the approved chocolates that I recommend to patients is Lily's chocolates. Made with erythritol or stevia, they have just the right amount of sweetness mixed with the bitterness of chocolate.

---

10. S.D. Anton et al., "Effects of Stevia, Aspartame, and Sucrose on Food Intake, Satiety, and Postprandial Glucose and Insulin Levels," *Appetite* 55, no. 1 (2010): 37–43.

According to some recent studies, erythritol does not change blood sugar or insulin levels when ingested. This is great for diabetics and people who are weight-loss resistant. It has also been shown not to feed bad bacteria in your mouth the way conventional sugar does, which contributes to tooth decay and cavities. This makes it a great choice for your kids.

The only challenge I've found with this sweetener is that it can give you gas when consumed in large doses. Some experts believe that it is damaging to your gut, but I haven't found enough research to support that. Use it in small doses or mix it with other sweeteners if you're going to put it in a recipe.

Glycemic Index: 0

Inulin

Not to be confused with insulin, inulin is a natural sweetener commonly extracted from chicory root. Inulin does a great job when mixed with other sweeteners. It adds sweetness, can caramelize like sugar, and typically doesn't add any aftertaste like other low-glycemic sweeteners can do.

One other benefit of inulin is that it can act like a prebiotic, feeding the good bacteria in your gut. Don't overdo it, though: inulin shouldn't cause you any gastric stress, but it can have a laxative effect if overconsumed.

Glycemic Index: 0

IMPORTANT NOTE

The sugars listed below should be used in moderation. They will spike your blood sugar higher than the ones listed above. I like to recommend the sweeteners below when you are in the maintenance phase of your Reset journey or when you're applying the 80/20 rule.

Bonnie has noticed that her daughter, who has type 1 diabetes, finds the sugars below tastier. She's therefore more willing to eat them. Every carb counts for a diabetic, so the following sugars are still great options.

Coconut Sugar

Coconut sugar is one of our family favorites. It's lower on the glycemic index than regular sugar, but it tastes very much like regular sugar. My kids like to bake a lot, and I found that they were very unsure of and resistant to baking with the above sweeteners. But coconut sugar was easy for them to use and pleased their palates. Coconut sugar is a 1:1 conversion with regular sugar in a recipe. For example, if a recipe calls for one cup of sugar, you can just swap it out for one cup of coconut sugar. This also makes it easy for your kids to use in a baking recipe.

Although coconut sugar tastes similar to regular sugar, there is a lot of controversy about this sugar because of its appearance of being a "health food." To make the right decision for your health, I think it's best to understand what coconut sugar really is.

Coconut sugar is not produced from coconuts. It is actually produced from the sap of the coconut trees, specifically the blossoms. The nectar is taken from the tree in a liquid state and then heated up to evaporate the liquid. The result is granules that are brownish and larger than those you would find in a standard table sugar. The taste is very similar to brown sugar. The challenge is that 70 percent of coconut sugar is identical to table sugar, so that's why I recommend you use it in moderation. I do believe that coconut sugar is a much better option than conventional sugar, but if you're diabetic or trying to lose weight, I would not overuse this sugar.

Glycemic Index: 35

Honey

Honey is another tricky ingredient—and by *tricky*, I mean it appears to be a health food, but it can still damage your blood-sugar levels. There's no doubt that honey is better than conventional sugar. In fact, when you buy the right kind of honey, it can have some tremendous health benefits.

But how do you know what the right kind of honey is? There are two things to look for: you want it in its purest form, so it should be raw and local. *Raw* means they didn't refine it, which would cause your sugar levels to spike. Good honey will say *raw* on the bottle. *Local* is also important because one of the benefits of local honey is that it can help allergies.

Because bees gather nectar from the flowers in your local area, the honey they make helps you build a stronger immune system against local pollens. If you're prone to sneezing during the springtime, a local raw honey is a great immune-boosting food to add into your weekly diet.

Again, be aware that honey does have a higher glycemic index and can keep you in a sugar-burning state, which will slow down your weight-loss progress.

Glycemic Index: 60

Maple Syrup

Maple syrup is derived from the sap of maple trees. For the most part, it's a natural, unrefined product. Compared to conventional refined sugar that offers absolutely no nutrients, maple syrup contains some important antioxidants and minerals, like zinc and manganese. There are also several well-known health benefits to maple syrup:

- Fights inflammatory disease
- Known to help protect against cancer
- Better sugar option for people with digestive conditions
- Mixed with coconut oil, can be beneficial to skin when applied directly

For years, I did a cleanse called the Master Cleanse, which is how I learned about the differences between maple syrups. The Master Cleanse is a detox where all you eat or drink for days is a mixture of freshly squeezed lemon, grade B maple syrup, and cayenne pepper in water. Why Grade B? Grade B is less refined and more packed with nutrients and antioxidants. When using maple syrup in your recipes, the best choice is organic, unrefined, grade B.

Again, be careful not to overdo maple syrup, as it's high on the glycemic index. See http://draxe.com/maple-syrup-nutrition/

Glycemic Index: 54

Dates

You'll start to see a trend here with many of our ingredients. I encourage you to buy fresh, natural, organic, non-altered, nature-made ingredients. By *non-altered*, I mean that not much has been done to the ingredient to change it from its original form. Dates fit well into that category, and they have proven to have many health benefits, including the following:

- Relief from constipation
- Decreased heart problems
- Better sexual function
- Reduced incidence of abdominal cancer
- Dates are rich in several vitamins and minerals, as well as fiber. They contain a large amount of calcium, sulfur (good for stimulating glutathione production), iron, potassium, phosphorous, manganese, copper, and magnesium. Many health specialists feel that eating one date a day is necessary for a balanced and healthy diet.

The downside of dates? They are high on the glycemic index.

Glycemic Index: 18 (1/4 cup)

GOOD OILS

There's no doubt a mental shift takes place when you first read *The Reset Factor* or start your Reset journey. Everything you have been taught about fat is completely wrong. If you're struggling to believe this, just stop and think about it. As a country, we went fat-free decades ago. Yet over the past few decades, have people become more or less obese? Have we seen more or fewer cases of cancer? What about heart disease and diabetes? When you do the research and look at the statistics, you'll see that all of these conditions are on the rise.

Your brain is 60 percent fat; in order for it to work right, it needs you to eat fat. The best way to have sustained energy is to eat more fat; your energy will last longer since fat is a better source of fuel than sugar. In fact, a study in *The Journal of the American Medical Association* recently revealed that a low-fat diet showed the greatest drop in energy expenditure plus increased insulin resistance when compared to a low-carbohydrate and low-glycemic-index diet.

If this is the first time you're hearing that fat is good and that you should eat lots of it, don't worry, you're not alone. It can be hard to begin to implement a healthy high-fat diet, and that's why you'll find lots of recipes in this book that are filled with good fats. We want you to have a large variety of options to get your good fat in.

So let's talk about oils. This is such a powerful place to start making changes in your diet. Pull out ALL harmful oils, like canola, vegetable, sunflower, and safflower oils. In Chapter 5, I listed the bad oils you're most likely to see. These oils will promote inflammation, make you weight-loss resistant, and put you on a fast path to disease. I cannot emphasize enough how important it is for you to stop consuming these oils.

So what oils should you add in? The following is a list of my favorite oils, many of which you'll find in the recipes in this book. Experiment with them. I recommend you throw out your bad oils immediately and replace them with good ones; this is a lateral change that's quite easy to make quickly.

Coconut Oil

If you haven't discovered the magic of coconut oil, now is the time. Studies have shown that coconut oil can be useful in curing and preventing diseases like type 2 diabetes, osteoporosis, mononucleosis, hepatitis C, herpes, biliary tract diseases, Crohn's disease, and cancer. In fact, in a study conducted by Adelaide University in Australia, researchers found that lauric acid, a saturated fat that is one of the main ingredients of coconut oil, was able to destroy 93 percent of colon cancer cells.[11]

Breaking down certain fats can be a complicated process for your body. Long-chain fatty acids like soybean oil take twenty-six steps to break down to use as fuel, whereas medium-chain fatty acids (MCFA) like coconut oils only take six. If you want the benefits that good oils give you, you want to eat as many medium-chain fatty acids as possible. Coconut oil is a fabulous source of MCFA.

Coconut oil is known to:

- Be easier to digest
- Not be stored readily as fat
- Work as an antimicrobial and antifungal (great for candida)
- Be smaller in size, allowing for easier cell permeability for immediate energy
- Build muscle
- Balance hormones
- Burn fat
- Prevent osteoporosis

- Reduce the symptoms of type 2 diabetes
- Prevent gum disease and tooth decay
- Reduce symptoms of gallbladder disease and pancreatitis
- Repair digestive conditions such as ulcers and ulcerative colitis
- Improve memory and brain function
- Improve energy
- Slow down the progression of Alzheimer's and dementia

There are a few things to know about cooking with coconut oil. First, coconut oil is a solid when colder than room temperature. If you put it in your smoothie, it will be a bit clumpy. Once you heat it up, it turns into a liquid. Also, it does have a coconut taste, so consider that when you use it in ingredients. People who really don't like a coconut taste will taste it in foods that have been cooked in coconut oil.

Avocado Oil

Next to coconut oil, avocado oil is the preferred oil in our household. Unlike olive oil, you can heat avocado oil at a high temperature and it won't turn into a bad fat. Avocado oil also has a very similar taste to olive oil, so most of the time, you won't notice any avocado taste when cooking with avocado oil.

Avocados are one of the healthiest foods you can eat.[12] Eating as little as one a week can improve your skin, balance your hormones, improve circulation, and help you lose weight. But the secret of this odd little fruit is in the oil. Here are some of the top health and beauty reasons I recommend you start cooking with this amazing oil:

- Keeps your heart healthy
- Great source of vitamin E
- Improves digestion
- Helps you lose weight
- Detoxifies your body
- Strengthens your skin
- Grows hair faster and fuller
- Reduces inflammation and itching
- Accelerates wound healing

---

11. J. K. Fauser et al., "Induction of Apoptosis by the Medium-Chain Length Fatty Acid Lauric Acid in Colon Cancer Cells due to Induction of Oxidative Stress," *Chemotherapy* 59, no. 3 (2013): 214–224.

12. Mark L. Dreher and Adrienne J. Davenport, "Hass Avocado Composition and Potential Health Effects," *Critical Reviews in Food Science and Nutrition* 53, no. 7 (2013): 738–50.

Avocado oil can cost more than olive oil, but places like Costco now carry large quantities at discounted prices.

Olive Oil

Is it time to give up on this oil? NO! There are still many great benefits to olive oil—you just don't want to heat it. When you heat olive oil over its smoking point (around 200 degrees), it turns into a harmful fat. So the trick with olive oil is to make sure you never heat it that high. This makes it a bad oil to use on anything that would go into the oven. You can use it in a pan on the stovetop, but just make sure you don't heat up the saucepan to the point where visible smoke rises from the olive oil.

The general rule I use is that for anything I cook in a pan or in the oven, I use avocado or coconut oil. For anything that is not heated, like salad dressings and spreads, I use olive oil. Organic extra virgin is the version of olive oil to get. This type of oil is extracted using natural methods and is standardized for purity and qualities like taste and smell. Olive oil that is truly extra virgin has a distinctive taste, and it's also high in phenolic antioxidants—the main reason olive oil is so beneficial. If you buy anything other than extra virgin, you're missing out on those antioxidants. The other important thing to recognize is that refined or "light" olive oils have often been extracted with solvents, treated with heat, or even diluted with cheaper oils like soybean or canola.

The following are some fabulous reasons you don't want to give up on this oil:

- Contains anti-inflammatory substances
- Protects against cardiovascular disease
- Lowers blood pressure
- Lowers LDL levels
- Lowers risk of cancer
- Can clear the plaque that builds up in the brain and contributes to Alzheimer's

Walnut Oil

Walnuts are an excellent source of Omega-3 fatty acids.[13] Although most of the research about walnuts has been done on the nut itself, walnut oil's popularity has grown over the past decade. If you want more variety in taste, this is a great oil to add to your diet. And Bonnie has used it in several of her recipes. Experiment with this oil, as it has many health and beauty benefits you don't want to miss out on, including the following:

- Fights wrinkles
- Helps treat psoriasis (apply topically or add to a bath)
- Great for your hair (fights hair loss, prevents dandruff, promotes hair growth)
- Reduces risk of cardiovascular disease
- Reduces belly fat
- Boosts blood vessels functioning

Walnut oil is best used uncooked, as it becomes bitter when heated.

Sesame Oil

When most people think of sesame oil, they think of Asian food. While sesame oil has a distinctive taste, more pungent than the other oils you cook with, don't count it out, as it has several great health benefits. The most important benefit is that it is packed with vitamin E, which is a powerful antioxidant that protects against heart disease and cancer. Sesame oil also contains magnesium, copper, calcium, iron, and vitamin B6, which are all important for good health.

Grapeseed Oil

When you think of this oil, think reduction of bad cholesterol in the arteries. It has a very light taste and can be used just as you would olive oil. Because it doesn't turn into a bad fat when heated at high temperature, this oil is preferable to olive oil when cooking at higher temperatures.

Flaxseed Oil

This oil comes from the flax plant, which is actually an herb. It's full of omega-3 fatty acids. In fact, flaxseed oil provides the highest concentration of omega-3 fats of any non-fish food. Since most people don't get enough omega-3s in their diet, try to incorporate this oil into your diet in as many ways as you possibly can. Omega-3s lower inflammation, make arteries more flexible, reduce blood clots, and even lessen your chances of a fatal heart attack. But don't heat this oil, as it destroys the omega-3s; in fact, be sure to keep it refrigerated.

---

13 . José Alberto Pereira et al., "Bioactive Properties and Chemical Composition of Six Walnut (Juglans regia L.) Cultivars, *Food and Chemical Toxicology* 46, no 6 (2008): 2103–11.

Pumpkin Seed Oil

Pumpkins aren't just for Halloween. The seeds offer an impressive cocktail of health- enhancing and disease-fighting effects. They are packed with tryptophan and essential fatty acids. Emerging evidence indicates that pumpkin seeds represent a potent functional food in the battle against heart disease, osteoporosis, bladder dysfunction, anxiety, and arthritis. But use this oil in moderation, as it does contain some omega-6 fatty acids, which most people are already getting in excess in their diet.

Hazelnut Oil

When eaten raw, hazelnuts can have a tremendous impact on your health, especially the health of your skin. Hazelnuts are high in catechins and tannins that can tone your skin. They also have astringent properties that can help you battle bad bacteria, both on your skin and in your gut.

Hazelnut oil has a deep distinctive flavor. It is great for spreads and salad dressings. You will see that Bonnie has used this oil in several of her recipes. The fun thing about using a different oil like hazelnut is that it will give your taste buds variety. The more health-enhancing foods you experiment with and enjoy, the more likely you'll be able to make the Reset way of health a lifestyle you can stick to for years to come.

DAIRY AND DAIRY SUBSTITUTES

For many people, understanding which dairy is healthy and which is harmful is confusing. I want to simplify it for you. Here are the basic concepts you need to know.

Pasteurized Dairy

This is what most people are drinking. Pasteurized dairy is a dead food, meaning it has no nutritional value—and it's not even high in calcium. I know this is counter to everything you have been taught. The reason for pasteurizing is to kill all the bacteria that could be present in the milk. When this is done, all the good bacteria and necessary enzymes like lactose are also killed. This makes it very difficult for your body to break down the molecules in dairy. The pasteurization process also increases the sugar content. It kills nutrients such as vitamin C and calcium. Yep, you read that right: pasteurized milk contains no calcium. If you're buying nonorganic pasteurized dairy, you're getting a dose of growth hormone and antibiotics as well.

Without the proper bacteria and enzymes, pasteurized cow dairy is very hard on the human digestive system and can lead to many health problems, such as acne, asthma, arthritis, autoimmune disorders, allergies, antibiotic resistance, osteoporosis, and cancer. I can't emphasize enough how harmful pasteurized milk is for your health, even if it is organic. Pasteurized milk is not recommended on the 45-Day Reset.

Raw Dairy

Raw dairy, on the other hand, is fantastic fuel for your body. Packed with omega-3 fatty acids, enzymes, good bacteria, and calcium, this food will provide great benefits for your body. Most people don't even notice a difference in taste compared to pasteurized dairy.

Numerous studies have documented the benefits of raw milk, and a great resource for more information on this subject is the Weston Price Foundation, a leader in raw milk for decades.

If you want the quick list of reasons to switch to raw dairy, here are just some of the benefits it gives you:

- Healthier skin, hair, and nails
- Stronger immune system
- Reduced allergies
- Increased bone density
- Weight loss
- More lean muscle

If you're having trouble wrapping your head around how you will live without dairy, I highly recommend raw dairy. The hardest part is finding it. You can find raw cheese quite easily, but finding raw milk is a little more challenging. Check out your local farmer's market or google "local raw dairy" and see if there's a food co-op or local farmer that will sell directly to you.

Goat and Sheep Dairy

Goat and sheep dairy are other great alternatives to cow dairy, if you can't find a raw source. Easier on the digestive system, goat's milk and sheep's milk are often better for lactose-intolerant people. These milks contain A2 casein, which the human body breaks down with more ease than the A1 casein found in most cow's milk. The only challenge with goat's milk and sheep's milk is that they are usually pasteurized, making them a dead food. If you can find unpasteurized versions of these milks, that would be the most optimal situation.

Coconut Milk

I'm a fan of anything coconut, one of the best dairy substitutes I know. Coconut milk and coconut water are packed with so many electrolytes that they can actually be used as an IV in the tropics when a person is severely dehydrated. The creamy texture and natural sweetness of coconut milk would make you think it was bad for you—but that's not the case at all. It's considered to be a "miracle liquid" because it has the power to build up the body's immune defenses and prevent disease.

Coconut milk contains the beneficial fat lauric acid, which is a medium-chain fatty acid. Remember how beneficial coconut oil is because of these MCFAs? Well, the same goes for coconut milk. And although coconut milk is primarily a saturated fat, don't expect it to raise your cholesterol levels and cause heart damage—it does the exact opposite. Coconut milk is known to lower blood pressure, lower cholesterol, and prevent heart attacks. Coconut milk is also a great option for lactose-intolerant people—and a great solution for a liquid in your smoothies.

When shopping for coconut milk, be sure to read the ingredients. Just as with nut milks, harmful fillers like carrageenan are sometimes added to coconut milk. A good rule of thumb is to look for your coconut milk in the refrigerated section—you'll most likely find the best coconut milk there. Also, make sure you get the unsweetened version. Added sugars will continue to promote disease in your body, not health. In Chapter 11: Reset Factor Kitchen Pantry, Bonnie has included three different ways for you to make your own coconut milk, which will be cheaper and fresher and ensure that what you're drinking is free from added chemicals.

Nut Milks

Personally, I like nut milks as dairy substitutes because they're packed with protein. The more protein and fat you eat, the more stable your blood sugar will be. There are two nut milks that you will see often: almond and cashew. Both are great alternatives to pasteurized cow dairy.

Most people have no idea that almond milk is more beneficial and nutritious than ordinary milk. It contains more nutrients and is not subjected to the same processing as cow's milk. It is an ideal alternative for those who are lactose intolerant and a much healthier alternative than soy milk. Like coconut milk, it is also surprisingly tasty and creamy.

The main warning I have about almond or cashew milk is to read the ingredients list! If the ingredients list is long or contains words that sound like a chemistry experiment, do your research before you buy it. Carrageenan is a common toxic ingredient you'll find in your nut milks.

This is why we have included several nut milk recipes. Nut milk is surprisingly easy to make and much fresher than the store-bought kind.

FERMENTED FOODS

I want to introduce you to one of the most helpful foods you can eat: fermented foods. You're going to see several recipes in this book for fermented foods, and here's why. Our gut bacteria is made up of literally thousands of different strains of good bacteria. Keeping this bacteria diverse and plentiful is crucial to preventing anxiety and depression, losing weight, killing candida, sleeping well, and having an abundance of energy. When you take a probiotic, at best you get thirty different strains of good bacteria—not a lot. And if you take that probiotic over and over again, you never add to the diversity of your microbiome. This is why I encourage you to try adding fermented foods into your diet.

What's so special about fermented vegetables and foods? Fermentation simply refers to an ancient technique and preservation method that naturally alters the chemistry of foods. The following are my favorite fermented foods:

Sauerkraut

This food is simple to make, tasty to eat, and packed with trillions of good bacteria—a must for anyone who is serious about repairing their gut. Bonnie has included many recipes in here that are great to add to eggs or any meat dish, and she even has a sweet one you can add to quinoa in the morning for breakfast.

Sauerkraut is a fermented cabbage that has been popular throughout central Europe for hundreds of years. It combines one of the healthiest foods there is—cabbage—with one of the most beneficial and time-honored food preparation methods ever used: fermentation.

I kid you not: a daily dose of this cabbage treat will repair your gut quickly and many times better than the strongest probiotic. But before you rush out and grab a jar of Bubbie's sauerkraut, make sure your sauerkraut is unpasteurized.

Water Kefir, *page 222*

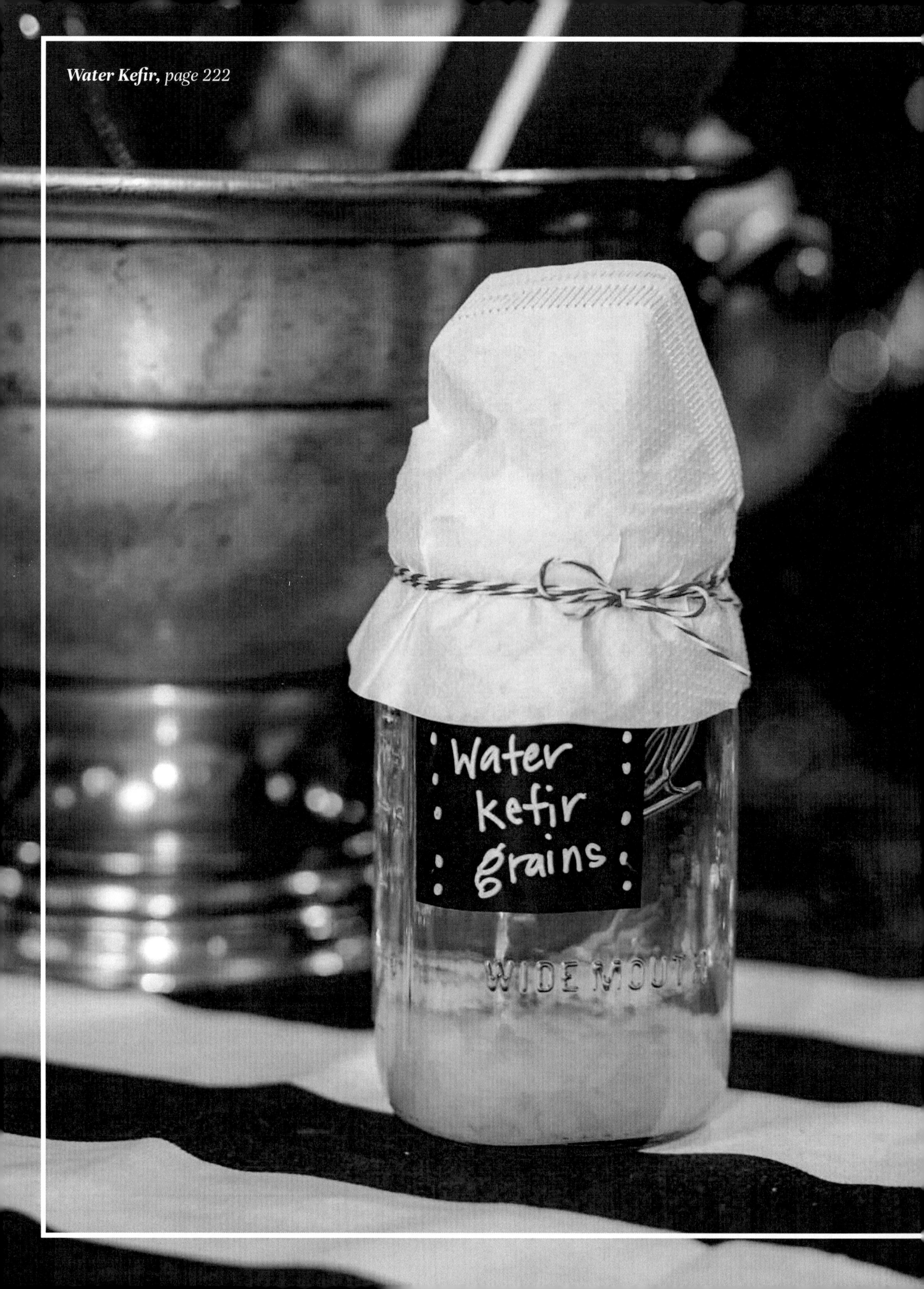

Just as with milk, when you pasteurize sauerkraut, you kill all the good bacteria.

Raw Kefir

Raw kefir is another probiotic-rich food you don't want to miss out on. Kefir is a unique cultured dairy product that is one of the most probiotic-rich foods on the planet. It has incredible medicinal benefits for healing issues like leaky gut. Its unique name comes from the Turkish word *keif,* which means "good feeling." For centuries, it has been used in European and Asian ancient medicine due to the wide variety of conditions it has been known to cure.

Kefir is fermented milk (cow, goat, or sheep milk). It tastes sour like yogurt but goes down more like milk. I like to put it in my smoothies, as it's high in B12, calcium, magnesium, vitamin K2, biotin, folate, enzymes, and of course, probiotics. Kefir is known to do the following:

- Boost immunity
- Heal inflammatory bowel disease
- Improve lactose digestion
- Kill candida
- Build bone density
- Fight allergies
- Support detoxification

It is the perfect food to add into your diet while on the 45-Day Reset. The one thing to be careful about with kefir is to make sure it's raw and has no added sugar. You'll find many yummy kefirs in your local health food store that appear to be healthy, but when you look closer, you'll see that they're packed with sugar and pasteurized, which means all the beneficial probiotics have been killed.

Kombucha

Surely you have heard of this hot new drink—you can find it everywhere. Kombucha is made from a sweetened tea that has been fermented by a symbiotic colony of bacteria and yeast called a SCOBY, or "mother." It's packed with probiotics—not as many as in kefir or sauerkraut, but still a healthy dose of good, diverse bacteria. And although kombucha starts off with yeast and sugar, the finished drink actually contains no yeast and very little sugar. In fact, one of its claims to fame is killing candida.

This "health elixir" has been around for more than two thousand years and has a rich anecdotal history of health benefits, like preventing and fighting cancer and combating arthritis and other degenerative diseases. It's easy to make at home, easy to find in your local supermarket, high in good probiotics, and low in sugar, so it's a perfect complement to your 45-Day Reset.

Here are some of the other things kombucha has a reputation for helping:

- Detoxification
- Joint care
- Digestion and gut health
- Boosting the immune system

What you need to look for when buying kombucha is the sugar content, as some kombucha's are higher in sugar than others. Keep your amount of sugar down, under 5 grams per bottle.

As you try these different recipes, you will be amazed at how your taste buds begin to change and your body begins to crave healthier options. Be open and willing to experiment. When I first tried sauerkraut, I was pretty sure that I would pass on adding it into my regular diet. But after I tried it a few times, my body started craving it.

You may surprise yourself.

CHAPTER 7

ACCELERATING YOUR RESULTS

As strongly as I feel the 45-Day Reset is the fastest path back to health, I also introduce other protocols to some patients to accelerate their results. When it comes to how fast a person can heal, it's important to understand that we've all been exposed to different stressors in our life. We also have different genetics, mixed with different toxic loads. This means that when you reset your health, you may have a different result from others.

I see this all the time with couples who go on the reset together. One will lose thirty pounds while the other loses eight. If this is you—you seem to have fewer results than others—remember you live in a unique body, with a unique set of circumstances. Comparison is not fair and will leave you discouraged. So don't give up! Consider trying some of the following protocols, which I have found helpful to accelerate anyone's results.

WEIGHT-LOSS RESISTANCE

Bottom line: some people lose weight fast and some take a long time. It really depends on how much damage has occurred in your body. We all have a gut, but how we've used that gut and the toxins it has been exposed to are vastly different. So when people embark on a program to reset their health, everyone's progress will vary. If you do the 45-Day Reset and feel you're not dropping weight quickly enough, apply one or both of the following strategies once the reset is over to speed up your results: putting your body into ketosis and/or fasting.

Putting Your Body into Ketosis

As mentioned earlier, our body burns energy from two sources: sugar and fat. If you want to lose weight for good, you need to train your body to burn fat. Getting yourself into a state of *ketosis* is the perfect way to do that.

The goals of ketosis are as follows:

- Switch your body from burning sugar to burning fat.
- Reduce inflammation around your cells.
- Retrain your cells to be sensitive to insulin.
- Improve your brain function.

So how do you get yourself into ketosis? There are three specific ways: lower your carbohydrate intake, increase your good fats, and do intermittent fasting.

1. Lower Your Carbs

The first step to getting into ketosis is to lower your carbohydrate load. You want to keep your carbohydrates under 50 grams per day. For most of you, this is significantly lower than what you've been doing (to give you a reference point, an apple contains 20 grams of carbohydrates). The best way to track your carbohydrate load each day is through an online tracker. My two favorite tools are the apps Carb Manager and Cronometer. If you start entering your food every day into either of these apps, you'll see exactly how many carbs you're getting.

Just tracking your carbs alone will shock you. Most people think they're eating lower carbs on the 45-Day Reset because they no longer eat grains, but carbs add up quickly. This is why I love having my patients track them. There is nothing more frustrating than thinking you're taking all the right steps to lose weight and then not getting results. Keeping your carbs under 50 grams per day is a key step to becoming a fat burner.

2. Increase Good Fats

The second step to getting into ketosis is to increase your good fat significantly. You want your daily fat intake to be 60 to 70 percent of your diet (you read that correctly!)—the hardest part for most people. It's hard for two reasons: first, fat fills you up, and thus, you'll notice you're not hungry; and second, you need to get really creative with how to get your fat in. I recommend to patients something called the 2-2-2 rule. This requirement is to take 2 tablespoons of MCT or organic coconut oil, 2 tablespoons of organic grass-fed butter, and 2 teaspoons of sea salt or Himalayan salt every day. Eating the two fats trains your body to burn fat, and the salt supports your thyroid and speeds up your metabolism. Beyond the 2-2-2 rule, you'll need to eat nut butters, raw nuts, avocados, etc., to get the good fat up in your diet. Bonnie has put into this book some great recipes that make it easier to do this.

One reason I love buttered coffee is that it's a fabulous way to get your good fat levels up. And it's tasty too!

3. Try Intermittent Fasting

The last trick to getting into ketosis is something called intermittent fasting. I wrote about this concept in *The Reset Factor*, but here's the short of it: go fifteen to eighteen hours without food. At first this may seem impossible, but when you do the math, you'll see it's not that hard. Here's how it works. If you stop eating dinner at eight o'clock at night and don't have breakfast until eleven o'clock the next morning, you've gone fifteen hours. You can still have your tea or coffee in the morning, and you can still drink detox water.

I like to have my buttered coffee in the morning and take my high-fat smoothie with me to work. I start drinking it around 11:00 a.m. and then wait until 1:00 p.m. to have my first significant meal.

A good way to measure if you're in ketosis is to get a ketone reader. (I like the Precision ketone reader.) Measure your ketones once a day (morning is usually best). You want your readings to be somewhere between 0.5 and 5.0. It can take several weeks of eating this way to get into ketosis, so don't get discouraged if your first readings are 0.2 or 0.3.

If you're diabetic and concerned about getting your body into ketosis, go back and read the chapter on navigating a nutrition label. What I am referring to above is called nutritional ketosis, not ketoacidosis.

Fasting

Fasting is getting a lot of attention right now—especially in the world of cancer. When you put your body into a fasting state for a short period of time, you signal the release of stem cells, improve hormone sensitivity, unblock receptor sites, and down-regulate inflammation of the cell membrane. What does that all mean to you? It means you heal faster.

One of my favorite fasts, especially for people with gut issues like SIBO and candida, is a bone broth fast. Bone broth has several nutrients that kill bad bacteria and yeast and repair leaky gut. For patients who have chronic fatigue, weight-loss resistance, candida, and hormonal imbalances, a bone broth fast will help immensely.

So how do you go about doing a bone broth fast? My favorite is a four-day bone broth fast followed by three days of probiotic-rich foods and drinks. For four days you drink only bone broth. No food. Water is OK. The fattier the bone broth, the better, so I don't recommend you buy the boxed bone broth you find at your health food store.

There are many online resources where you can get high-quality bone broth. Here are some of my favorites:

- Au Bon Bone
- Bonafide (Whole Foods carries this)
- Arizona Grass Raised Beef Company

Here's what a typical bone broth fast looks like:

Days 1 to 4: Beef Stock Only (NO SUPPLEMENTS)

- Consume at least 8 to 12 cups of broth per day, and more if desired.
- Make sure your bone broth is from grass-fed organic bones.
- Consume no food during the four days of the broth fast.
- Don't consume any gum, coffee, or tea.
- You may drink filtered/reverse-osmosis water—no tap—although you may not need or want to due to your drinking the broth.
- Note: Because you are consuming only liquids, be aware that you will have fewer bowel movements than normal during this phase.
- Begin creating a meal plan for when you end the fast.

Days 5 to 7: Breaking the Fast

- Begin your recommended supplements regimen.
- Start soft foods that are approved on the 15-Day Detox, such as smoothies with unsweetened almond milk or coconut milk, low-sugar fruits like blueberries, and avocados, steamed vegetables, squash, zucchini, and blended vegetables.
- Add to your diet LOTS of fermented vegetables, such as sauerkraut and kimchi.

- Drink 2 cups of sauerkraut juice (like Gut Shot from Farmhouse Cultures).
- Raw kefir in smoothies is also recommended. (Kefir has to be raw, so check labels.)
- Organic tea and coffee can be added.

Day 8 and Beyond

- Follow the 30-Day Habit Reset guidelines in Chapter 3.
- For the next thirty days, continue to stay away from grains, processed foods, sugar, and alcohol.

You have reset your microbiome, killed yeast, and fertilized your gut with lots of great bacteria, so be cautious about what you put into this great new healthy gut you've created. The more probiotic-rich foods you eat and the fewer toxins you put into it over the next thirty days, the more you'll set your results.

What to Expect during Your Fast

It's normal to have detox symptoms, especially during the first three days of this cleanse. The symptoms usually consist of mild to severe headache, fatigue, digestive issues, and skin rashes or breakouts. These symptoms are usually mild, and they disappear as the fast continues. A white tongue is usually present during this cleanse as well.

You may also experience any of the following positive symptoms:

- An increase in energy and focus
- More radiant skin from the collagen of the broth
- Weight loss
- An increased ability to adapt to stress
- Improved digestion
- Less brain fog (more clarity)
- An overall greater sense of well-being

If you feel incredibly weak and dizzy while on this fast, I recommend stopping the fast. Many people are adrenal fatigued, and their bodies can only handle a day or two of the fast. With patients who have this strong reaction, I tell them to try one-day bone broth fasts every two weeks until their body is strong enough to handle a four-day fast.

If you're diabetic, you absolutely need to be coached through this fast. Please consult your doctor before embarking on a fast.

GUT REPAIR

If you want to get well, many of you are going to have to fix your gut. Too many of you have unknowingly destroyed your gut through antibiotic use, years on birth control, and eating genetically modified and processed foods. It's not your fault. You weren't taught that many of these chemicals would destroy your gut. If you're unclear about how the gut plays a role in your overall health, I highly recommend you go back and read *The Reset Factor*. The whole book is about that. Once you see how important gut health is to feeling great, losing weight, getting out of pain, and managing many of the diseases you have been diagnosed with, you can do things differently.

How would you know if your gut was damaged? Testing is by far the best way. One of the tests I frequently run in my office is an organic-acids test. It tells me if a patient has too much bad bacteria or yeast. I've run several hundreds of these tests in the past year alone, and 90 percent of them showed damage to the gut. Something is destroying everyone's gut. The best places to look for the cause are your pantry, refrigerator, and medicine cabinet. Anything you put in your mouth will either build a healthy gut or destroy it.

If you feel that you have severe gut damage, and if it's still present after the 45-Day Reset, then the following are some additional protocols I've used with patients that work well for candida, SIBO, and leaky gut syndrome. You can also find me on social media or call my office to get more one-on-one help with these protocols.

Candida

Bone broth fast — This is one of the fastest ways I know to kill candida and restore gut balance.

Antifungals — There are three supplement brands that I often use to kill candida: Designs for Health, Bioray, and Systemic Formulas. These companies have protocols that will help you kill the yeast in your gut and that are very helpful in making sure you get the right supplements for your condition. So reach out to them. They have doctors on staff who will answer your questions. You can also find the antifungals I use on my website, www.familylifechiropractic.com.

Eliminate harmful foods — If you think you have candida, you need to completely eliminate sugar, bread, beer, and wine. Those foods will feed the yeast and continue to make your condition worse. If you do the above steps to kill candida but continue to eat foods that promote its growth, you will never get ahead of the rapidly growing yeast.

SIBO

Bone broth fast — Once again, this is a fast path to killing bad bacteria. For my patients who have SIBO, I strongly emphasize a three-day probiotic-rich food cleanse. Sauerkraut alone will help you replenish the good bacteria in your gut. Remember, sauerkraut has trillions of good bacteria in it. The best probiotic in the world doesn't even begin to touch that amount of beneficial bacteria.

Aloe shot —This protocol has worked wonders for many of my patients suffering from SIBO. You need to get aloe vera juice or gel and sovereign silver. Put a tablespoon of each in a glass and drink it, three times a day, away from food. Do this for two weeks only. For many people suffering with gut issues, this is a miracle cure.

Leaky Gut Syndrome

This is a major issue for so many people, and they don't even realize it. A great book I encourage you to read about leaky gut is Dr. Josh Axe's *Eat Dirt,* which contains some helpful protocols for healing this condition. I've found the following protocols also help leaky gut:

1. *4-Day bone broth fast* — See a trend here? This is why I love bone broth fasting. It's a powerful way to repair the gut.

2. *Collagen* — One reason I love the 15-Day Detox is that I can get so many great nutrients into a smoothie to heal my body—including collagen. Among my favorite powdered collagens is GI Revive by Designs for Health.

3. *Restore* — This is a new product that has come on the market (restore4life.com) since I wrote *The Reset Factor.* This powerful liquid has proven to repair the microholes that form with a leaky gut condition. I put patients on this product for ninety days, as it takes time to see the results. This is also a product I highly recommend you take before you go out to eat. Most restaurants serve food that is genetically modified. Tightening those microholes before you eat restaurant food is incredibly helpful.

HEAVY METAL DETOX STRATEGIES

In Chapter 5, "Ingredients That Will Destroy Your Health," we addressed heavy metals, which cause serious health problems for many people—although most don't even know it. Weight-loss resistance, depression, anxiety, learning disabilities, insomnia, chronic fatigue, and even chronic pain can all be due to heavy metal toxicity. In my office, we have a four-step process to determine a person's heavy metal and neurotoxicity levels; it involves a neurotoxic questionnaire, a visual test, and two urine tests. Many doctors will do hair tests to determine metal toxicity, but these only tell you what metals your body is trying to get rid of. Urine tests are hands-down the best way to test for metal toxicity.

Once you identify that you have heavy metal toxicity, there is a very specific protocol to follow. It can take months, even years, to detox these metals, and the protocol is far more complicated than I can explain here. But as discussed earlier, the most important thing to know is that there are three phases to detoxing metals: the prep phase, the body phase, and the brain phase. If you're under the guidance of a doctor to help you detox these metals, be sure he or she is doing all three of these phases. Detoxing metals can be dangerous if not done right but life changing if done correctly.

Next to repairing the gut, detoxing metals can be the most rewarding experience. For many of our patients, removing metals is a crucial piece of their health puzzle. Once those metals are removed, their symptoms finally resolve.

ALLERGIES

Allergies are an immune-system issue. The immune system is controlled by two other systems in your body: your nervous system and your gut. If you want to get over your allergies—and you can—you need to fix these two systems. Here are the protocols I use for allergies:

1. *Check the top vertebra (atlas) in your spine.* The upper cervical area of your spine is built differently than the rest of the bones in your body—and there's a reason for that: it's protecting your brainstem. Your brainstem controls respiration, digestion, hormone production, and immunity. If the top vertebra is out of alignment, it will impact those functions. An imbalanced immune system is a common side effect of a misaligned atlas. This will make it harder for you to fight pollens, dust, cat dander, etc. I have seen patients who

have suffered with allergies for years helped tremendously by a chiropractic adjustment. If you have allergies, the chiropractor needs to be your starting point.

2. *Fix your gut.* Once you've had your spine checked, start looking at what you can do to repair your gut. The 45-Day Reset will help tremendously. Staying away from sugar, wheat, and dairy will also make a major difference for you. Increase your probiotic foods, and be sure you're taking a high-quality probiotic that has over 50 billion CFUs.

3. *Increase your vitamin C.* I've found this to work incredibly well. Start by taking 1,000 mg of vitamin C a day. Each day, increase your intake by 1,000 mg. Do that until you begin to notice that you're having loose stools. Once that happens, back down 1,000 mg and stay at that dosage until your allergies subside. I find that most patients who suffer from allergies need somewhere between 3,000 and 5,000 mg of vitamin C per day to help boost their immunity.

CHRONIC FATIGUE

Increased energy is a common result many people get from the 45-Day Reset. But if you are severely adrenal fatigued or have been diagnosed with Epstein Barr Virus (EBV), you'll need to do more than just the 45-Day Reset. Here are my some of the protocols I recommend for chronically fatigued patients.

1. *Don't guess, test.* Everyone gets chronic fatigue for a different reason. For my patients with high EBV counts, most of the time we find a major issue in the gut. Eighty percent of the immune system lives in the gut, so if your gut is damaged, you won't be able to have a strong enough immune response to fight the virus. For people who are adrenal fatigued, the gut is not as crucial a player. Adrenal-fatigued patients have typically overused their adrenals so the adrenals become less efficient. The easiest and cheapest way to test your adrenals is by doing an orthostatic blood pressure reading. Your holistic doctor should know how to do that test. There are also spit tests you can do to help you see just how adrenal fatigued you are.

2. *Repair your gut.* If you have chronic fatigue or EBV, follow my above strategies for gut repair. A bone broth fast followed by a probiotic cleanse is an incredible starting point, even before you do the 45-Day Reset. Several of my patients have gotten their life and energy back just from doing that seven-day protocol.

3. *Stop stimulating your adrenals.* Typically, people who are adrenal fatigued drink more and more coffee or energy drinks to keep up. That is a slippery slope. Resist the urge to increase your caffeine load. When you lack energy, it's hard to imagine giving up coffee completely. A great starting point is to just stop increasing the amounts and work on other strategies, like the next few, to get your energy back.

4. *Get a chiropractic adjustment.* There are many conditions that I think you'd be crazy to try and heal with nutrition only. Adrenal or chronic fatigue is one. The bones of the spine protect the nerves that carry information from your brain to your organs. If there is a misalignment of or damage to these bones, those nerves will get pinched. A pinched nerve doesn't always feel painful. In fact, you have to have 40 percent of a nerve pinched before you notice pain. Whenever I start working on a patient's spine, the most common first result they get is more energy. That's because the brain can begin to see the needs of the body and do a better job at healing injured or depleted areas.

5. *Take an adrenal supplement.* This is another must for adrenal-fatigued patients. There are many good supplements out there that will support your adrenals and give them the nutrients they need. A good adrenal supplement is high in B vitamins, vitamin C, zinc, and selenium—all nutrients your adrenals need to function properly. Glandular supplements with bovine tissue and herbs can also be very helpful. My favorite adrenal supplements are Ga Adrenal Supplement by Systemic Formula and Loving Energy by Bioray. Both have worked wonders for my patients.

6. *Make sleep a priority.* Last, you need sleep to repair your adrenals or to fight EBV. Take naps if you have to. Be sure to get in bed before 10:00 p.m., as our body does its best repairing between 11:00 p.m. and 3:00 a.m. You want to make sure you are in a deep REM sleep by 11:00 p.m. Also, many people feel they can get away with less than seven hours of sleep. I'm here to tell you, you can't. I have researched this topic over and over again, and the bottom line is that the human body needs sleep—and it needs seven to nine hours of sleep a night. If you are chronically fatigued, you have to begin to make sleep a priority or you will never heal.

DIABETES

First, let me state that there is a dramatic difference between type 1 and type 2 diabetes. Having said that, both types of diabetes will benefit from the guidelines set out in the 45-Day Reset. We have had numerous type 2 diabetics whose doctors took them off their Metformin after they followed the Reset protocols. Bonnie will be the first to tell you that stabilizing her daughter's blood sugar became much easier as she started preparing foods with higher fat content and fewer carbohydrates.

The long-term use of insulin can lead to several severe conditions, such as cardiovascular disease, neuropathy, kidney damage, eye damage, foot damage, hearing impairment, and Alzheimer's disease. Minimizing the amount of insulin a diabetic has to take not only helps the body out immediately, but can be a life-saving strategy for the long haul.

Here's what we learned about modifications to the 45-Day Reset that will support diabetics:

1. *More food with your two smoothies.* We have found that many diabetics need to eat a small meal with their smoothie. Bonnie tested several smoothies with her daughter and found that if she also gave her something to chew on, like chicken breast or salad with carrots, it was helpful.

2. *Chromium supplement* (200–400 mcg/day). Chromium is a trace mineral that improves the action of insulin and helps move glucose and other nutrients into the cells. Chromium doesn't cause the body to make more insulin; it just helps insulin work better. At least fifteen well-controlled clinical trials examining the effects of supplemental chromium on patients with diabetes, insulin resistance, and other blood sugar abnormalities have shown that this key mineral improves glucose metabolism.

3. *Magnesium* (500–1000mg). For type 2 diabetics, magnesium has been shown to decrease insulin resistance, helping to keep blood sugars in check.

4. *Vanadium* (50–300mg). One of the most effective supplements for diabetes is vanadium. It has been proven to lower blood sugar by mimicking insulin and improving the cell's sensitivity to insulin. Studies have shown a 20 percent reduction in average fasting blood sugar after taking 50 mg of vanadium twice a day for four weeks.

CANCER

Cancer is a scary and complicated disease. But once you understand how the human body develops cancer, you will see that you have more control over this disease than you think.

There are three things to know about cancer:

1. *A cancer cell was once a healthy cell*; something just attacked it and changed it into an unhealthy cell. That "thing" is normally a toxin.

2. *Ninety-five percent of cancers are due to lifestyle and environment.* This is good and bad news. It's good because if something you did caused it, you can change much of your lifestyle and stop the production of more cells. This is also crucial information if you're worried about getting cancer; only 5 percent of cancers are genetic. If your family members had cancer and you don't want to get cancer, don't live the same lifestyle as they did.

3. *You have to heal the cells if you're going to get well.* There are three things that destroy cells: bad fats, sugar, and toxins. This is why I love the 45-Day Reset — it removes bad fats, lowers your sugar, and begins to remove the toxic load your cells have been under.

If you want to prevent cancer, the principles I teach in the 45-Day Reset and this book are a great guide to doing that. If you have a cancer diagnosis, I have a few recommendations. First, get a book called *The Cancer Killers* by Drs. Charles Majors, Ben Lerner, and Sayer Ji. It has the protocols in it that Dr. Majors used to reverse four brain tumors naturally. Dr. Majors is a personal friend and mentor of mine and an amazing example of how tenacity, persistency, and a well-executed plan can heal you. Another resource I recommend is *The Truth About Cancer* series. There's a website, and you can purchase Ty Bollinger's 11-hour docuseries, which will open your mind to how cancer develops in the first place, why natural treatments for cancer are becoming popular, and why they are extremely effective.

AUTOIMMUNE CONDITIONS

If you have an autoimmune condition, you need to look at healing your gut and detoxifying heavy metals. Autoimmune diagnoses are growing as fast as cancer diagnoses. When we start seeing an upswing in diseases, why don't we ask why? This continues to baffle me. Why is the body attacking itself? What has irritated the immune system so much that it has started attacking the body's own cells?

A great place to start is to look at the immune system itself. From this point forward, whenever you're sick, your allergies flare up, or your immune system feels weak, you need to think about your gut and nervous system. These two systems control your immune system. In fact, 80 percent of the immune system is controlled by the gut alone. Dr. Daniel Pompa, author of *Cellular Detox Diet* and founder of the True Cellular Detox program, says that an autoimmune condition starts with a genetic expression you carry that gets turned on by stressors (physical, emotional, and chemical). Once this gene is turned on, if your gut microbiome is damaged, you won't have enough immune power to turn the gene off.

So how can you help an autoimmune condition? Here are some crucial steps anyone with an autoimmune condition needs to take:

1. *Add fermented foods into your diet.* There are literally trillions of good bacteria in fermented foods such as sauerkraut, kimchi, and raw kefir. Restoring the microbiome of your gut will be a powerful step in turning off the autoimmunity gene that got turned on and restoring balance to your immune system.

2. *Intermittent fasting.* You need to give the gut a break. Lessening the amount of food that goes into the gut will give the gut time to heal. You can reference intermittent fasting in the section above.

3. *Start a daily habit of apple cider vinegar.* Apple cider vinegar will start to kill bad bacteria and create an environment in your gut where the good bacteria in your fermented foods can thrive. I like the detox water recipe that we outline in Part 2.

4. *Bone broth fast.* The ultimate bad bacteria killer. Every person with an autoimmune condition would benefit from a bone broth fast followed by a probiotic cleanse.

5. *True Cellular Detox.* A stressor (a toxin, trauma, or infection) is often a trigger that turns on a gene that initiates an autoimmune condition. Detoxing these stressors and the damage they have created can be crucial in turning off that gene. This is why my patients with autoimmune conditions go through a very thorough detox protocol

called True Cellular Detox. This is another protocol that is hard to explain in this book, but it's important that you know it exists. If you are suffering from an autoimmune condition that is not improving, you need to find a doctor who is trained in True Cellular Detox. You can call my office or go to www.truecelluardetox.com to find a local doctor trained in this protocol.

THYROID

Ah, the thyroid. I have a practice full of people suffering with thyroid conditions. Mark my words, over the next decade, you're going to start hearing of more and more people with thyroid problems—especially Hashimoto's Disease, which is a fancy name for your body attacking its own thyroid. Once again, your attention is best put on discovering *why* your body would attack its own thyroid.

The first thing to understand about the thyroid is that it is the canary in the coal mine. What that means is that when the thyroid starts to malfunction, it's a sign of two imbalances:

- Gut damage
- Toxic overload

You're going to have to repair your gut and pull toxins out of your cells if you want to get your thyroid working well again. The great news is that you can do a lot of things naturally to improve your thyroid function—things that will work quickly. My patients with thyroid conditions do extremely well on the 45-Day Reset, so start there. Once you're past the 15-Day Detox, add in the following:

1. *Iodine.* The thyroid needs iodine to function normally. Most people are deficient in iodine and would benefit greatly from taking an iodine supplement.

2. *Selenium.* This is another crucial nutrient the thyroid needs and most people are greatly lacking.

3. *Heavy metal detox.* Remember how I mentioned that many of you have heavy metals that are destroying your health? A common problem with a malfunctioning thyroid is that it has been exposed to heavy metals. Often, heavy metals get into the bloodstream through a leaky gut and start destroying the thyroid. The receptor sites for cells of the thyroid get blocked, causing thyroid hormones to go out of balance.

4. *Fix your gut.* In some situations, your thyroid is working just fine, but it's your gut that's damaged. Once secreted by your thyroid, your thyroid hormones go into the gut for absorption into the bloodstream. If your gut is damaged, your thyroid can secrete these hormones, but your body won't absorb them properly.

5. *Know your cervical curve.* I mentioned this in *The Reset Factor.* You need to have the proper curve in your cervical spine in order for the proper information to get from your brain to your thyroid. Thousands of patients in my office have seen improvement in their thyroid function when they restore their cervical curves. The only way to know if you have the proper curve in your neck is through an X-ray. Find a local chiropractor and have him or her check your curve.

DEPRESSION AND ANXIETY

Every day I hear a new patient complain about depression and anxiety. There appears to be an epidemic of people starting to suffer from these symptoms. Within the last year, I have noticed a new trend of patients with anxiety, and at younger and younger ages. When trends appear, I start asking myself why. And once again, this issue has led me to the gut.

The gut produces neurotransmitters. A neurotransmitter is a chemical messenger that carries neurological information from one cell to another. Two neurotransmitters you may be familiar with are serotonin and GABA. Serotonin makes you happy and GABA calms you. If your gut is damaged, you will not produce enough of these neurotransmitters, which can contribute to depression and anxiety. Again, the 45-Day Reset is a great starting point for taking the toxic food that destroys your gut out of your system. Along with the 45-Day Reset, here are some areas I would recommend looking at:

1. *Bone-broth fast.* I know I sound like a broken record, but it really works to repair the gut.

2. *5-HTP.* I love this supplement, and my patients have had great results with it. 5-HTP is a precursor to serotonin. Serotonin makes you happy. You cannot get it in food, so you have to get it in supplement form. Since serotonin helps regulate mood and behavior, 5-HTP can have a positive effect on sleep, mood, appetite, and pain sensations.

I hope you find these protocols helpful. If you have a health condition that has been going on for a while, I strongly recommend that you get coaching from someone who is familiar with natural healing. When I use these protocols with my patients, everyone's path back to health is a little different. It's beneficial to have someone to help you navigate through the different phases of healing that your body will go through.

Another important concept to realize is that healing takes time. We have been so misled by the medical community when it comes to how quickly a body can heal from a chronic disease. We have been trained to take a pill and expect results to start happening almost instantaneously. This need for immediate results has left many people frustrated and hopeless.

Seeing results from the above protocols takes time. The more severe your condition, the longer it will take to heal. I tell patients who have chronic conditions to expect it to take six months to a year before your body will feel like it did years ago. In fact, there's a principle in the natural world that says it takes one month of healing for every year a disease has existed. With the right protocols and a good health coach, you will heal. I see patients come back from the worst conditions all the time. So keep the faith!

For a list of all of my favorite products and tests, go to the store page on my office website: www.familylifechiropractic.com.

CHAPTER 8

THE HEALING POWER OF SUPPLEMENTS

I have a lot of strong opinions about supplements — so get ready!

The first thing you need to know about supplements is that it's important to be very specific about which ones you take and why. You need to understand what supplements your body needs, and you need to be clear about the outcome you're hoping to achieve.

There are two ways to figure that out. One is by your symptoms. Now, I warn you—this can be a slippery slope. Many people reach for a supplement recognizing that it could help one of their symptoms. Then they take the supplement and it doesn't "solve" their health problem. So they go on to the next quick-fix supplement, hoping that will do it. And the same thing might happen again.

So what's the problem? There are several reasons a supplement doesn't work. One, you have the wrong supplement for what your body needs. Two, you're not taking a high enough dose. Three, the supplement isn't of high enough quality. And four, your body needs more than just that one supplement to "fix" the problem it's dealing with. Remember, if you want to reset your health properly, you need a multi-therapeutic approach. One supplement is not likely to solve all your health problems.

This leads me to my second point, which you saw in the previous chapter: test, don't guess. This is what I do in my office. I look at patients' symptoms, their health history, and what systems in their body appear not to be working properly—and then I test. I have several urine and blood tests that will tell us if a patient has a hormonal imbalance, heavy metal toxicity, too much yeast in his or her gut, too much bad bacteria, low glutathione levels, vitamin deficiencies, neurotransmitter imbalances, or low antioxidant levels. This makes it really easy for me to be sure patients don't waste their money on the wrong supplement by getting them the exact supplement their body needs to help them feel better.

If you don't have access to that type of testing, don't worry. The second best way to approach your supplements is to follow a proven protocol, like the 15-Day Detox. The supplements used for this program are the ones I know will be most helpful in resetting your health. I have taken much of the guesswork out of it for you; follow the supplements I outlined in the 15-Day Detox chapter closely and you WILL see a result.

As I mentioned before, the supplements I included in the 15-Day Detox were discovered after years of trial and error. These are some of the greatest supplements I know of to reset your health. These supplements are meant to be used during the detox only, but after you finish the bottle, you can determine if you need more based on what symptoms you're still experiencing (or by testing, if you've gone through that process).

This chapter contains details on each of the supplements I recommend for the 15-Day Detox and why. These include probiotics, vitamin D3, turmeric, N-acetyl cysteine, milk thistle, alpha-lipoic acid, omega-3 fatty acids, green chlorophyll superfood, nutrient-rich protein powders, glutathione, and L-glutamine.

PROBIOTICS

Remember that there are trillions of good bacteria in the gut? If you have been exposed to antibiotics, GMO foods, birth control pills, or chemical-laden foods, you may no longer have an abundant supply of good bacteria. Replenishing these bacteria is key to resetting your health. Most people have been exposed to one or more of the above toxins, which is why I have you take a probiotic during your detox.

When picking the right probiotic, you need to look for a few things, including the following:

1. *CFU (colony forming unit) count.* This is usually in the billions. Low doses of CFUs are not very helpful. For the detox, you want a higher dose, somewhere between 50 and 100 billion CFUs. Once the detox is over, typically you can reduce the dosage to 15–25 billion CFUs. Again, it depends on your symptoms and what you're trying to accomplish.

2. *Strains of bacteria.* A good probiotic will tell you how many strains of bacteria it has. The higher the number, the better. I have seen probiotics as high as 30+ strains.

This means there is more diversity of bacteria. Since you have thousands of different strains in your gut, the more diverse, the better.

3. *Rotate your probiotic every ninety days.* Many people take the same probiotic over and over again. You need to vary it. Remember: Diversity is key. I like to switch back and forth between two or three different brands for my patients.

Two frequently asked questions about probiotics are the following:

Can I give them to my kids? Yes! There are lots of powders and small tablets that are perfect for kids. If your child has allergies, anxiety, or skin issues, probiotics are fantastic natural tools to help those conditions.

Do they have to be refrigerated? Not necessarily. It depends on the company. Every company processes its probiotics differently. If you're ordering from a company that is not refrigerating its probiotics, I would ask why and how best to store them.

Recommended dosage: 50 billion CFUs /30+ strains

VITAMIN D3

Vitamin D is one of the maintenance supplements I recommend everyone take for long-term health and prevention of disease. And it's a crucial nutrient you need to help prevent cancer. In fact, having the proper vitamin D level can slash your chances of getting cancer by 77 percent.[14] There are very inexpensive ways to test your vitamin D levels, so getting your levels checked is a great starting point.

Many people ask, can't I just get Vitamin D from the sun? There are several problems with that, including the following three main ones:

1. After the age of thirty, our bodies become less efficient at turning sunlight into vitamin D_3 (the active form of vitamin D).

2. According to the Vitamin D Council, many variables determine whether you get enough vitamin D from the sun: time of day, skin color, amount of skin exposed, how long you expose your skin, and how close you live to the equator. This makes it hard to calculate whether you're getting adequate amounts of the vitamin.

3. If you use sunscreen, you completely block your body's ability to make vitamin D from the sun.

So it's not as easy as just popping into the sun for a while. This is why I highly recommend a vitamin D supplement. Be sure you always get vitamin D_3; it's a more bioactive and usable form of vitamin D, and it's far superior to vitamin D_2.

Recommended dosage: 5,000 IU

TURMERIC

Turmeric is quickly becoming my favorite supplement. Nearly seven thousand peer-reviewed scientific articles have been published evaluating its effectiveness. The secret to turmeric's healing power is a chemical called *curcumin.* Unfortunately, curcumin is poorly absorbed into the bloodstream. There is one way around this: consuming black pepper with your turmeric. Black pepper contains a substance called *piperine* that enhances the absorption of curcumin by 2,000 percent. Here are some of the health benefits turmeric is reported to have:

- Natural anti-inflammatory
- Powerful antioxidant that helps fight cell damage by free radicals
- Improves brain function and lowers risk of brain disease
- Lowers risk of heart disease
- Helps prevent cancer
- Helps arthritis symptoms
- Helps alleviate symptoms of depression

---

14. Joan M. Lappe et al., "Vitamin D and Calcium Supplementation Reduces Cancer Risk: Results of a Randomized Trial," *American Journal of Clinical Nutrition* 85, no. 6 (2007): 1586–91.

Can you see why it's my favorite supplement? I also like nutrients that are easy to find in food, which turmeric is. Check your local health food store for raw organic turmeric. We juice with it in our house and even cut up the root and give it to our dogs. The only challenge with trying to get adequate turmeric from your foods is that you most likely won't get enough of it to reach a therapeutic level. So I still think taking a supplement with black pepper added is the best way to get the reported health benefits. And I often recommend combining higher doses of turmeric with omega-3 fish oil to lower inflammation in the body for people with acute and chronic injuries. I call it my natural Advil.

Recommended dosage: 225 mg

N-ACETYLCYSTEINE (NAC)

Remember the benefits of glutathione that I talked about earlier in this book and in *The Reset Factor*? Well, glutathione is naturally made in the mitochondria of your cells. Its main purpose is to attach to toxins and get them out of you. Unfortunately, if your body has been exposed to a lot of toxins, your glutathione stores are most likely depleted. It's hard for your body to keep up with the toxic demands, so supplementing with glutathione becomes a critical part of resetting your health. But one challenge is that glutathione taken orally is not as effective as glutathione produced naturally by your cells. So I have looked for as many ways as possible for you to stimulate your own glutathione production during your 45-Day Reset.

Adding certain nutrients to your diet will get your cells producing glutathione again. One of those nutrients is N-acetylcysteine (NAC). According to a study done at Stanford University, chronic illness like HIV infections, COPD, chronic infections, metabolic disorders, and genetic defects have severe glutathione deficiencies. NAC has been used successfully to treat those deficiencies and improve the quality of life and well-being of a patient with those conditions.

NAC also has the following benefits:

- Fights flu infections
- Helps fight infections like Helicobacter pylori—the bacterial culprit behind stomach ulcers that has been linked to malignant gastric cancers

- Helps numerous neurological conditions, such as Parkinson's, Alzheimer's, and dementia
- Improves athletic performance by reducing muscle fatigue and improving respiration

Recommended Dosage: Start at 600 mg and work up to 3,000 mg. Take with vitamin C for an added antioxidant effect.

PROTEIN POWDERS

The first thing you have to know about protein powders is that not all protein powders are equal. This is definitely an area where you want to make sure you're getting the highest-quality product possible. In some cases, that may mean you buy the more expensive one; when it comes to protein powders, cheaper often means less effective.

I have found that drinking smoothies is one of the fastest ways to turn your body from a sugar burner to a fat burner. So you'll be drinking a lot of smoothies during your 45-Day Reset, and here are some key things to know about choosing the right protein powder for your smoothies:

1. *Make sure you like the taste of it.* If you don't like the taste of the powder, it will be difficult to drink two smoothies a day during your detox. At first, your willpower will push you through, but my experience has been that after a while, obstacles and distractions will pull you off course. My patients who say, "I love the smoothies," do best with the detox and often ask if they can continue drinking them for a longer period. I want to help you find a way to love your smoothies so that resetting your health is easy. Finding a protein powder that you like the taste of is a good place to start.

2. *Look at the sugar content.* Remember, we're working to stabilize your blood sugar, so you want to take in lower-sugar foods during your 45-Day Reset. Look at the nutrition label on the protein powder you're considering and go straight to the sugar content. You want to see a low number there, like 2 or 3 grams per scoop. Anything higher is too much sugar.

3. *Grass-fed versus plant-based powders.* There are two different styles of protein powders that are suitable for the 45-Day Reset: grass-fed whey and plant protein. Let's look at the pros and cons of each.

Plant Protein Powder

Plant protein powders are a great solution for vegetarians. These usually come from peas or hemp, both of which are great sources of protein. Plant protein powders also usually have added probiotics and enzymes in them, which makes them ideal for repairing the gut.

What you have to look out for with plant proteins is sugar content—especially with pea proteins. Also, make sure all the ingredients are organic. Several popular brands that patients have brought me look as if they have amazing ingredients, but none are organic. I have even reached out to some companies and asked about the organic source of their ingredients; their response is, "We try to buy organic whenever possible." That is code for "No, it's not organic." Be sure you read the labels of any protein powder before you purchase.

Grass-Fed Whey Protein Powder

Grass-fed whey protein powder serves a different purpose for your body from that of plant proteins. The unique quality of grass-fed powder is that it can stimulate your body's own glutathione production. Keeping your glutathione levels high is crucial to the detox process.

But one obstacle you'll encounter with grass-fed whey protein is the quality of the powder. This is definitely a case of cheaper not being better. Make sure you're getting organic whey protein from cows that have not been injected with antibiotics or growth hormones. If it's not mentioned on the label, I highly recommend e-mailing the company and asking. Again, if they give you an ambiguous answer like "most of the time," that means no.

How do you choose which protein powder is best for you? I like my patients to use both. Since you're going to be doing a lot of smoothies during your reset, you want variety. Not only does it help prevent boredom, but you'll also get the probiotic benefit of the plant protein and the glutathione benefit of the whey protein if you use both.

Avoid harmful ingredients. You will quickly see that the 45-Day Reset can become a way of life. Smoothies are a key part of that. If you get the combination right with your smoothie, you can reset your gut, nourish your liver, and turn your body into a fat-burning machine. To make sure that you're not drinking a glass full of chemicals with your smoothies, you'll want to avoid a few harmful ingredients you'll sometimes find in protein powders. These include the following:

Soy Protein Isolate

This is one of the worst ingredients you'll find in a protein powder. An important nutrition concept to know is that nonorganic soy is genetically modified. GMO foods are a fast path to leaky gut syndrome. Since soy is a GMO food, it also means it's sprayed with glyphosate. Glyphosate has been linked to the following:

- Cancer
- Infertility
- Reproductive damage

Soy also contains isoflavones, which can suppress thyroid function. When the thyroid is suppressed, a whole host of problems can happen, including the following:

- Insomnia
- Anxiety and mood swings
- Difficulty losing weight
- Difficulty conceiving a child
- Digestive problems
- Food allergies

The 45-Day Reset is about getting your health back on track. If you were to add this harmful ingredient into your smoothies every day, you would be doing the exact opposite. Be sure to read the ingredients on your protein powders and power bars, and avoid this ingredient at ALL costs.

Whey Protein Isolate

All whey protein isolates are highly processed and devoid of nutritional cofactors, including alkalizing minerals, naturally occurring vitamins, and lipids. This renders them deficient, acidifying, and a liability to your health.

Here are some other reasons you want to stay away from whey protein isolate:

1. Many whey protein isolates add chemicals and detergents to restore flavor. They include genetically modified soy lecithin and chemical surfactants, like polysorbate 80 and propylene glycol, which are used in soap.

2. They can contain hidden sources of MSG, such as malodextrin, hydrolyzed proteins, and caseinates.

3. They have a damaging form of protein in them that is more harmful to your health than rancid bad fats.

4. Many cheap whey protein isolates are produced from acid cheese; they're byproducts of acid processing, which is a cheap way to separate whey from the curd.

5. Most whey protein isolate products are rated below pet foods because of the inferior quality of the protein.

If you're going to use a whey protein powder, be sure it is whey protein *concentrate* from a grass-fed whey source.

MILK THISTLE

Milk thistle has been used for over two thousand years as a tool to detoxify the body. Milk thistle draws out of your body many of the harmful toxins that contribute to cancer, high cholesterol, diabetes, kidney stones, skin damage, and gall bladder disorders. It is as equally powerful an antioxidant as vitamin C and E in slowing the aging process and fighting free-radical damage.

One of the greatest benefits of milk thistle is that it preserves glutathione levels in your body. Poor diet, medications, stress, pesticides, traumas, infections, and pollution all deplete your glutathione levels. You need high levels of glutathione in your body to be able to detoxify properly. Milk thistle helps increase glutathione levels. Milk thistle also strengthens the liver cell walls, buffering them from invading toxins, and it supports liver regeneration. If you want to support your liver and pull toxins out of your body, you need to supplement with milk thistle.

Here are some of the top reasons to take milk thistle:

- Powerful liver detoxifier
- Decreases your risk for cancer
- Can help lower cholesterol
- May help prevent type 2 diabetes
- Helps prevent gallstones
- Slows the aging process
- Boosts skin health

Suggested dosage: 50–425 mg

ALPHA-LIPOIC ACID

Cancer cells are created in your body when free radicals begin to attack healthy cells. Antioxidants like vitamins C and E are crucial for protecting healthy cells from free-radical attack. But other nutrients are also key to protecting your cells from free-radical damage. One of these is alpha-lipoic acid (ALA). ALA helps stabilize the cellular wall, neutralizes free-radical damage, protects the mitochondrial wall, ensures ATP production for energy, regenerates glutathione, and reduces cellular inflammation.

Alpha-lipoic acid has been reported to have the following properties:

- Increases insulin sensitivity
- Works with B-vitamins to help produce energy from proteins, carbohydrates, and fats
- Helps in the treatment of diabetic neuropathy, liver ailments, and glaucoma
- Protects brain and nerve tissue
- Helps reverse symptoms of lupus and rheumatoid arthritis
- Chelates heavy metals

Suggested dosage of alpha-lipoic acid: 50 mg

GREEN SUPERFOOD POWDER WITH CHLOROPHYLL

Here's a general nutrition tip I like to give all my patients: eat greens—and lots of them! There are so many benefits to adding greens into your diet, including the following:

- Increases immune function
- Possesses anti-aging properties
- Improves digestion
- Reduces cravings for sweets
- Improves heart heath
- Alkalizes your body to protect you against cancer
- Decreases inflammation
- Contains antihypertensive properties

Getting greens into the diet is a major challenge for many people. In fact, in a crazy- busy life, it's almost impossible to get enough greens to reap the benefits mentioned above. The

45-Day Reset was meant to be easily implemented into the busiest of lives. This is why I recommend you add a green superfood powder into your smoothies.

When choosing a green powder to add to your smoothies, there are a few key things to look for. First, it needs to be certified organic. The last thing you want is a smoothie full of pesticides. Second, it should not be sweetened with sugar. Most great green powders are sweetened with stevia. Third, the more variety, the better. If you can find a green superfood powder with several nutrient-packed foods—like camu camu, wheat grass, spirulina, chlorella, and blue-green algae—your body will love you.

Chlorella is a key nutrient your green powder should have. Along with slowing the aging process, improving immunity, balancing hormones, and improving circulation, chlorella has a powerful weight-loss component. In a study published in the *Journal of Medicinal Food*, researchers stated, "Chlorella intake resulted in noticeable reductions in body-fat percentage and fasting blood glucose levels." As your body loses weight, toxins are released. It is incredibly important to flush these toxins out of your system as quickly as possible. Chlorella will surround the toxins and heavy metals that get released, facilitating their elimination and preventing reabsorption.

Suggested usage: 1 scoop/day

OMEGA-3 FATTY ACIDS

Did you know that having a deficiency in Omega-3 fatty acids could kill you? According to a study done by Harvard University, Omega-3 fatty acid deficiency is one of the top ten causes of death in America.

Omega-3 fatty acids are crucial for all cell function. The outer membranes of your cells need these essential fats to breathe properly. If you are deficient in omega-3 fatty acids, the cell membrane will become rigid and inflamed. This makes it incredibly difficult for toxins to get out of your cells and nutrients to get into your cells.

Because of their powerful effect on your cells, fish oils have been used by many health professionals to treat the following conditions:

- Heart disease
- ADHD
- Anxiety
- Depression
- High cholesterol
- Inflammatory bowel disease
- Arthritis
- Alzheimer's
- Autoimmune disease
- Macular degeneration
- Eczema
- Diabetes
- Cancer
- Weakened immunity

The other important concept to know about omega-3 fatty acids is that you need to have a good balance between omega-3, -6, and -9 fatty acids. Many Americans' health problems can be traced back to having an imbalance of omega-3 and omega-6 fats. Due to the large amounts of bad fat that most Americans eat, the average American has a 20:1 ratio of omega-6 to omega-3 fats; a healthy ratio is around 2:1.

There are great ways to test your fatty acid balance. In my office, I do a blood spot test that will tell me exactly if you are deficient in omega-3 and high in omega-6, and whether your ratios are out of balance. Knowing these numbers is critical to keeping your cells healthy.

One question I get a lot is, how can I get omega-3 fatty acids into my foods? The following are some great sources of omega-3 and should be incorporated into your daily menus:

- Mackerel
- Oysters
- Herrings
- Cod liver oil
- Sardines
- Anchovies
- Flaxseeds
- Chia seeds
- Walnuts

If you're like me and know that you will struggle to get the above foods into your diet on a routine basis, I highly recommend a supplement. When looking for a high-quality supplement, make sure it's mercury free and/or pharmaceutical grade.

Suggested Usage: 3–5 grams

L-GLUTAMINE

Repairing your leaky gut is a key part of resetting your health. As I have discussed several times throughout this book and in *The Reset Factor*, microholes can form in your gut, leading to a whole host of chronic problems.

It is helpful to stop eating foods that create leaky gut syndrome, like wheat, genetically modified foods, and harmful inflammatory oils. But once you have removed those, you need to make sure you implement strategies that help repair those holes. L-glutamine is one of those nutrients that will begin to heal a leaky gut.

What is L-glutamine? It's an amino acid produced in your body. It makes up 61 percent of your skeletal tissue. It has a powerful repairing effect on musculoskeletal tissue, making it a helpful nutrient to repair the tissue of your intestinal lining. Because of its effectiveness in building muscle, body builders use it a lot to help repair their muscles after an intense workout.

Here are some of the many proven benefits of L-glutamine:

- Assists in muscle growth
- Improves cell hydration, thus reducing recovery time from a workout
- Increases levels of naturally occurring growth hormone
- Repairs mucosal lining of small intestine—especially helpful in diverticulitis, ulcers, and leaky gut syndrome
- Calms your moods, improves mental clarity, and increase alertness

As powerful as L-glutamine is, there is one condition I strongly recommend you don't use L-glutamine with: cancer. Unfortunately, cancer cells use L-glutamine as fuel. If you have a cancer diagnosis, I recommend you use a collagen or bone broth–type supplement to repair your gut, not L-glutamine.

Suggested usage: 3–5 grams

GLUTATHIONE

You already know how I feel about glutathione: it's the most important molecule you need to stay healthy and prevent disease. Yet most people have never even heard of this powerful antioxidant. Many experts believe that your glutathione levels are key to preventing cancer, heart disease, Alzheimer's, and dementia, and to slowing the aging process. More than eighty-nine thousand medical articles have been written about this incredible antioxidant.

The good news is that your body naturally produces glutathione. You may have noticed in the above supplements that key nutrients like milk thistle, N-acetylcysteine, and alpha-lipoic acid help your body produce more glutathione. The bad news is that poor diet, pollution, toxins, medications, stress, trauma, aging, infections, and radiation all deplete your glutathione levels. In this day and age, supplementing with glutathione is a crucial step in helping your liver detoxify.

Glutathione acts like sticky fly paper, clinging to toxins and pulling them out of your system. It is a critical component to helping the immune system do its job and minimizing the damage that can occur from free radicals.

According to Dr. Mark Hyman, MD, author of *Eat Fat, Get Thin*, glutathione deficiencies can be found in people with:

- Chronic fatigue syndrome
- Heart disease
- Cancer
- Chronic infections
- Autoimmune disease
- Diabetes
- Autism
- Alzheimer's
- Parkinson's disease
- Arthritis
- Asthma
- Kidney problems
- Liver disease

MULTIVITAMINS

There are two types of supplements: target and supportive. Target supplements work to get a specific result, such as repairing your gut or detoxing your liver. Many of the supplements I have listed in the 15-Day Detox are target supplements.

But once you've finished detoxing, there are a few supplements I feel your body benefits from taking all the time. A multivitamin is one of those. This is because the fruits and vegetables you're eating today are being grown in soil that's been depleted of vitamins and minerals. Improper farming practices have massively depleted our soils of nutrients. When plants are repeatedly grown on the same land, the soil loses nutrients faster than they can be replaced. Over time, the plants have fewer nutrients to support growth.

Fertilizers contain just enough nutrition for the plant to survive until harvesting, but not enough to support human health. This results in plants that have 75 percent fewer micronutrients. In addition to the lack of nutrients in the plant itself, most fruits and vegetables are not harvested fresh. They sit on trucks, shelves, and counters for weeks before being eaten. Over time, the nutrient content of these plants decreases.[15]

IODINE

Iodine deficiency is an epidemic in this country. Over the last thirty to forty years, our iodine intake has declined 50 percent (it's been removed from our food supply), while the incidence of toxins and halogens such as bromine, fluorine, chlorine, and percholorate has dramatically increased in our food, water, and medicines. When consumed, these halogens block iodine receptor sites and make it impossible for cells to use the little iodine they are exposed to.

Your thyroid needs iodine to function properly. In fact, iodine is so important to the thyroid that even the names of the different thyroid hormones reflect the number of iodine molecules attached: T4 has four attached iodine molecules and T3 has three, showing what an important part iodine plays in thyroid biochemistry.

Iodine has four important functions in the body:
- Stabilization of metabolism and body weight
- Brain development in children
- Fertility
- Optimization of the immune system (iodine is a potent antibacterial, antiparasitic, antiviral, and anticarcinogenic agent)

With the fall in iodine intake, there has been a simultaneous increase in rates of thyroid disease, breast cancer, fibrocystic breast disease, prostate cancer, and obesity.

I hope this helps you understand why I have chosen the above supplements for your 15-Day Detox.

Supplements can be incredibly powerful tools for resetting your health. I know that it can be overwhelming to understand where to start and which ones to take. Start with the above list. These are some of the best nutrients I know to get your health back on track quickly.

Every once in a while, someone asks me if he or she absolutely needs to take the supplements while on the detox. I cannot emphasize enough the power of the supplements I have chosen to add during the 15-Day Detox. They will accelerate your results. When you start giving your body the resources it needs to detoxify, you will heal.

---

15. Dave Asprey, "Why Getting Your Nutrition Only from Food Is a Bad Idea," *Bulletproof*, https://www.bulletproofexec.com/why-you-need-supplements/

CHAPTER 9

HOW TO SUCCEED AT EATING OUT DURING YOUR 45-DAY RESET

I know this seems like a funny topic to have in a cookbook. After all, aren't recipes something you use for cooking and eating at home?

As I mentioned earlier, this book was born out of necessity. When thousands of people went through the 45-Day Reset, we could see the necessity not only for great tasting recipes you could make at home, but also for guidelines for eating out.

Most people find that they don't eat out while doing the 15-Day Detox part of the reset. Remember that the 15-Day Detox is there to turn your health around as quickly as possible. The closer you follow the recommendations laid out in the detox phase, the better the results you'll get. But once you're into the 30-Day Habit Reset part of the program, it gets much easier to eat out—once in a while. When you do eat out, here are my recommendations.

CHOOSE A RESTAURANT WISELY

There are two ways to pick a restaurant: by the number of food options it offers that will help you succeed at the 45-Day Reset and by the number of temptations it has that could pull you away from your healthy path.

My family loves to eat out at a wonderful burger place. I love this restaurant for a variety of reasons. Not only can everyone in my family find food choices they love to eat, but the place also offers several organic and grass-fed meat options. They do a burger wrapped in lettuce instead of a bun. This makes it really easy to find something to eat that tastes great and supports all family members' health.

But there is one thing that destroys me every time at this restaurant: sweet potato fries. I absolutely love sweet potato fries. Although sweet potatoes are allowed on the Reset Program, the oils the restaurant uses in these fries are bad oils. As we discussed earlier, bad oils cause inflammation in your body.

Now I know what you're thinking: one meal, one order of fries — could it really be that harmful? My answer is yes.

If you're trying to change a health condition, you need to follow the 45-Day Reset exactly as it's laid out. One meal with bad oils can cause an immediate inflammatory reaction and can set you back. But once you've completed the 45-Day Reset, one plate of fries won't set you back—as long as you're following the 80/20 rule and you love how your body is functioning and feeling.

So think ahead about what will be on the menu at a restaurant you're going to. Will there be healthy options for you to pick? Will there be temptations you can't overcome? You want to relax and enjoy your meal, not feel guilty because you picked the wrong thing—or worse yet, feel like it's taking all your strength to resist your favorite food.

When I'm following the 15-Day Detox, I avoid our favorite burger joint because I know I don't have enough strength to pass on the sweet potato fries. When I'm following the 80/20 rule, I happily go there with my family.

DECIDE AHEAD OF TIME WHAT YOU'RE GOING TO EAT

Before you even step inside the restaurant, decide what you're going to eat. Even if you don't know the exact menu, most menus have a similar breakdown of food. I walk into a restaurant knowing that I will never eat the bread they put on the table and that I'd rather live in a body that feels great than have the thirty seconds of pleasure a dessert would bring my taste buds. I make the decision to avoid both before I ever set foot in the restaurant—and I'm clear about my decision. I also know that I will most likely choose a food from the salad or entree section, and I know if I will be having a glass of wine or not. The key is to have a plan before you walk in.

One of the reasons people fail at their diets is they don't have a clearly defined path. They try to use willpower to make food choices. Willpower doesn't work—planning ahead does. When you have a clear path and you know what you're going to eat or not eat, it becomes effortless to succeed at health.

BE LASER FOCUSED ON THE MENU

Once you sit down with the menu, be laser focused on it. Don't let your eyes wander and look at all the yummy options others are eating, which your brain will tell you that you must have. Remember your commitment to yourself. Again, the idea is to eat foods that support your health and your commitment to the 45-Day Reset. Typically, the appetizer and dessert sections will have options that can quickly pull you off track. The pasta section is another area that will deplete you of good health.

Get in and get out as fast you can—that's my menu philosophy. The more you linger over a menu, the more temptations will appear and the more your mind will start bargaining with you. Pick your food thoughtfully—food that will support you on your reset path. Then close the menu.

TURN AWAY TEMPTATIONS

I love bread as much as the next person, but I don't love what it does to my body. When I first decided to go grain-free, I did not have enough willpower to let a basket of bread sit on the table and not eat it. So every time a waiter would bring the basket, I would ask him or her to take it away. At first, it was hard; I was sad to see the basket leave my table. But I found it was the only way to ensure that my brain didn't get the best of me and convince me that it was OK to eat the bread "this one time."

Same goes with desserts. I was recently at a restaurant with my staff when our waiter brought us a tray of desserts. The waiter thought he was bringing us this amazing gift and that we would be so happy. He launched into a detailed description of each dessert. I finally had to politely tell him that we weren't interested. The longer he stayed there and the more details he gave us about the sugary treats, the harder it became for us to resist dessert.

Whether they bring the dessert menu or a dessert tray, the sooner you let your servers know you won't be having dessert, the more likely you'll be to stick to the health plan you came in with.

DON'T LEAVE HOME HUNGRY

My last recommendation for eating out is to not leave for the restaurant hungry. What? Isn't that the whole point of eating out? Well, yes and no.

Eating out can be a social event, as well as a time to feed yourself. How many times have you walked into a grocery store hungry and walked out with food you don't normally eat? The same thing happens at a restaurant. If you go in extremely hungry, you're likely to make a bad choice. Your taste buds will make the decision for you, and you won't stick to the plan you committed to before you entered the restaurant.

You don't have to eat a lot before you go—just don't go in famished. Have some raw vegetables, a handful of nuts, or an apple before you leave the house.

HEALTH HAZARDS OF EATING OUT

OK, I'm going to be frank because I don't know any other way to be. Even though I've given you some good suggestions for making eating out healthy, it still poses many dangers to your health—dangers that you have no control over. In fact, my patients who eat out often never get lasting results with their nutritional changes.

There are two main reasons for this. First, most food in America is genetically modified. In *The Reset Factor*, I talk about how harmful genetically modified foods are to your gut. To give you a summary, GMO foods are not only sprayed with glyphosate (which, as we pointed out earlier, is the same chemical used in the weed killer Roundup), but most GMOs also have a toxin in them called BT toxin. When ingested, these two toxins will destroy the lining of your gut and kill healthy bacteria. So unless the restaurant you're eating at says they're organic or non-GMO, you're getting a plate full of glyphosate every time you eat out. You can't control that.

The second reason eating out poses the threat of harm to you is that most restaurants use bad oils to cook with. Very few restaurants are up to speed on good oils versus bad oils. Most restaurants cook with vegetable or canola oil—bad oils—and olive oil. (Remember, olive oil turns to a bad fat when it's heated.)

Here's the challenge I see with patients as they work so hard to reset their health: They do all the right things at home but then eat out, often thinking that they're making smart choices. Then they don't get the health result they want and become frustrated. If you are in a serious health crisis, I highly recommend that you follow the 45-Day Reset exactly as it is laid out and don't eat out for the forty-five days. If you want to prevent disease and feel better than you do now, follow the 80/20 rule. Eighty percent of the time, eat at home, consuming the high-quality foods you know will build you a healthy body. Eat out only twenty percent of the time.

EATING AT A FRIEND'S HOUSE

This issue has come up several times when I'm coaching someone to achieve better health: How the heck do I socialize and go to a friend's house to eat? Some people don't want to draw attention to themselves or create a fuss. I have several recommendations for handling invitations to your friend's house for dinner:

1. Be proud of the changes you're making.

Don't be shy. Let people know why you want to be healthier, what you're experiencing, and how excited you are to be on this journey. Most people will want to know more, and many will even want to join you on the 45-Day Reset.

2. Let the host know ahead of time.

Tell the friend who invited you what you're up to and that you'd love to come over, but tell them that you're on a new health program that has specific guidelines. Offer to bring something; if you bring a food you can eat, you won't be any trouble at all.

My husband and I did this recently. We were invited over to some good friends' house for dinner, but we were one week into our 15-Day Detox. These were friends of ours who have great taste in wine and always serve an amazing meal. So I just let them know ahead of time what our restrictions were. They had no problem with it at all. We even brought several bottles of Kombucha to drink and share instead of wine.

There is no greater joy in life than living in a body that feels fantastic. Everything in your life will flourish when your health is in a great place. I know that some of the advice that I give in this book may seem rigid, but I want you to get to that place where your health is not holding you back from living life to the fullest. If you follow the 45-Day Reset exactly as it is laid out, your body will repair itself. Hang in there, reach out if you need help, and know that as you work these healing principles, over time your health will be reset. Bonnie and I are cheering you on!

Be a trend setter and bring a bottle of homemade kefir water to the next dinner party you are invited to. It's bubbly like champagne and sweet like soda, so adults and kids alike will love it! What a great way to share healthy probiotics with your family and friends!

Who knew that giving the gift of a balanced digestive micro-flora could be so fun?

Second fermentation kefir water flavored with sour cherry & lime elixir (page 203)

THE
RESET FACTOR
KITCHEN

CHAPTER 10

SHOPPING GUIDE

Once you begin to understand which foods you need to avoid and which ones you need to add to your diet, it's time to go to the grocery store. No doubt this can be an overwhelming experience at first—especially when you're reading labels, trying to understand what ingredients mean, and venturing into new places in the store.

This guide is meant to simplify the experience for you.

GENERAL GUIDELINES

Here are some general tips you'll want to follow:

1. Give yourself enough time.

The first time you go looking for your Reset Factor–approved foods, it will take you much longer than a usual trip to the grocery store. Be sure to account for that. The people who have found the 45-Day Reset the easiest are those who planned ahead, got the right food, and were the most prepared.

2. Don't go hungry.

This may be the simplest advice you've ever heard, but going to the grocery store hungry is a recipe for disaster. Not only do you buy more than you need, but you'll be tempted by your old favorite foods.

3. Stick to the perimeter of the store.

If you stop and think about it, every food that is harmful to your health lives on the shelves in the middle of the store. The packaged, chemical-laden foods don't need refrigeration — and they can sit on a shelf for months and not rot. Remember that if a food has a long shelf life, it will shorten yours.

Next time you go to the store, what you're going to do is make a huge U. When you walk in, go to the right or left and stay in the outside aisles of the store. You'll find the foods on the outside of the store are produce, meat, dairy, and anything that needs to be refrigerated. If you're following the 45-Day Reset exactly as it's designed, you'll notice that you only need a few things in those center aisles.

In my office, I do a Reset Dinner for families in my community. At this dinner, I teach this perimeter rule to kids, along with how to read labels. Kids grab onto these concepts easily, so teach your kids.

4. Read labels.

I've mentioned this several times, but it's such an important nutrition concept that I must say it again. You have to read labels to know what is in a food. Get in the habit of looking at the label of every food you put in your cart. One guideline I use with labels is that the longer the list of ingredients, the more likely it has a chemical in it. Sometimes I pick up a food and immediately see a longer-than-normal list; I put it back, knowing that it's most likely a processed food.

5. Buy more food without labels.

The best foods are the ones without a label. These are nature-made foods. One question you can ask yourself when trying to decide if a food is the right choice for you is, Is this food manmade or did nature make it? Foods without labels are always nature made.

6. Look out for tricky labeling.

Don't be pulled into labels that say "low fat," "low carbs," "all natural," or even "gluten- free." Remember, you want chemical-free foods. Even if the front of a package has a catchy phrase that says what you're looking for, be sure to turn it over and read the ingredients.

"Gluten-free" is a great example of this. Just because it says "gluten-free" doesn't mean it's healthy. Since gluten-free has become so popular, more companies are making gluten-free products packed with sugar and other harmful ingredients. I call these foods gluten-free junk food. You want to avoid these.

7. Buy organic.

Yes, organic food can be a little more expensive—but it's worth it. Only when something is labeled certified organic can you be sure that it's free of pesticides and harmful chemicals that have been added to the soil and/or the product.

8. Organic and non-GMO doesn't always mean healthy.

This is the same idea as point #6 above. If a product is organic, that's a great starting point. But other questions I would want to know are: How much sugar is in this item? Does the ingredients list contain words I don't recognize? What kind of oils are used in this food product?

It's exciting when you first start to decipher these labels. Just don't get so excited about a product's being organic that you forget to look at the ingredients.

9. Always be on the lookout for toxic ingredients.

Anything that ends in an -ose is a sugar. Neurotoxic ingredients often appear as "hydrolyzed" or "autolyzed." Hydrogenated or partially hydrogenated oils are a fast path to disease and weight-loss resistance. And artificial ingredients build cancer. You always want to be on the lookout for these.

10. Know your oils.

Oils can be the most frustrating things on labels. You will definitely pick up certain foods and be so excited that they seem to meet all the Reset Rules—and then notice that they contain a bad oil. This happens all the time. And it's frustrating, because the food looks great but the oils are not. This happens with premade hummus a lot. Hummus is a great food to have while on your 45-Day Reset—and there are many tasty options for hummus out there. But when you look closely, most of them have canola oil in them. I have only been able to find one brand that has olive oil (the Hope brand). So be careful about what oils you're putting in your body.

ADDITIVES TO AVOID

The following is a quick list of ingredients you want to avoid. We went into these in great detail in Chapter 5: Ingredients That Will Destroy Your Health, but I want you to have a summary that you can take with you to the store, if necessary.

A great resource for this kind of information is an organization called Maximized Living, which has over four hundred Maximized Living offices throughout America. Maximized Living is a group of wellness doctors who are giving people the tools they need to live healthier lives. Many Maximized Living offices do an event called Shop with the Doc, where the doctor takes you into your local store and teaches you how to find foods that build your health. The list below was adapted from their shopping list. Check out www.maximizedliving.com to find an office local to you.

Artificial Food Coloring —This is found in processed foods, cereals, fruit snacks, drinks, etc. It may contribute to nerve damage, hyperactivity, and learning disabilities, and it also has carcinogenic effects.

Artificial Flavors — This is a "catch-all" phrase that allows companies not to include all ingredients in their lists. It often indicates that the food contains MSG, glutamates, or other additives.

Artificial Sweeteners — These include aspartame (Nutrasweet, Equal) and sucralose (Splenda). They're found frequently in drinks, puddings, yogurt, ice cream, popsicles, etc. Not only are they filled with toxins, but they are also highly chlorinated. Studies show links to impaired brain development and brain damage, nervous system disruption, MS-type symptoms, tremors, seizures, weight gain, etc.

BHA/BHT — These are found in many processed foods containing fats. They are generally used to keep fats from becoming rancid. They have been shown to cause liver and kidney damage, infertility, immune system suppression, cancer, etc. BHT is banned in England.

Canola Oil — Often found in processed foods (including "health foods"), this is a manmade, genetically modified oil made from rapeseed oil. It's processed at very high temperatures and contains trans fats. It inhibits enzymes, suppresses the immune system, and has been linked to kidney, heart, thyroid, and adrenal problems.

Carrageenan — Often found in soy milk and dairy products, it's generally safe but can cause intestinal discomfort. Some studies show it to destroy human cells, especially mammary, intestinal, and prostate cells.

Caramel Coloring — Commonly found in colas, meats, and sauces, it's often produced with ammonia and is shown to cause cancer in the laboratory.

Corn Syrup and High-Fructose Corn Syrup — Found frequently in drinks, condiments, tomato products, breads, cookies, crackers, syrups, etc., these are highly associated with blood sugar issues, depression, fatigue, hyperactivity, tooth decay, weight gain, etc.

Free Glutamates/MSG — These are known brain toxins! They are commonly found in baby formula, low-fat milk, candy, gum, drinks, protein bars, soups, and processed foods. They are always found in autolyzed yeast, calcium caseinate, gelatin, glutamate, glutamic acid, hydrolyzed corn gluten, hydrolyzed protein, hydrolyzed soy protein, monopotassium glutamate, monosodium glutamate, pea protein, plant protein extract, sodium caseinate, textured protein, yeast extract, yeast food, and yeast nutrient. They may also be found in barley malt, bouillon, broth, carrageenan, citric acid, malt extract, malt flavoring, maltodextrin, natural flavors, natural chicken flavoring, natural beef flavoring, pectin, protease, protease enzymes, soy protein, soy protein concentrate, soy protein isolate, soy sauce, stock, whey protein, whey protein concentrate, and whey protein isolate.

Fructose/Dextrose/Sucrose (Sugar) — These may be corn based. They can cause gastrointestinal issues and elevated triglycerides, and they have been shown to be tumor-inducing.

GMO Foods—This term refers to foods that have been altered through genetic engineering. Such foods are contained in many packaged foods and in the produce section. Long-term effects have not been researched enough.

Hydrogenated Vegetable Oils — These include soy, safflower, corn, vegetable, and canola. They are associated with heart disease, cancer, elevated cholesterol, etc.

Maltodextrin — This is sugar, usually corn based, and may contain free glutamates.

Modified Food Starch — This is found in many packaged foods. It is chemically processed and not adequately tested.

Nitrites — These are found in many processed meats and are used to prevent botulism. They are powerful cancer-causing agents (especially pancreatic).

Propylene glycol (a chemical found in antifreeze) — This is found in many drinks, popsicles, etc. Side effects include skin and eye irritation, nervous system disorders, and kidney failure.

Sorbitol — This is often corn-based. It can cause gastrointestinal distress, bloating, diarrhea, and pain. DO NOT GIVE TO CHILDREN.

Soy and Soy Ingredients — These are typically genetically modified. They contain enzyme inhibitors and toxins, and they mimic estrogen. They depress thyroid function and the immune system, and they inhibit mineral absorption. NOTE: Fermented soy products are OK and much healthier.

TBHQ — This is a form of butane (yes, really). Found in many fast foods, especially chicken nuggets, it is highly toxic to humans.

GUIDELINES FOR BUYING THE BEST

Coldwater Fish	Wild Pacific or Alaskan is best.
Small Fish	Anchovies, sardines in olive oil.
Eggs	Eggs from free-range, hormone-free, and antibiotic-free chickens are better than eggs from caged, injected chickens fed organic foods or omega-3s.
Raw Cheese	Packed with enzymes and probiotics, this is your best cheese choice. (Beware of rice and soy alternatives.)
Beef	100% grass fed or green fed—and you must ask! Some farms grain feed the animals "at the end," which is still not desirable. This alters their vitamin E content and fatty acid ratios. Please note that "organic" does NOT mean grass fed. Check with local farms, co-ops, and online sources.
Chicken	Free-range, hormone-free, and antibiotic-free are best. "Free from antibiotics" and "Naturally Raised" are steps in the right direction.
Turkey	Free-range, hormone-free. Look for natural turkey "bacon" without nitrites or sugar.
Whey Protein	Whey from raw milk from a grass-fed cow is best, as it is the least harmful. (Most commercial brands are heated at high temperatures and may contain excitotoxins and/or artificial sweeteners).
Protein Supplement/ Complete Meal Replacement	Avoid commercial soy and whey products. Acceptable plant-based products should either be fermented soy, sprouted rice, or hemp-seed based.
Egg Protein	Great for baking—it can also substitute with or for eggs or egg whites. If not available, use whey protein plus 1 egg (best and most similar-tasting substitute).
Shelled Hemp Seeds	Incredible protein source for salads. Produces a complete meal. 4 tablespoons = 2 grams of protein.
Raw Nuts and Seeds	Look for raw and consider organic. Often available at bulk food stores. Store in the fridge to maintain the integrity of the fats.
Olive Oil, Olives, Grape Seed Oil	Extra virgin is best. EVOO should be in a dark container to block the light.
Coconut Oil	Coconut oil is the ideal oil for cooking, baking, and frying, as it does not denature with high heat. Extra virgin is best; virgin or non-virgin is acceptable for greasing the pan.
Coconut Flakes	Toasted flakes are delicious on a salad or as a snack.
Coconut Flour	Great alternative to grain flour for baking and thickening sauces, and great in smoothies.

Coconut Butter	Not for cooking but for eating!
Coconut Milk	Full-fat coconut milk is thicker than watered-down versions. This is a personal preference.
Flaxseeds, Flaxseed Meal	Ground flax meal is great on salads, in oatmeal, and as a healthy substitute for flour in baking.
Flaxseed Oil, Cod Liver Oil	Do NOT heat!
Hemp Seed Oil	Best ratio of essential fatty acids. Mix into salad dressings, smoothies, oatmeal—everything!
Fish Oil (Supplement)	Look for fish oil that has been formulated to eliminate any contamination. Fish oil with essential fats in the optimal ratio is idea.
Nut Butters (almond, macadamia)	Raw is best but can be difficult to find.
Tahini	Raw is best.
Yogurt	Full-fat, plain, organic. Raw is best, if available. NO SUGAR!
Butter	Organic, grass fed. Raw is best, if available.
Milk	Full-fat, organic is a bare minimum (non-homogenized is even better; non-pasteurized is best if available).
Amasai	Cultured dairy product from A1 casein-free cows, with superior probiotics. Honey and berry flavors are good.
Chocolate (cacao)	Pure chocolate contains no sugar—mix or melt down with stevia and/or cinnamon. Use in yogurt, smoothies, or with nuts/berries for a dessert or snack. Look for 100% chocolate cubes ("baker's chocolate") or chocolate powder.
Vegetables	Organic is best. Veggies with the highest pesticide loads should be bought organic.
Green Drinks	Great substitute for essential veggies if lacking in your diet—and great for kids! Watch out for additives in commercial brands.
Starchy Vegetables	Organic is best.
Beans	Dried, in bulk or in bags—organic is best.
Canned Beans	No salt added is preferred. Look for BPA-free cans.

Refried Beans,	Flavored brands are also available, using healthy spices.
Whole Grains, and Whole Cereals	Must be "whole grain, sprouted, or stone ground."
Whole-Grain Breads, Bagels, English Muffins, etc.	Every grain ingredient on the label must read "whole grain, sprouted, or stone ground." (Must freeze this type of bread.)
Mayonnaise	Most substitutes readily available in grocery stores (including some brands of mayo substitute) are made with canola oil and/or soy products. Grapeseed oil and olive oil–based spreads are acceptable.
Salad Dressings	Most store brands use rancid oils—copy the ingredients and make your own healthy dressings with acceptable replacement ingredients! Hemp seed oil has the ideal ratio of omega-3s and -6s.
Tamari	Fermented soy product, excellent substitute for traditional soy or steak sauce. It's a great wheat-free version of soy sauce.
Marinades	Bragg's Liquid Aminos (or Liquid Soy) is a healthy form of soy—and great for meat.
Herbs and Spices	Herbs in bulk are most economical. Organic spices are best. Look for individual "blends" (Greek Seasoning, Herbs of Provence, and Salad Sprinkles). Gomasio (sesame seeds with garlic, sea salt, and/or seaweed) is also great on salads and veggies.
Salsa	Look for no-sugar salsas. Organic is best.
Tapenade	Also very easy to make at home.
Salt	The words *sea salt* aren't great enough! Generic sea salt may contain 2% additives, including sugar. Check the labels! Some of the best, unrefined sea salts are Celtic sea salt and Himalayan salt. You will see flecks of color in the salt, which indicates the minerals are unprocessed and intact.
Stevia	Look for stevia without unnatural preservatives and additives. Brands come in a variety of tastes and concentrations.
Xylitol	Some people prefer the taste of xylitol over stevia. Be sure to use a xylitol that is derived from birch, not corn, and one that does not contain corn-based additives. Use in small quantities only to avoid digestive distress. No salt added is preferred.
Water	The majority of your fluid consumption should come from water! Check into solutions for getting pure water into your home and body.
Sports Recovery Drinks	These drinks should come from pure sources only and be used pre– and post–"surge-style and endurance workouts." Avoid commercial sports drinks, which contain processed sugar and artificial colorings. A great substitute for sports recovery drinks is coconut water. It is naturally packed with electrolytes.

CHAPTER 11

RESET FACTOR KITCHEN PANTRY

Almond Milk

Coconut Milk – 3 Ways

Cashew Cream

Nut Butter – 4 Ways

Raspberry Chia Jam

Coco-Cacao Bliss

Avocado Garlic Aioli

Un-ketchup

Low-Carb Honey Mustard

Barbeque Sauce

Health Teriyaki Sauce

No-Sugar Pizza Sauce

Bone Broth – 2 Ways

Coconut Sugar Simple Syrup

ALMOND MILK

YIELD: 4 CUPS

CARBS:
8 grams per 8-ounce serving
(Note: Adding more dates increases the carb count by 1.25 grams per serving per date..)

PREP TIME:
Overnight
(soak nuts for 8 to 12 hours)

TOTAL TIME:
Overnight + 10 minutes

INGREDIENTS:

– 1 cup raw almonds,
  soaked overnight

– 3-½ cups filtered water

– ½ teaspoon almond extract

– 3 Medjool dates

OPTIONAL INGREDIENTS:

– 1 whole vanilla bean or 1/2
  teaspoon vanilla extract in place
  of almond extract

– Additional dates (5g carbs each)

DIRECTIONS:

1. Place almonds in a covered glass jar or bowl and fill with 2 to 3 cups of filtered water. Soak overnight (8 to 12 hours) at room temperature to soften them. When the nuts have expanded to 1-1/2 times their original volume, drain and rinse well with filtered water.

2. In a Vitamix or powerful blender, add the almonds (and any optional ingredients you desire) and pulse the nuts so they break up a bit. Add 3-1/3 cups of filtered water and blend, on low speed at first, gradually working your way up to the highest setting and then blending for 1 minute.

3. Over a medium-size bowl, pour the almond mixture into either a nut milk bag (and squeeze the milk out) or a fine-mesh strainer (and press out the nut milk with a spoon). Discard the pulp or save it for added protein and fiber for your smoothies and sauces.

4. Using a funnel, transfer the milk to a sealed container and store in the refrigerator for up to five days. The milk will separate, so shake well before using.

_____

TIPS & TRICKS: *Presoaked almonds will keep in your refrigerator for up to five days, if you want to save time and soak several batches together in advance.*

15-Day Detox Approved (without the dates)/30-Day Habit Reset Approved/Gluten-Free/Diabetic Friendly/Kid Approved

DR. MINDY'S NOTES

One of the major challenges many people face on the 45-Day Reset is finding high- quality almond milk. Most almond milks contain carrageenan, which is toxic. This milk is easy to make and tastes better than any milk I've found in the grocery store. Be adventurous and give this recipe a try. You'll be happy you did!

COCONUT MILK
3 WAYS: CANNED, SHREDDED, AND MANNA

#1. USING CANNED COCONUT

YIELD: **5 1/2 CUPS**

CARBS:
2 grams per 8-ounce serving

PREP TIME:
5 minutes

TOTAL TIME:
5 minutes

INGREDIENTS:

– 4 cups filtered water

– 1 13.5-ounce can coconut milk

DIRECTIONS:

1. Blend in a Vitamix or powerful blender for 1 minute. Serve.

———————

TIPS & TRICKS: *Please choose organic ingredients and cans that are BPA-free.*

#2 USING SHREDDED COCONUT

YIELD: **5 1/2 CUPS**

CARBS:
5 grams per 8-ounce serving

PREP TIME:
5 minutes

TOTAL TIME:
5 minutes

INGREDIENTS:

– 4 cups filtered water

– 2 cups unsweetened shredded coconut

DIRECTIONS:

1. Blend in a Vitamix or powerful blender for 1 minute. Strain and serve.

#3. USING COCONUT MANNA

YIELD: **4 CUPS**

CARBS:
16 grams per 8-ounce serving

PREP TIME:
5 minutes

TOTAL TIME:
5 minutes

INGREDIENTS:

– 3 cups filtered water

– 1 cup manna

DIRECTIONS:

1. Place the jar of coconut manna in a bowl of hot water until it softens (about 15 minutes). When soft, place the manna and water into a Vitamix or powerful blender.

2. Blend for 1 minute. Serve.

———————

TIPS & TRICKS: *To speed up the process of softening the manna, you may want to change the hot water half way through.*

SPECIAL DIET INFORMATION:

15-Day Detox Approved/30-Day Habit Reset Approved/Gluten-Free Diabetic Friendly/Kid Approved

DR. MINDY'S NOTES

This is a great milk option for those of you who have nut allergies or dairy allergies. As you'll see throughout this book, coconuts are healing. We want you using coconuts in as many of your foods as possible. High in saturated fat, coconut nourishes your brain. It's also sweet, so it makes your taste buds happy.

CASHEW CREAM

YIELD: 24 FLUID OUNCES

CARBS:
*4 grams per fluid ounce
equal to 2 tablespoons or 1 ice cube)*

PREP TIME:
Overnight (soak nuts for 8 to 12 hours)

TOTAL TIME:
Overnight + 10 minutes

INGREDIENTS:

- 2-½ cups cashews, soaked overnight
- 3 cups purified water for soaking
- 1-½ cups purified water for blending

OPTIONAL INGREDIENTS:

- 2 tablespoons maple syrup (26g carbs)
- 1-1/2 teaspoons vanilla extract

DIRECTIONS:

1. Using a Vitamix or powerful blender, start with 1/2 cup of water and then gradually thin it out in order to achieve the desired thickness. Mix all ingredients until thick and creamy.

TIPS & TRICKS: *If you choose to add the optional ingredients, keeping the mixture thick and dense will allow you to use this as a fruit topping.*

I like to make this in advance and store it in ice cube trays in the freezer—then it's available for quick use when making soups or other dishes in which I need only a small amount of cashew cream. If you choose to add 2 tablespoons of maple syrup, the carb count will increase 2g carbs per fluid ounce or "ice cube.

SPECIAL DIET INFORMATION:

15-Day Detox Approved (without maple syrup)/30-Day Habit Reset Approved/Gluten-Free/Diabetic Friendly/Kid Approved

DR. MINDY'S NOTES

If you're looking for a rich, sweet-tasting cream, this recipe is for you! This would be great to add to your smoothie for more protein and good fat. If you use this recipe while on the 15-Day Detox, be sure to skip the maple syrup, as it will spike your blood sugar too quickly. You will also notice that this cream is kid approved—so don't be shy to use this cream in smoothies for your kids.

 NUT BUTTER
4 WAYS: ALMOND, PISTACHIO, CASHEW, AND NUT BUTTER OF THE GODS

#1. ALMOND NUT BUTTER YIELD: **2-1/4 CUPS (18 2-TABLESPOON SERVINGS)**

CARBS:
4 grams per 2 tablespoons (1 ounce)

PREP TIME:
30 minutes

TOTAL TIME:
30 minutes

INGREDIENTS:

– 3 cups almonds

OPTIONAL INGREDIENTS:

– 1/4 cup coconut oil (for creaminess when using a Vitamix)

DIRECTIONS — 2 METHODS:

Using a Vitamix (for a chunkier texture):

1. Add almonds and pulse. Use the tamper to keep the almonds moving toward the center of the blade.

2. Once the almonds start to get pulverized, add the coconut oil to help in the blending process.

3. Transfer the almond butter to a sealed glass jar. The nut butter will store in the fridge for up to two weeks.

Using a powerful food processor (for a creamier texture):

1. Using the S-blade of your food processor, place the almonds in the processing bowl. Secure the lid and allow to process for a few minutes, stopping and scraping down the sides as needed throughout the process.

2. The almond butter is ready when the oils have released, and the resulting butter is very smooth and creamy. The more time blending, the smoother the texture will be.

3. Transfer the almond butter to a sealed glass jar. The nut butter will store in the fridge for up to two weeks.

TIPS & TRICKS: *I prefer the chunkier texture of the nut butter made in the Vitamix.*

SPECIAL DIET INFORMATION:

15-Day Detox Approved/30-Day Habit Reset Approved/Gluten-Free/ Diabetic Friendly/Kid Approved

DR. MINDY'S NOTES

Nut butters are fantastic sources of energy, and they also curb your appetite. Packed with protein and good fat, they make incredible snacks. If you add the coconut oil, you will notice that your skin will be moister when you eat this nut butter on a regular basis.

#2. PISTACHIO NUT BUTTER

CARBS:
7 grams per 2-tablespoon serving

PREP TIME:
5 minutes

TOTAL TIME:
5 minutes

INGREDIENTS:

- 3 cups raw pistachios, shelled
- 2 tablespoons coconut oil
- 3 teaspoons orange blossom water
- 2 teaspoons raw honey
- 1/2 teaspoon sea salt
- 1/2 teaspoon ground cinnamon
- 1/8 teaspoon ground cardamom

SPECIAL DIET INFORMATION:

15-Day Approved (without the honey)/30-Day Habit Reset Approved/Gluten-Free/Diabetic Friendly/Kid Approved

DIRECTIONS:

1. In a food processor, add the pistachios and pulse the motor for 3 to 5 minutes until the nuts are finely ground. Add the other ingredients and continue to pulse until fully incorporated.

2. Once you've achieve the desired nut butter consistency, check the flavor to make sure it is to your liking and adjust accordingly.

3. Transfer the pistachio butter to a sealed glass jar. The nut butter will store in the fridge for up to two weeks.

TIPS & TRICKS: *I prefer making this recipe in a food processor because it provides creamier results.*

DR. MINDY'S NOTES

Who doesn't love pistachios? I highly recommend that you find better ways to get more fats into your diet—and this is one of them! The more good fats you eat, the lower your inflammation levels. Good fats nourish your brain and help your body burn fat too. But we don't want you to get burned out eating the same thing over and over, so adding pistachios into your weekly routine is a great idea.

#3. CASHEW NUT BUTTER

CARBS:
10 grams per 2-tablespoon serving

PREP TIME:
10 minutes

TOTAL TIME:
10 minutes

INGREDIENTS:

- 2 cups raw cashews
- 1/4 cup organic coconut oil

TIPS & TRICKS: *This is a great substitute for peanut butter cookies!*
Serve with a nice glass of delicious RFK Almond Milk to make it complete.

SPECIAL DIET INFORMATION:

30-Day Habit Reset Approved (in moderation)/Gluten-Free/Diabetic Friendly/Kid Approved

DIRECTIONS:

1. Using a powerful blender or a Vitamix, blend all ingredients until creamy.

DR. MINDY'S NOTES

Anytime you eat a good fat with sugar, you slow down the absorption of the sugar in your body. This is one of the reasons I love these cookies. With the grass-fed butter and cashew butter, you get a serious dose of good fat. Remember, good fat makes you thin, nourishes your brain, and fills you up. A helpful health tip on this one is to line your baking sheet with parchment paper; aluminum baking sheets can contribute to your heavy metal toxic load, so anytime you bake cookies, be sure to line the sheet with parchment paper to minimize your aluminum exposure.

CONTINUE »

» *NUT BUTTER continued*

#4. NUT BUTTER OF THE GODS

YIELD: 3-1/2 CUPS (2 TABLESPOON SERVINGS)

CARBS:
6 grams per 2-tablespoon serving

PREP TIME:
5 minutes

TOTAL TIME:
25 minutes

INGREDIENTS:

- 2 cups raw almonds
- 1 cup raw cashews
- 1 cup raw pecans
- 1/2 cup coconut oil
- 2 Medjool dates, pitted

DIRECTIONS:

1. Place all ingredients except the coconut oil in a Vitamix. Start pulsing to break the nuts into smaller pieces.

2. Use the plunger to keep the nuts down and moving towards the blades for processing.

3. Add the coconut oil and continue pulsing and using the plunger (take frequent breaks so the engine doesn't overheat). During these breaks, turn the machine off and move the ingredients around in the blades to readjust the mixture.

4. Once the nut butter is the consistency you desire, transfer the nut butter to a sealed glass jar. The nut butter will store in the fridge for up to two weeks.

TIPS & TRICKS: *I like the rougher texture I get when making this recipe in a Vitamix. For a smoother texture, you may want to consider using a food processor, which can require less coconut oil.*

SPECIAL DIET INFORMATION:

15-Day Detox Approved (without the dates)/30-Day Habit Reset Approved/Gluten-Free/Diabetic Friendly/Kid Approved

DR. MINDY'S NOTES

This is my favorite nut butter recipe, hands-down! If you're trying to decide which of these nut butters to make first, I recommend trying this one. If you are on your 15-Day Detox, skip the dates. This butter makes a great snack when spread on green apples.

RASPBERRY CHIA JAM

YIELD: ABOUT 1 CUP (16 1-TABLESPOON SERVINGS)

CARBS:
5 grams per 1-tablespoon serving (1/2 ounce)

PREP TIME:
2 minutes

TOTAL TIME:
2 minutes + 10 minutes wait time

INGREDIENTS:

- 10 tablespoons RFK Just Raspberry Syrup
- 3 tablespoons chia seeds

DIRECTIONS:

1. Mix raspberry syrup/puree and chia seeds in a small storage container.

2. Let rest for 10 minutes.

3. It's ready to enjoy!

TIPS & TRICKS: *I love this recipe! It's like magic!*

SPECIAL DIET INFORMATION:

15-Day Detox Approved/30-Day Habit Reset Approved/Gluten-Free/ Diabetic Friendly/Kid Approved

DR. MINDY'S NOTES

This recipe will blow your mind—you'll think you're eating a sugary jam! Chia seeds have so many beneficial qualities. They are gelatinous, which means that they hook on to toxins in your body. Plus, they're one of the most antioxidant-rich foods you can eat. Spread this on the waffle recipe from Chapter 12—your kids will love it! I also like to take a spoonful of nut butter with this jam on top to satisfy my sweet tooth.

COCO-CACAO BLISS
HEALTHY NUTELLA ALTERNATIVE

YIELD: 17 OUNCES (34 1-TABLESPOON SERVINGS)

CARBS:	PREP TIME:	TOTAL TIME:
3.5 grams per 1-tablespoon serving	*30 minutes*	*35 minutes*

INGREDIENTS:

– 15 ounces coconut manna

– 5 tablespoons raw cacao powder

– 2 teaspoons raw honey

DIRECTIONS:

1. Warm the coconut manna in hot water for about 15 to 20 minutes to melt. (Make sure no water gets into the jar.)

2. Pour manna into a medium-size bowl and stir in the cacao powder and honey until fully integrated.

3. Pour mixture back into the original manna jar or a decorative storage container of your choice. Allow the recipe to cool to room temperature for a few hours before putting the lid back on.

4. This can stay unrefrigerated for a couple of weeks in a cool pantry.

5. Enjoy as you would store-bought Nutella.

SPECIAL DIET INFORMATION:

15-Day Detox Approved (without the honey)/30-Day Habit Reset Approved/Gluten-Free/Diabetic Friendly/Kid Approved

DR. MINDY'S NOTES

I don't know about you, but if I were to put a jar of Nutella in front of my kids, they would down the whole jar. But the Nutella you find in the store is packed with high-fructose corn syrup and other harmful ingredients. So this fabulous treat makes a great substitute for Nutella. We purposely tested many of the recipes in this book on our kids to see if they were as good as we had hoped. This one was a winner!

AVOCADO GARLIC AIOLI

YIELD: APPROXIMATELY 3-1/2 CUPS (28 2-TABLESPOON SERVINGS)

CARBS:
0 grams per 2-tablespoon serving

PREP TIME:
30 minutes

TOTAL TIME:
30 minutes

INGREDIENTS:

- 6 cloves garlic, crushed
- 4 eggs, room temperature
- 3 cups avocado oil
- Juice from one lemon
- 1 teaspoon sea salt
- 1 teaspoon Dijon mustard
- 1-1/2 teaspoon dry mustard

DIRECTIONS:

1. In a blender, combine garlic and eggs until mixture is smooth.

2. Add Dijon mustard and dry mustard and incorporate into mixture.

3. Add 1/4 cup avocado oil and blend until it emulsifies. Add oil 1/4 cup at a time, three more times. Once emulsification has clearly taken, the rest of the oil can be slowly added while the blender is on. Season with salt and lemon juice to taste.

TIPS & TRICKS: *The emulsification process works best if all ingredients are at room temperature. It might sound counterintuitive, but if it's not thick enough, add more oil and keep blending.*

SPECIAL DIET INFORMATION:

15-Day Detox Approved/30-Day Habit Reset Approved/Gluten-free/ Diabetic Friendly

DR. MINDY'S NOTES

Missing sandwiches? Here's a great spread to put on sandwiches so you can bring them back into your diet. (Check out the RFK Gone-Nuts Loaf for one of the best grain-free breads I have ever tasted.) Spread this yummy aioli sauce on a piece of RFK Gone-Nuts Loaf and put some sliced turkey on it and perhaps a slice of raw cheese. Add some microgreens and you have an amazing-tasting sandwich that will build your health.

Un-Ketchup (left) and Barbecue sauce (right)

UN-KETCHUP

YIELD: APPROXIMATELY 3-1/4 CUPS (52 1-TABLESPOON SERVINGS)

CARBS:	**PREP TIME:**	**TOTAL TIME:**
2.5 grams per 1-tablespoon serving	*5 minutes*	*25 minutes*

INGREDIENTS:

– 12 ounces tomato paste

– 1/4 cup raw honey

– 3/4 cup apple cider vinegar

– 3/4 cup water

– 1 teaspoon sea salt

– 1/2 teaspoon onion powder

SPECIAL DIET INFORMATION:

30-Day Habit Reset/Gluten-Free/
Diabetic Friendly

DIRECTIONS:

1. In a saucepan, whisk together all ingredients until smooth.

2. Over medium heat, let the mixture come to a slight boil.

3. Reduce heat and simmer for 10 to 15 minutes so flavors meld together. Turn off the heat and cool. Transfer to a glass container. Refrigerate.

TIPS & TRICKS: *This Un-ketchup will last for several weeks.*

DR. MINDY'S NOTES

When Bonnie first started learning how to cook for her family the Reset Factor way, she kept mentioning how hard it was to find some staple pantry items, like ketchup, without sugar. As I mentioned, this book was created out of necessity. One of the first recipes she wanted to master was ketchup. Not only is this recipe healthy, but it tastes better than most ketchups I've tried.

BARBECUE SAUCE

YIELD: 6 CUPS (48 2-TABLESPOON SERVINGS)

CARBS:
4 grams per 2-tablespoon serving

PREP TIME:
10 minutes

TOTAL TIME:
20 minutes

INGREDIENTS:

- 24 ounces tomato paste
- 1-1/4 cups balsamic vinegar
- 1/4 cup apple cider vinegar
- 12 whole chipotle peppers in adobo sauce
- 3 cloves garlic, crushed
- 2 tablespoons maple syrup
- 2 tablespoons Dijon mustard
- 1-1/2 teaspoons ground cardamom
- 1 teaspoon ground ginger
- 3-1/2 teaspoons ground cumin
- 1 teaspoon sea salt
- 1 teaspoon ground pepper
- 1-1/2 cups water
- 3 gloves garlic, crushed

DIRECTIONS:

1. In a Vitamix or powerful blender, blend all ingredients with a few pulses and then pour the mixture into a medium saucepan.

2. Place on the stove and simmer for ten minutes, then set aside to cool. Store in a glass container in the refrigerator.

TIPS & TRICKS: *This sauce can keep in the refrigerator for up to thirty days. It's important not to skip the cooking, because this is when the flavors all blend together.*

SPECIAL DIET INFORMATION:

15-Day Detox Approved (without the maple syrup)/30-Day Habit Reset Approved/Gluten- Free/Diabetic Friendly

DR. MINDY'S NOTES

Finding a healthy barbecue sauce is nearly impossible. So we put Bonnie on the job of creating one that was easy to make, tastes great, and fits all the requirements of The Reset Factor. She knocked it out of the park with this one!

Honey Mustard (left) and Avocado Garlic Aiol (right, page 99)

LOW-CARB HONEY MUSTARD

YIELD: 5 CUPS

CARBS:	**PREP TIME:**	**TOTAL TIME:**
Approximately 1/2 gram per teaspoon	5 minutes	15 minutes

INGREDIENTS:

- 2 cups erythritol
- 1-1/2 cups dry mustard
- 2 cups apple cider vinegar
- 3 large eggs, beaten
- 1/2 cup honey

DIRECTIONS:

1. In a medium-size saucepan, whisk the erythritol and mustard together, gradually adding in the vinegar and eggs until fully blended.

2. Cook the mustard over medium heat, whisking constantly, for 12 to 15 minutes or until thick and smooth. Remove from heat and whisk in the honey. Let cool and store in a glass container.

TIPS & TRICKS: *Honey mustard is one of our families favorite condiments, but it's traditionally packed with sugar. This recipe substitutes erythritol for the sugar because it's a 0 on the glycemic index and it tastes even better than the store-bought versions! This mustard can keep in the refrigerator for up to 30 days.*

SPECIAL DIET INFORMATION:

15-Day Detox Approved/30-Day Habit Reset Approved/Gluten-Free/ Diabetic Friendly

DR. MINDY'S NOTES

Bonnie has come up with another amazing staple for your pantry with this mustard. If you start reading labels, you'll see that some of the most harmful ingredients are in store-bought mustard. Making your own is the healthiest way to go.

HEALTHY TERIYAKI SAUCE

YIELD: 10 FLUID OUNCES

CARBS:
7 grams per fluid ounce (2 tablespoons)

PREP TIME:
5 minutes

TOTAL TIME:
10 minutes

INGREDIENTS:

- 1/2 cup coconut aminos
- 1/4 cup fresh orange juice (or water)
- 1 tablespoon honey
- 2 tablespoons ginger (fresh grated)
- 3 garlic cloves (pressed or minced)
- 1/8 teaspoon chili flakes

OPTIONAL INGREDIENT:

- 2 teaspoons tapioca flour (if you want your sauce to be thicker)

DIRECTIONS:

1. In a small saucepan over medium heat, mix all ingredients except the tapioca flour. If you are using tapioca flour, mix it with 2 tablespoons of cold water and add the mixture into the teriyaki sauce; cook to your desired thickness.

2. Simmer the sauce until thickened. Use immediately or store in a glass container in the refrigerator.

SPECIAL DIET INFORMATION:

30-Day Habit Reset Approved/ Gluten-Free/Diabetic Friendly/Kid Approved

DR. MINDY'S NOTES

When you pick sauces out at the store, you really have to read labels, as many sauces are high in sugar. You can take a healthy meal with organic ingredients and ruin it by adding a sauce that's high in sugar or chemicals. Whenever possible, make your own sauce. This is a great one!

NO-SUGAR PIZZA SAUCE

YIELD: APPROXIMATELY 2-1/2 CUPS (20 2-TABLESPOON SERVINGS)

CARBS:	**PREP TIME:**	**TOTAL TIME:**
3 grams per 2-tablespoon serving	15 minutes	30 minutes

INGREDIENTS:

- 14 ounces tomato sauce
- 6 ounces tomato paste
- 1-1/2 teaspoon avocado oil
- 1-1/2 teaspoon ground Herbes de Provence
- 1/4 teaspoon sea salt
- 1/4 teaspoon finely ground pepper

DIRECTIONS:

1. In a medium saucepan, mix all ingredients over medium heat until flavors are melded together (about 15 minutes).

2. Cool and store in a glass container in the refrigerator for up to 2 weeks.

_____

TIPS & TRICKS: *I save time by making a double batch of this recipe because it stores well in the fridge and I make this pizza at least once a week. Don't make too much of it, though, because since there aren't any preservatives (this is a good thing), this sauce will eventually spoil (this is also a good thing, too, because real food spoils).*

SPECIAL DIET INFORMATION:

15-Day Detox/30-Day Habit Reset/
Gluten-Free/Diabetic Friendly

DR. MINDY'S NOTES

If you must buy tomato sauce or tomato paste at the grocery store, choose those that come in a box or a glass jar. You want to avoid cans, as they can carry toxins such as BPA. Bonnie made a smart choice by putting avocado oil in this sauce, as olive oil turns to a bad fat when you heat it. You'll find as you start to look for healthy versions of pizza sauce in your grocery store that most of them have bad oils in them. Make a jar of this sauce and have it ready at all times in your refrigerator.

BONE BROTH

2 WAYS: THERAPEUTIC AND CULINARY

#1 THERAPEUTIC

YIELD: **6 TO 8 CUPS**

CARBS:
0 per serving

PREP TIME:
5 minutes

TOTAL TIME:
48 hours (mostly cooking time)

INGREDIENTS:

- 2 pounds bones from a healthy source (grass-fed beef bones are best)
- 2 tubers of turmeric
- 3 cloves of garlic
- 2 tablespoons apple cider vinegar

DIRECTIONS:

1. Wash the bones and place in the bottom of a slow cooker.
2. Peel the turmeric and cut into large pieces.
3. Peel the garlic and place the whole cloves in a slow cooker.
4. Add enough water to fill to the top of the slow cooker.
5. Add apple cider vinegar.
6. Place on medium heat for the first hour. Periodically watch for any foam that might appear at the beginning of cooking. Scrape this foam off as you see it form.
7. After one hour, turn down the heat to low and let the broth cook for 48 hours before you drink it.

TIPS & TRICKS: *It used to be hard to find quality bones, but due to bone broth's popularity, it is getting easier. If you are making bone broth for therapeutic reasons, I recommend grass-fed beef bones. You most likely will have to ask for them at the butcher's counter of your local health food store. If you use chicken, making this broth takes bones from 2 to 3 chickens. Chicken feet are also great to use, as they create a more healing gelatinous soup.*

SPECIAL DIET INFORMATION:

15-Day Detox Approved/30-Day Habit Reset Approved/Gluten-Free/Diabetic Friendly/

DR. MINDY'S NOTES

I have a pot of this broth cooking on my countertop at all times. If you are going to do a bone broth fast, this is the recipe to use. You will see an oil that forms on the top of this broth. This oil is incredibly healing, and not only will it help kill bad bacteria in your gut, but it will leave your skin glowing. Bone broth is packed with collagen to repair even the worst leaky-gut situations. You can find several great versions of bone broth at your local health food store, but making it is easy and whole lot less expensive.

CONTINUE »

#2 CULINARY

YIELD: **10 CUPS**

CARBS:
0 grams

PREP TIME:
45 minutes

TOTAL TIME:
45 minutes + 24 to 48 hours

INGREDIENTS:

- 7 to 8 pounds grass-fed beef bones
- 3 yellow onions, cut into 8 wedges
- 8 carrots, peeled, cut into 2-inch pieces
- 4 inches fresh turmeric, peeled and grated
- 1/3 cup raw apple cider vinegar
- 6 cloves garlic
- 6 ounces tomato paste

OPTIONAL INGREDIENTS

- 2 chicken feet (for extra gelatin)

DIRECTIONS:

1. Preheat oven to 375°F
2. Using a large roasting pan, roast the bones until golden brown (about 45 minutes).
3. When the bones are nice and brown, transfer them to a 6-quart slow cooker or large stock pot, and turn it on. Fill the pot halfway with water.
4. Using the same roasting pan as you used for the bones, roast the vegetables along with salt and pepper and the tomato paste, which should be stirred evenly among the vegetables. Roast for 20 minutes, then add to the slow cooker and add water to cover.
5. Cook for 24 to 28 hours. Remove bubbles at the top when they form.

TIPS & TRICKS: *Bone broth makes a perfect liquid to braise meats in (like the pot roast and pulled pork recipes in this book). You can also reduce bone broth to make gravy.*

SPECIAL DIET INFORMATION:

15-Day Detox Approved/30-Day Habit Reset Approved/Gluten-Free/ Diabetic Friendly

DR. MINDY'S NOTES

Nothing heals your gut as fast as bone broth. It's easy to make, will help repair a leaky gut, and will fill you up. If you're looking for more ways to get good fat into your body, bone broth is a great addition to your daily meals. The culinary version of bone broth will have a richer, deeper flavor than the therapeutic recipe. Both of them have a therapeutic benefit.

COCONUT SUGAR SIMPLE SYRUP

YIELD: APPROXIMATELY 12 OUNCES (72 1-TEASPOON SERVINGS)

CARBS:
6 grams per teaspoon

PREP TIME:
10 minutes

TOTAL TIME:
10 to 15 minutes

INGREDIENTS:

– 2 cups coconut sugar
– 2/3 cup water

DIRECTIONS:

1. Add ingredients to a medium saucepan on medium heat to melt all the sugar granules. (Avoid an active boil because the syrup will burn.)

2. Once all the granules are melted, take the syrup off the heat and cool. Once cool enough to handle, transfer the syrup to an airtight container using a funnel. Store syrup in the refrigerator.

TIPS & TRICKS: *For storage, I like to use recycled French lemonade bottles with clip tops. This syrup has a wide variety of uses, from sweetening your coffee to any recipe that calls for molasses. Try the RFK Not Your Average Spice Cookies...they are the bomb!.*

SPECIAL DIET INFORMATION:

30-Day Habit Reset Approved (in moderation)/Gluten-Free/Diabetic Friendly (in moderation)/Kid Approved

DR. MINDY'S NOTES

Coconut sugar is lower on the glycemic index than regular sugar. This means it won't contribute to weight-loss resistance. Although it's recommended to take all sugar out of your diet for the 15-Day Detox, once you transition to the 30-Day Habit Reset, this is a great substitute for regular sugar—a substitution you may find enjoyable for life! Bonnie always has a bottle of this simple syrup in her refrigerator, ready to go for any recipe that may require it. My kids love coconut sugar as well.

CHAPTER 12

MORNING FARE

Waffles – 3 Ways

Guilt-Free Blueberry Muffins

Cinnamon Quinoa Breakfast Cereal

Almond Kefir Scones

Low-Carb Tater Tots

Granola

Crustless Kitchen Sink Quiche

Bacon-Avo-Egg

WAFFLES
3 WAYS: REGULAR, CHOCOLATE, AND APPLE CINNAMON

YIELD: APPROXIMATELY 4 CUPS (16 2-FLUID OUNCE WAFFLES)

CARBS:
9 grams per 2-fluid ounce waffle

PREP TIME:
20 minutes

TOTAL TIME:
25 minutes

INGREDIENTS:

- 3 cups blanched almond flour
- 1/4 cup shredded coconut, unsweetened
- 1 teaspoon baking powder
- 1/4 teaspoon sea salt
- 1/2 teaspoon ground cinnamon
- 2/3 cup coconut milk
- 5 eggs, yolks and whites separated
- 1/4 cup maple syrup
- 2 teaspoons vanilla extract
- 1/3 cup grass-fed butter, softened

FLAVOR VARIATIONS:

For Chocolate Waffles, add:

- 1/4 cup raw cacao powder (adds 1g carb per waffle)

For Apple Cinnamon Waffles, add:

- 1 teaspoon cinnamon
- 2 cups shredded green apple (adds 3g carbs per waffle)

DIRECTIONS:

1. Turn on your waffle iron to the desired setting.
2. In a medium-sized bowl, combine all the dry ingredients (almond flour, shredded coconut, baking powder, cinnamon, and salt) until evenly mixed. (If you're making the chocolate version, add the cacao powder here.)
3. In a separate large bowl, cream the liquid ingredients, except the egg whites (coconut milk, maple syrup, vanilla, egg yolks, and butter). If you're making the apple cinnamon version, add the additional cinnamon and shredded apple here.
4. In a third medium bowl, beat the egg whites to a soft peak.
5. Gently fold the egg whites into the other liquid ingredient mixture.
6. Gently fold the dry ingredients into the creamed liquid ingredients until fully incorporated.
7. Using a 2-ounce ladle, position a dollop of batter onto the center of the waffle square. Cook per waffle iron instructions (approximately 4 minutes).

TIPS & TRICKS: *A Belgian waffle iron makes these waffles crispy every time! Enjoy with RFK Just Raspberry Syrup and sliced raw almonds.*

DR. MINDY'S NOTES

I kid you not, these waffles are some of the best I have ever tasted. It's hard to believe they're grain free. But that's not the best part: They're also packed with protein and antioxidants that won't make your blood sugar spike!

Waffles and Just Raspberry Syrup (page 166)

GUILT-FREE BLUEBERRY MUFFINS

YIELD: 12 MUFFINS

CARBS:
Approximately 20 grams per muffin

PREP TIME:
15 minutes

TOTAL TIME:
50 to 55 minutes

INGREDIENTS:

- 3 cups almond flour, finely ground
- 1 tablespoon xanthan gum
- 1 teaspoon baking powder
- 1/2 teaspoon sea salt
- 6 large eggs
- 1-1/2 cups frozen blueberries
- 1/2 cup raw honey
- 2 teaspoons almond extract

DIRECTIONS:

1. Preheat oven to 350°F. Lightly butter silicon baking cups or line your traditional muffin tin with paper liners.

2. In a medium-size bowl, combine all dry ingredients.

3. In a separate bowl, beat the eggs and then mix in the honey and almond extract.

4. When your oven is ready, gently fold in the frozen blueberries—but use as little as possible because the blueberries will stain the batter as you fold them in (this discoloration will disappear during baking). Do not over-stir the blueberries—you should avoid breaking them because they should burst in your mouth when you eat the finished muffin!

5. Bake at 350°F for 35 to 40 minutes or until an inserted toothpick comes out clean. Don't take them out too early as they need to bake all the way through. Let them cool before storing in the refrigerator.

TIPS & TRICKS: *Keep the frozen blueberries in the freezer until ready to use. I recommend silicon muffin molds as they make cleanup easier and you don't lose valuable muffin on the paper—these muffins are too good to waste.*

SPECIAL DIET INFORMATION:

15-Day Detox Approved (without the honey)/30-Day Habit Reset Approved/Gluten-Free/Diabetic Friendly

DR. MINDY'S NOTES

I'm up for anything that starts with "Guilt-Free." These muffins will satisfy your cravings for a blueberry muffin but won't set your health back. Remember that good fat will nourish your brain and force your body to burn fat for fuel, so spread a big pat of grass-fed butter on these muffins.

CINNAMON QUINOA BREAKFAST CEREAL

YIELD: 4 CUPS (8 1/2-CUP SERVINGS)

CARBS:	PREP TIME:	TOTAL TIME:
15 grams per 1/2-cup serving	5 minutes	20 to 25 minutes

INGREDIENTS:

- 1 cup quinoa
- 2 cups almond milk or water
- 1 teaspoon ground cinnamon
- 1/2 teaspoon freshly ground nutmeg
- 2 tablespoons flaxseed
- 2 tablespoons maple syrup

DIRECTIONS:

1. Run water over quinoa through a fine-mesh strainer and then place in a medium saucepan.

2. Add all other ingredients and bring to a boil.

3. Once boiling, reduce heat and simmer 15 to 20 minutes or until tender and all liquid has been absorbed. Remove from heat and fluff with a fork.

TIPS & TRICKS:

Serve this with your choice of toppings: coconut milk, nuts, berries, green apple, green macha tea, chia seeds, shredded coconut, nut butter, or RFK Coconut Probiotic Topping—the list is endless!

SPECIAL DIET INFORMATION:

15-Day Approved (without maple syrup)/30-Day Habit Reset/Gluten-Free/Diabetic Friendly

DR. MINDY'S NOTES

Start your day with quinoa, one of the great superfoods. Quinoa seeds are 14 to 18 percent protein. Quinoa contains the nine essential amino acids in the required proportions. Tender leaves and flower heads of the quinoa plant contain high levels of vitamin A and antioxidants such as carotene and lutein. Antioxidants remove harmful free radicals from the body, thus protecting it from degenerative neurological diseases, cancers, and aging. Quinoa grains are good sources of vitamin E, vitamin B, and essential fatty acids such as linoleic. The grains are also rich in dietary fibers and minerals such as magnesium and iron. Magnesium ensures a smooth flow of blood by relaxing the blood vessels. Iron is needed for the formation of red blood cells.

ALMOND KEFIR SCONES

YIELD: 8 SCONES

CARBS:	**PREP TIME:**	**TOTAL TIME:**
19 grams per scone	15 minutes	35 minutes

INGREDIENTS:

- 2 cups almond flour
- 1/2 cup arrowroot flour
- 2 teaspoons baking powder
- 1 teaspoon kosher salt
- 2 eggs
- 2 tablespoons maple syrup
- 2 teaspoons almond extract
- 4 tablespoons cold grass-fed butter
- 1/2 cup milk kefir
- 1/2 cup sliced almonds

DIRECTIONS:

1. Preheat the oven to 350°F.

2. In a large mixing bowl, whisk together the almond flour, arrowroot flour, baking powder, and salt. Cut butter into chunks and cut it into the flour mixture using fingers, a pastry cutter, or a food processor, until the chunks are the size of small peas.

3. In a small bowl, whisk together the eggs, maple syrup, almond extract, and kefir. Add the wet ingredients to the dry ingredients until just combined. Stir in the sliced almonds, then transfer the dough to a lightly floured piece of parchment paper on a flat work surface. Form into a 10-inch circle.

4. Cut the dough into 8 wedges and place parchment on a baking sheet. Bake for 20 minutes, rotating halfway through, until golden brown and cooked through. Cool on a wire rack and serve.

TIPS & TRICKS: *Serve with grass-fed butter and RFK Raspberry Chia Jam!*

SPECIAL DIET INFORMATION:

30-Day Habit Reset Approved/
Gluten-Free/Diabetic Friendly

DR. MINDY'S NOTES

Anytime you add raw kefir to your meal, you help your gut out. This scone will taste just like the grain-filled scones you're used to. Spread some RFK Raspberry Chia Jam on it—and you have yourself a serious breakfast health food!

LOW-CARB TATER TOTS

YIELD: 40 1-OUNCE TATER TOTS

CARBS:
4 grams per 1-ounce tater tot

PREP TIME:
30 minutes

TOTAL TIME:
40 minutes

INGREDIENTS:

- 8 cups cauliflower, riced (equal to 2 large or 3 small cauliflower heads)
- 2 whole eggs + 2 egg whites, beaten
- 1/4 cup fresh goat chevre
- 1 cup raw Parmesan cheese
- 1 tablespoon ground Herbes de Provence
- 1/2 teaspoon sea salt
- 1/2 teaspoon finely ground pepper

DIRECTIONS:

1. "Cauliflower rice" is made by pulsing raw cauliflower in a food processor or Vitamix; after a few minutes of pulsing, the texture will resemble rice. In a 6-quart stock pot or saucepan, boil cauliflower rice in about 2 inches of water until tender, about 8 to 10 minutes. Drain through a fine strainer. Transfer the cauliflower rice to a nut milk bag or fine-weave dish towel. Wearing plastic gloves to protect your hands from the heat, squeeze all the moisture out of the cauliflower rice. After squeezing the water out, you should be left with approximately 4 cups of compact cauliflower. Cool cauliflower on a baking sheet in the fridge (or freezer for faster results) for 15 minutes.

2. In a large bowl, mix the cooked, strained, and cooled cauliflower; beaten eggs; chevre; Parmesan cheese; and spices. Use your hands if necessary to get a consistent texture.

3. Prepare a baking sheet with parchment paper or a Silpat nonstick baking sheet.

4. Prepare the coconut flour for rolling and coating the tater tots by placing it in a shallow pan.

5. Spoon out 2 tablespoons of mixture. Roll in the coconut flour to coat and make it a little easier to handle the tots.

6. Place on the prepared baking sheet and continue to form your tater tots.

7. Spray all sides of the tater tots with spray avocado oil. Bake for 10 to 15 minutes at 400°F.

SPECIAL DIET INFORMATION:

30-Day Habit Reset Approved/ Gluten-Free/Diabetic Friendly

DR. MINDY'S NOTES

Bonnie worked her magic again with this recipe. You will forget that you're living a grain-free life while you're dining on these fabulous tots. Cauliflower is one of those key foods that will stimulate your glutathione production, so be sure to give yourself two helpings of this tasty treat.

GRANOLA

YIELD: 12 CUPS (24 1/2-CUP SERVINGS)

CARBS:	**PREP TIME:**	**TOTAL TIME:**
22 grams per 1/2-cup serving	20 minutes	40 minutes

INGREDIENTS:

3 cups rolled oats

3/4 cup sunflower seeds

3/4 cup sesame seeds

3/4 cup cashews

3/4 cup unsweetened, dried cranberries

3/4 cup coconut milk powder

2/3 cup pumpkin seeds

2/3 cup ground flaxseed

2/3 cup walnuts

2/3 cup sliced almonds

1/2 cup pecans

1/4 cup buckwheat groats

1 tablespoon ground cinnamon

1 cup avocado oil

1/4 cup coconut oil

1/4 cup raw honey

1/4 cup RFK Coconut Sugar Syrup

DIRECTIONS:

1. Preheat oven to 375°F.

2. Prepare a baking sheet lined with parchment paper, lightly oiled with coconut oil.

3. Bring oils, honey, and coconut syrup to a light boil. Remove from heat and cool.

4. In a large bowl, mix all dry ingredients together.

5. Once the liquid ingredients have cooled, pour over the dry ingredients and mix thoroughly.

6. Turn out the granola mixture onto the prepared baking sheet. Bake at 375°F for 15 to 20 minutes, tossing the mixture at the halfway point to make sure it doesn't burn. The granola is done when it shows signs of being toasted (light golden brown and nutty smell).

TIPS & TRICKS: *This recipe is RFK approved for a special treat when you just have to have your granola fix!*

SPECIAL DIET INFORMATION:

30-Day Habit Reset Approved (occasionally)/Gluten-Free/Diabetic Friendly

DR. MINDY'S NOTES

When you start your 45-Day Reset, you may think you'll need to give up some of your favorite treats like granola. Well, think again. Not only is this granola grain free, but it's packed with protein and good fats.

CRUSTLESS KITCHEN SINK QUICHE

YIELD: **APPROXIMATELY 6 CUPS (12 1/2 CUP SERVINGS)**

CARBS:
3 grams per 1/2-cup serving

PREP TIME:
35 minutes

TOTAL TIME:
65 to 70 minutes

INGREDIENTS:

- 1 cup diced onion, sautéed until clear

- 3 cups (total) of whatever you have in your kitchen, such as:

- 1 cup frozen organic spinach, thawed, squeezed, finely diced

- 1 cup diced bacon, cooked

- 1 cup diced roasted red bell peppers

- 3 cups (total) of whatever cheese you have, such as:

- 1-1/2 cups shredded goat cheddar cheese

- 1-1/2 cups shredded raw Parmesan cheese

- 8 large eggs, beaten

- 1/2 teaspoon salt

- 1/2 teaspoon pepper

- 1 teaspoon of the herb of your choice (mine is Herbes de Provence)

DIRECTIONS:

1. Preheat oven to 350°F.

2. Prepare an oiled baking dish (8" x 8" square).

3. Prep your ingredients: thaw, squeeze, and chop the spinach. Sauté the onion. Cook and chop the bacon. Dice the roasted bell pepper. Grate the cheeses.

4. Beat the eggs and add the salt, pepper, and spices.

5. In a large bowl, mix all the ingredients together.

6. Pour into a baking dish. Bake for 30 to 40 minutes or until a toothpick comes out clean in the center.

TIPS & TRICKS: *As long as you keep the proportions the same in this recipe, you can experiment with different ingredients. This quiche never gets boring!*

SPECIAL DIET INFORMATION:

30-Day Habit Reset Approved/
Gluten-Free/Diabetic Friendly

DR. MINDY'S NOTES

Remember how I mentioned you need to get more good fats? Well, this recipe is packed with good fats. The great thing about eggs is that they have all the nutrients you need to build bone, muscle, and ligaments. This is the type of breakfast that not only tastes great but will keep you full all day long.

BACON-AVO-EGG

YIELD: 4 SERVINGS

CARBS:
15 grams per serving

PREP TIME:
20 minutes

TOTAL TIME:
30 minutes

INGREDIENTS:

– 4 large eggs

– 4 large avocados

– 16 slices bacon

– 1/4 cup raw apple cider vinegar

– 1 teaspoon salt

– 1/2 teaspoon pepper

DIRECTIONS:

1. Halve the avocados and discard the seeds. Scoop a small amount of avocado out of the center to make a little more room for the poached egg that will go inside. Carefully peel off the avocado skin. Set aside.

2. In a saucepan, bring 3 to 4 inches of water to a boil along with 1/2 teaspoon of salt and apple cider vinegar. Poach for 5 minutes.

3. Carefully place a poached egg into each avocado and close it inside. Wrap each avocado with approximately 4 slices of bacon.

4. On high heat, sear the bacon on the outside of the avocado, rotating it slowly until it's crispy and golden brown all around. Leaning the avocado along the edge of a curved pan is a great way to sear the curved areas. Once the bacon starts to cook and get crisp, it will create a shell and hold the avocado together and the egg inside.

5. Serve immediately.

TIPS & TRICKS: *The acid in the water from the vinegar is what helps keep the egg together while poaching. The trick to searing the bacon-wrapped avocado is high heat: It has to be hot and fast; otherwise, the texture of the soft avocado underneath will be compromised. Serve this delicious dish over a salad of mixed greens, sliced heirloom tomatoes, freshly chopped parsley, and crumbled feta cheese. Top it off with RFK Citrus Burst salad dressing.*

SPECIAL DIET INFORMATION:

15-Day Detox Approved/30-Day Habit Reset/Gluten-Free/Diabetic Friendly

DR. MINDY'S NOTES

This may be the most perfect recipe ever discovered. Avocados, in my opinion, are one of the tastiest good fats around. Not only is this recipe packed with protein, but it will look beautiful on your plate.

Fish in Parchment Paper, *page 129*

CHAPTER 13

THE MAIN DISH

PIZZA WITH HERBED CAULIFLOWER CRUST

YIELD: 1 8-SLICE PIZZA

CARBS:
18 grams per slice (1/8 th of pizza)

PREP TIME:
40 minutes

TOTAL TIME:
1-1/2 hours

INGREDIENTS:

– RFK Pizza Sauce (1/2 recipe)

– 8 cups cauliflower, riced (equal to 2 large or 3 small cauliflower heads)

– 2 whole eggs + 2 egg whites, beaten

– 8 ounces fresh goat chevre

– 1 tablespoon ground Herbes de Provence

– 1/2 teaspoon sea salt

– 1/2 teaspoon finely ground pepper

Suggested Toppings:

– 1 pound spicy ground sausage, crumbled and cooked

– 1 pound grated cheese, grated

– 1-1/2 cups RFK Caramelized Onions

DIRECTIONS:

1. Preheat oven to 400°F.

2. If you choose to top your pizza with caramelized onions, start cooking those first (in a 350°F oven).

3. Rice your cauliflower. "Cauliflower rice" is made by pulsing raw cauliflower in a food processor or Vitamix; after a few minutes of pulsing, the texture will resemble rice. In a 6-quart stock pot or saucepan, boil the cauliflower rice in about 2 inches of water until tender, for about 8 to 10 minutes. Drain through a fine strainer. Transfer the cauliflower rice to a nut milk bag or fine-weave dish towel. Wearing plastic gloves to protect your hands from the heat, squeeze all the moisture out of the cauliflower rice. After squeezing the water out, you should be left with approximately 4 cups of compact cauliflower.

4. In a large bowl, mix the cooked cauliflower, beaten eggs, chevre, and ground spices. Use your hands if necessary to get a consistent texture.

5. Choose the shape of your pizza crust. This recipe is enough "batter" to make one large rectangular pizza crust using a 1/2-sheet pan (approximately 13" x 18"). Line the baking sheet with ovenproof parchment paper. Spread batter evenly; no matter what shape you choose, keep the dough about 1/3" thick.

6. Bake for 35 to 45 minutes at 400°F. The crust should be firm and lightly golden brown when finished.

7. If you haven't already made your RFK Pizza Sauce, this is the perfect time to make it!

8. When the crust is ready (slightly brown on top and cooked through), top generously with pizza sauce, your choice of cheese, and your other favorite toppings. Our favorite combo is goat cheese mozzarella, ground pork sausage, caramelized onion, and Parmesan cheese.

9. Return the pizza and toppings to the 400°F oven for 10 to 12 minutes (or until the cheese is melted and slightly brown around the edges).

SPECIAL DIET INFORMATION:

30-Day Habit Reset Approved/ Gluten-Free/Diabetic Friendly/Kid Approved

TIPS & TRICKS: *Save time and cook the onions while you're preparing the cauliflower. Make the pizza sauce and grilled onions in advance. I always have caramelized onions in my fridge because I use them in so many dishes; they add depth of flavor and a touch of sweetness without any carbohydrate-laden sugars.*

When you first hear "cauliflower crust pizza," you think, how can that be possible? Well, Bonnie not only made it possible, she made its taste amazing! Everyone loves pizza, yet pizza is one of those foods that will spike your blood sugar fast. Pizza also will put you into a weight-loss-resistant state. Remember that cauliflower will stimulate glutathione production in your body and goat cheese is much easier for the human gut to digest than cow's milk cheese. We do a Sunday night pizza night in my family, and this recipe is a family favorite!

caramelized onions (page 147)

BRAISED BEEF IN BONE BROTH

YIELD: APPROXIMATELY 12 CUPS (24 1/2-CUP SERVINGS)

CARBS:
2 grams per 1/2-cup serving

PREP TIME:
15 minutes

TOTAL TIME:
3 to 8 hours

INGREDIENTS:

- 8 pounds organic grass-fed beef
- 4 to 4-1/2 cups beef bone broth (see RFK Bone Broth)
- 1 onion, peeled and cut into 8 wedges
- 12 ounces tomato paste
- 2 cups baby carrots (or 3 to 4 large carrots, cut into 2-inch chunks)
- 4 stalks celery, cut into 2-inch-long chunks
- 1 tablespoon ground Herbes de Provence
- 4 to 5 cloves garlic, whole
- 1 tablespoon sea salt for searing
- 1 tablespoon ground pepper for searing

DIRECTIONS:

1. You can braise 4 ways. Here are the fastest to slowest methods: pressure cooker, stovetop, oven, or slow cooker. I prefer the slow cooker method (mine is 6-1/2 quarts), so that's what these directions are for.

2. Start warming up the bone broth in your slow cooker. Sometimes, I boil the bone broth first to help kick-start it.

3. Prepare to sear your beef by sprinkling salt and pepper on all surfaces. Heat a large frying or sauté pan on medium-high heat and sear each side of the meat until lightly golden brown. This is an important step because you're doing two things that are going to make your final dish delicious: sealing in moisture and creating flavor. All the crusty bits are full of flavor that will transfer to your braising liquid.

4. Place the meat, all the vegetables, the Herbes de Provence, and the garlic cloves in the slow cooker. You can braise this for 4 to 8 hours. I go the whole 8 hours so the meat is as tender as possible and ready to eat when I'm finished with my workday.

5. Before serving, you can choose to take some sauce to serve with your braised beef by transferring 1-1/2 cups of the sauce to a saucepan. In a small glass, mix a small amount of warm liquid with 1 to 2 teaspoons of arrowroot; use a small whisk to blend. Then incorporate this mixture into the sauce you've set aside in the saucepan. This premixing technique minimizes clumping.

TIPS & TRICKS: *I use a 6-1/2 quart slow cooker—and I love it! I get up early and prep for dinner, and it's ready when I'm finished with my workday. I also love leftovers. Braised meats only get better the longer the flavors meld together—and it's like having a free meal that I didn't have to invest time in. This is why this recipe is made to feed a small army: We eat some, I freeze some, and sometimes, I give some away! I use baby carrots in my braised recipes because they're a shortcut that saves me time. Also, I can get organic ones, so I'm not forced to settle for lower-quality ingredients.*

SPECIAL DIET INFORMATION:

15-Day Detox Approved/30-Day Habit Reset Approved/Gluten-Free/Diabetic Friendly

Bone broth is one of the most healing foods you can eat. It can become boring and a bit monotonous just to drink it by the cup. Bonnie has come to the rescue again with this braised beef recipe. Be sure to get your tomato paste in a jar, as cans often contain a chemical called BPA that will trigger a weight-loss-resistant state in your body. Grass-fed beef is high in omega-3 fatty acids that will lower inflammation in your body, and the bone broth is filled with glycine and collagen that will repair your leaky gut. If you're living with chronic pain, this will be an incredibly healing food for you.

Braised Beef in Bone Broth with Turneric Cauliflower (page 138)

PULLED PORK IN BONE BROTH

YIELD: APPROXIMATELY 12 CUPS (24 1/2 CUP SERVINGS)

CARBS:	**PREP TIME:**	**TOTAL TIME:**
2 grams per 1/2-cup serving	15 minutes	3 to 8 hours

INGREDIENTS:

– 6 pounds pork shoulder

– 2 tablespoons ground cumin

– 1 medium organic yellow onion, cored

– 3 to 4 bay leaves

– 2 tablespoons ground Herbes de Provence

– 8 cups RFK Bone Broth

– 1/2 teaspoon cayenne pepper

– 1/4 cup chopped cilantro

– Juice of two lemons

DIRECTIONS:

1. You can braise 4 ways. Here are the fastest to slowest methods: pressure cooker (1 hour), stovetop (3 to 4 hours), oven (4 to 8 hours), or slow cooker (also 4 to 8 hours). I prefer the slow cooker method (mine is 6-1/2 quarts), so that's what these directions are for.

2. Prepare to sear your pork shoulder by sprinkling salt and pepper on all surfaces. Heat a large frying or sauté pan on medium-high heat and sear each side of the meat until lightly golden brown. This is an important step because you're doing two things that are going to make your final dish delicious: sealing in moisture and creating flavor. All the crusty bits are full of flavor that will transfer to your braising liquid.

3. Boil all liquids and spices together before putting the mixture into the slow cooker.

4. Put liquids, meat, and onion into the slow cooker and cook for 8 hours. Note that the liquid should just cover the meat.

5. When you're finished cooking, you can set aside some of the bone broth to mix in with the shredded meat, but first you'll want to thicken it a little bit with some arrowroot powder. This is done by mixing a little hot liquid with a teaspoon of arrowroot powder at a time, thoroughly blending then adding this back to your reserved liquid for sauce.

6. Remove the meat from the slow cooker and shred, using two forks, and add the thickened sauce.

7. Serve with RFK Barbecue Sauce, RFK Caramelized Onions, and/or RFK Cauliflower Tortillas.

SPECIAL DIET INFORMATION:

15-Day Detox Approved/30-Day Habit Reset Approved/Gluten-Free/ Diabetic Friendly

DR. MINDY'S NOTES

Another great bone broth recipe! Your gut will benefit from as many different ways you can get bone broth into you as possible. Pork is one of those meats I recommend you eat in moderation. The pig doesn't have sweat glands, so it holds in toxins more than any other animal. Be sure you buy organic pork to minimize your toxic load.

BOLOGNESE SUGO

YIELD: APPROXIMATELY 12 CUPS (24 1/2-CUP SERVINGS)

CARBS:	**PREP TIME:**	**TOTAL TIME:**
4 grams per 1/2-cup serving	20 minutes	1 hour

INGREDIENTS:

- 2 large red onions, diced
- 2 tablespoons avocado oil
- 3 pounds ground grass-fed beef
- 2 tablespoons ground Herbes de Provence
- 2 teaspoons salt
- 1 teaspoon ground pepper
- 1/2 teaspoon cayenne pepper
- 1 cup beef bone broth
- 6 ounces tomato paste
- 4 cloves garlic, crushed
- 57 ounces chopped tomatoes

DIRECTIONS:

1. In a large stock pot (8 quarts or larger), sauté the onions in the avocado oil until clear (about 10 minutes).

2. At the same time, in a sauté or frying pan, cook the ground beef, breaking it into small pieces. Drain the fat and add the meat to the onions in the stock pot.

3. Add all the other ingredients, stirring well to incorporate.

4. Simmer for 45 minutes so the flavors have time to meld together.

TIPS & TRICKS: *Sugo in Italian means "sauce." In my house, we just call this favorite "sugo." POMI-brand boxed tomatoes are recommended, and look for tomato paste in a jar as opposed to a can.*

Serving suggestion: *Serve over Explore Asia–brand Organic Edamame Spaghetti noodles. These noodles are grain free, high in protein, and about half the carbs of normal spaghetti noodles. These noodles can be found at some Costco stores and on Amazon.com.*

SPECIAL DIET INFORMATION:

15-Day Detox Approved/30-Day Habit Reset Approved/Gluten-Free/Diabetic Friendly

DR. MINDY'S NOTES

Another great way to get grass-fed beef and bone broth into your diet. Remember that grain-fed beef contributes to high cholesterol, but grass-fed beef does the opposite. You can't categorize these two beefs as the same food. One harms your health and one helps your health.

LEMON GINGER SALMON

YIELD: 12 4-OUNCE SERVINGS

CARBS:
2 grams per serving

PREP TIME:
30 minutes

TOTAL TIME:
1-1/4 hours

INGREDIENTS:

– 1 large salmon filet
(2-1/2 to 3 pounds)

– 2 tablespoons organic miso,
low sodium

– 1 to 2 tablespoons sesame oil

– 1 tablespoon coconut aminos

– 4 tablespoons fresh ginger, grated

– 1/2 teaspoon fresh turmeric, grated

– 2 teaspoons minced garlic

– 2 teaspoons raw honey

– Juice from 2 large lemons

– Zest from 3 large lemons

DIRECTIONS:

1. Preheat oven to 350°F.

2. Prepare a large baking dish (the one I use is 15") by adding a little oil to the bottom of the pan before you lay the salmon skin-side down. (This will prevent the skin from sticking.)

3. Mix all ingredients together into a thick sauce. Pack the sauce on top of the salmon; the thick, zesty part of the sauce will stay on top and create a crust during the baking process, and the juices will slide to the bottom of the pan, giving flavor and moisture to the rest of the fish.

4. Bake at 350°F for approximately 45 minutes or until the salmon starts to brown on the top and is cooked through in the thickest part of the filet.

TIPS & TRICKS: *If your filet is too long for your baking dish, you can cut off the small tail end of the salmon and place it in the empty space in the baking dish; it does not have to be cooked in one piece. Watch the thinner areas of the salmon to make sure they don't overcook and get dry; if you need to, you can take these parts out early.*

SPECIAL DIET INFORMATION:

15-Day Detox Approved (without the honey)/30-Day Habit Reset Approved/Gluten-Free/Diabetic Friendly

DR. MINDY'S NOTES

This recipe is filled with anti-inflammatory properties. Salmon is packed with omega-3 fatty acids that nourish the outer membranes of your cells and lower inflammation in your body. Make sure that you get wild salmon, not farm fresh. Turmeric contains many anti-carcinogenic and anti-inflammatory qualities. Ginger will aid in digestion. If you're looking for a meal that will heal your body from the inside out, this is the one!

FISH IN PARCHMENT PAPER

YIELD: 8 2-OUNCE SERVINGS

CARBS:
1 gram per serving

PREP TIME:
30 minutes

TOTAL TIME:
45 minutes

INGREDIENTS:

- 8 fish fillets (trout, salmon, halibut, sea bass, or cod)
- 16 ounces haricots verts (thin green beans)
- 2 yellow bell peppers, thinly sliced
- 1 red onion, thinly sliced
- 4 large tomatoes, diced
- 4 tablespoons capers, drained
- 3 lemons, sliced
- 2 lemons, juiced
- 1/2 cup basil, thinly sliced
- 1/4 cup avocado oil
- 1 teaspoon sea salt
- 1 teaspoon ground pepper
- 1/2 teaspoon cayenne pepper

DIRECTIONS:

1. Preheat oven to 400°F. Prepare 8 17-inch squares of parchment paper.

2. Divide haricots verts, bell peppers, onion, tomatoes, and capers evenly among the 8 squares of parchment. Place one fish fillet on top of each and drizzle lemon juice and a little avocado oil over each piece of fish. Top with 1 to 2 lemon slices, salt, pepper, and a dash of cayenne. Bring parchment paper sides up over mixture; double-fold the top and sides to seal, making airtight pockets. Place pockets on a baking sheet.

3. Bake at 400°F for 15 to 20 minutes; your thermometer should register 140° to 145° when inserted through paper and into the fish. Place each packet on a plate and cut open. Sprinkle fish with basil. Serve immediately.

TIPS & TRICKS: *The parchment paper keeps the fish moist, as well as keeping all the flavor in! This dish is a winner with dinner guests, too, because it looks fancy when you serve it in the parchment paper.*

SPECIAL DIET INFORMATION:

15-Day Detox Approved/30-Day Habit Reset Approved/Gluten-Free/ Diabetic Friendly

DR. MINDY'S NOTES

Not only is this meal low in carbs, but it's high in healthy oils. Fish oils will greatly benefit your health by lowering inflammation in your body. With less inflammation, your aches and pains will go away, you'll lose weight, and your energy will skyrocket.

Breadcrumb-Free Crab Cakes topped with Steve P's Kickin' Corn Salad (page 141)

BREADCRUMB-FREE CRAB CAKES

YIELD: 6 CRAB CAKES

CARBS:	**PREP TIME:**	**TOTAL TIME:**
8 grams per crab cake	30 minutes	50 minutes

INGREDIENTS:

- 1 pound responsibly sourced crab meat, cooked
- 1/2 head cauliflower, riced, steamed, and water extracted (1 cup when finished)
- 5 eggs
- 6 tablespoons coconut flour
- 3 tablespoons RFK Garlic Avocado Aioli
- 1/4 cup curly parsley, finely chopped
- 1/4 cup green onions, chopped
- 1/2 teaspoon sea salt
- 1/4 teaspoon ground pepper
- 1/2 teaspoon cayenne pepper
- 1/2 teaspoon paprika
- 1 teaspoon fresh dill
- Lemon juice to taste
- 2 tablespoons avocado oil or coconut oil (for searing)

DIRECTIONS:

1. Preheat oven to 350°F.

2. In a Vitamix or food processor, rice the cauliflower. Steam for 10 minutes. Squeeze excess liquid out, either with cheesecloth, a kitchen towel, or a nut butter bag. (I like to prepare the whole head of cauliflower and save half for another time, in the freezer.) Set aside to cool.

3. In a small bowl, whisk together the eggs, RFK Garlic Aioli, and spices.

4. In a medium bowl, gently fold cold (otherwise, it will cook the eggs) cauliflower with the egg mixture and coconut flour until evenly mixed. (The cauliflower and the coconut flour give the finished crab cakes a nice, crispy outside.)

5. Gently fold in the crab meat, being careful not to break up the meat too much. (It's nice when the finished crab cakes have large chunks of meat in them.)

6. Cool the mixture in the fridge for 15 minutes. Preheat oven to 350°F at this time.

7. Make patties the size of your choice. (I prefer approximately 1 inch thick and 3 inches across.)

8. On medium-high heat, pour oil into a cast-iron (recommended) pan. When the pan and oil are hot, add the crab cakes, being careful not to overcrowd the pan (this will cause steaming, not searing). Cook about 3 minutes to a golden brown, then flip and cook another 3 minutes.

9. Place pan-fried crab cakes on a baking sheet and transfer to the preheated oven to cook through (12 to 15 minutes).

TIPS & TRICKS: *Serve over mixed greens with half an avocado filled with RFK Fermented Salsa or RFK Steve P's Kickin' Corn Salad.*

SPECIAL DIET INFORMATION:

15-Day Detox Approved/30-Day Habit Reset Approved/Gluten-Free/Diabetic Friendly

DR. MINDY'S NOTES

There are some foods that you love and think you'll never be able to eat again once you're on the 45-Day Reset. These include crab cakes. I know my kids love a good crab cake, but I don't love that they're often filled with high-carb breads and fillers. This recipe changes all of that, turning your crab cakes into a healthy, delicious meal.

ROASTED LEG OF LAMB

YIELD: 20 4-OUNCE SERVINGS

CARBS:
0 grams per serving

PREP TIME:
15 minutes (best if marinated 2 days)

TOTAL TIME:
1 hour (plus marinating time)

INGREDIENTS:

- 5 pounds boneless leg of lamb
- 8 sprigs fresh rosemary
- 2 lemons, zest and juice
- 1 tablespoon minced garlic
- 1/4 cup avocado oil
- 2 teaspoons salt
- 1 teaspoon ground pepper

DIRECTIONS:

1. Place everything in 2 (for extra strength) 10-gallon clear plastic garbage bags. Take extra care when placing the rosemary sprigs to make sure they don't puncture the plastic bag. Get all the air out of the bag and tie a knot at the top; this makes sure that the entire leg of lamb gets marinated.

2. Place the lamb in a bowl or dish (just in case it leaks) in the fridge for 4 hours or up to 2 days.

3. When ready to cook, you can do so on the grill (medium heat for 45 minutes or until done) or start it on the grill to get color and then finish it in the oven (375°F) for 45 minutes or until done.

SPECIAL DIET INFORMATION:

15-Day Detox Approved/30-Day Habit Reset Approved/Gluten-Free/Diabetic Friendly

DR. MINDY'S NOTES

Lamb is another great meat to eat grass fed. Remember that grass fed means high in omega-3 fatty acids. Omega-3s nourish the outside membranes of your cells (all 72 trillion of them) and lower inflammation. When your cell membranes are rich in omega-3 fatty acids, they allow toxins out and nutrients into the cells much more efficiently. This means a happy and healthy body and mind. Be sure you get your lamb grass fed to get the additional health benefit.

ROASTED PORK LOIN

YIELD: 12 5-OUNCE SERVINGS

CARBS:
0 grams per serving

PREP TIME:
15 minutes (best if marinated for 2 days)

TOTAL TIME:
1-1/2 hours (plus marinating time)

INGREDIENTS:

– 4 to 5 pounds boneless pork loin

– 2 tablespoons fresh rosemary, finely chopped

– 1 tablespoon garlic, minced

– 2 tablespoons avocado oil

– 1 tablespoon lemon zest

– 2 tablespoons lemon juice

– 2 teaspoons sea salt

– 1 teaspoon ground pepper

– 1/8 teaspoon cayenne pepper

DIRECTIONS:

1. Combine all ingredients in 2 (for extra strength) 10-gallon clear plastic garbage bags. Marinate for 4 hours to 2 days (the longer, the better the flavor).

2. When ready to cook, preheat oven to 425°F.

3. Place the loin in a roasting pan with rack for 20 minutes at 425°F. Then reduce heat and roast for 1 hour or until the juices run clear and the internal temperature reaches 155°F.

4. Remove the meat from the oven and allow it to rest for 10 minutes before slicing and serving.

TIPS & TRICKS: *Marinating always makes things taste better—it just takes a little planning in advance. I like to serve this dish with RFK Green-Apple Applesauce . . . yum!*

SPECIAL DIET INFORMATION:

15-Day Detox Approved/30-Day Habit Reset Approved/Gluten-Free/Diabetic Friendly

DR. MINDY'S NOTES

You'll forget that you're on a healthy eating plan when you eat this meal. Be sure you get organic pork to minimize toxins. Garlic and cayenne pepper are great foods to help build a strong immune system. Sea salt is a key nutrient your thyroid needs to function properly.

THE BEST ROASTED CHICKEN

YIELD: 4-6 servings

CARBS:
0 grams per serving

PREP TIME:
10 minutes

TOTAL TIME:
55 minutes

INGREDIENTS:

- 1 whole chicken
- 3 lemons, sliced
- 5 sprigs fresh rosemary
- 1 teaspoon sea salt
- 1/2 teaspoon ground pepper
- Dash paprika

DIRECTIONS:

1. Preheat oven to 375ºF.

2. Prepare roasting pan by covering it with parchment paper and tucking the edges between the drip pan. Create a bed of lemon slices and rosemary sprigs to put the chicken on for roasting.

3. Butterfly your chicken by removing the spine. You can do this either with sturdy kitchen shears or a knife. By removing the spine, you can flatten the chicken out on a roasting pan so it cooks more evenly and in less time, all the while staying moist on the inside and crispy on the outside. Place the chicken on top of the lemons and rosemary. Sprinkle with salt, pepper, and paprika.

4. Roast for 45 to 55 minutes or until the juices run clear.

TIPS & TRICKS: *Serve with RFK Sweet Hot Habanero Sauce—and your chicken will never be dry and boring again!*

SPECIAL DIET INFORMATION:

15-Day Detox Approved/30-Day Habit Reset Approved/Gluten-Free/ Diabetic Friendly/Kid Approved

DR. MINDY'S NOTES

My family loves a roasted chicken for dinner. We lead a fast-paced life and often go to our local health food store and buy one already cooked in the heated food section. But one thing that has always bothered me is that the roasted chicken sits in a plastic container under heat lamps all day long. That plastic has to leach out into the chicken. Bonnie has made this chicken recipe not only easy, but also as yummy as those store-bought roasted chickens. With zero carbs and lots of great spices, this recipe is sure to be a family favorite.

HEALTHY CHICKEN NUGGETS

YIELD: 48 chicken nuggets

CARBS:
5 grams per chicken nugget

PREP TIME:
20 minutes

TOTAL TIME:
45 minutes

INGREDIENTS:

- 8 hormone-free chicken breasts, boneless, skinless
- 4 eggs, beaten
- 3 cups quinoa flour
- 2 teaspoons garlic powder
- 2 teaspoons sea salt
- 2 teaspoons ground black pepper
- 1 cup coconut oil

DIRECTIONS:

1. Cut the chicken into nugget-shaped pieces (about 6 nuggets per chicken breast).

2. In a shallow dish, mix the flour, garlic powder, salt, and pepper thoroughly. Dip the chicken pieces individually into the beaten eggs, then coat each side lightly with the flour mixture. Shake off excess flour before placing on a plate and continue until all the chicken has been coated.

3. Liberally coat a large nonreactive skillet or saucepan (cast iron is my favorite) with coconut oil. You want to use enough so that the chicken nuggets don't have dry spots, but not so much that they're soggy.

4. Start sautéing the nuggets on each side until golden brown. You may need to pause between batches to quickly clean the pan because there will be small bits that remain in the pan; those have a tendency to burn if not removed, making the conditions less than ideal for the fresh nuggets.

5. You'll know that your nuggets are done when they're golden brown and no longer pink in the center.

TIPS & TRICKS: *The nutrition data for this recipe includes the full amount of the breading ingredients. The actual amount of the breading consumed will vary.*

SPECIAL DIET INFORMATION:

30-Day Habit Reset Approved/
Gluten-Free/Diabetic Friendly/Kid
Approved

DR. MINDY'S NOTES

What kid doesn't love a chicken nugget? But chicken nuggets bought frozen at the store are often filled with GMO flours that will destroy your gut and toxin-packed chicken that will create an inflammatory response in your body. Bonnie has changed all that for you by creating this easy-to-make, healthy, and yummy recipe. Try her ketchup recipe with these nuggets and you'll have a meal that your kids will love and that will build them a healthy body.

CHAPTER 14

SIDE DISHES

ROASTED TURMERIC CAULIFLOWER

YIELD: SERVES 8 TO 12

CARBS:
4 grams per 1/2-cup serving

PREP TIME:
10 minutes

TOTAL TIME:
55 minutes

INGREDIENTS:

- 2 large heads cauliflower
- 1/3 cup avocado oil
- 1-1/2 teaspoon ground turmeric
- 1 teaspoon sea salt
- 1/2 teaspoon pepper
- 1 pair disposable plastic gloves (for prep)

TIPS & TRICKS: *Any leftovers are great served cold on a salad!*

DIRECTIONS:

1. Preheat oven to 350°F.
2. Remove the tough core from the cauliflower and break the rest into 3-inch florets.
3. Mix the turmeric, salt, and pepper in a small bowl and reserve.
4. In a large rectangular baking dish, drizzle oil over the cauliflower and toss to evenly distribute the oil. (This is where I like to use the gloves so my hands don't turn bright yellow!) Continue tossing while sprinkling the spices evenly over the cauliflower.
5. Roast in the oven for 45 minutes, mixing and tossing twice during cooking time to ensure even cooking.
6. Enjoy with steak, chicken, salmon, shrimp—almost anything!

SPECIAL DIET INFORMATION:

15- Day Detox Approved/30-Day Habit Reset Approved

DR. MINDY'S NOTES

Cauliflower is great for detoxification, and turmeric lowers inflammation. This recipe is a great substitute for roasted potatoes.

GREEN BEANS WITH CARAMELIZED SHALLOTS

YIELD: 10 SERVINGS

CARBS:
4 grams per 3 1/2 ounce serving

PREP TIME:
35 minutes

TOTAL TIME:
45 minutes

INGREDIENTS:

- 2 pounds haricots verts (thin green beans)
- 1 cup sliced almonds
- 15 shallots
- 2 tablespoons avocado oil
- 2 tablespoons grass-fed butter
- 1 teaspoon salt
- 1/2 teaspoon pepper

DIRECTIONS:

1. Prepare the shallots by peeling and slicing thinly. In a medium frying pan, sauté them in 1 tablespoon oil until they caramelize and are golden brown (this may take 30 minutes—add more oil if necessary). Stir occasionally, but not too often; the shallots need time to cook, and if you stir too often, the caramelization doesn't have time to happen. But at the same time, keep a watchful eye on them so they don't burn. Once caramelized, reserve the shallots in a bowl.

2. Prepare to blanch the beans. Boil enough water to submerge the beans in an 8-quart stock pot. While the water is heating, trim both ends of the beans. Prepare an ice-water bath to cool the beans after blanching in the water. Blanch the beans in the water for about 3 minutes. Remove quickly and place in the ice-water bath to cool and stop the cooking process. Once cool, remove the beans from the ice water bath, drain, and reserve.

3. Lightly toast the sliced almonds in a frying pan on medium heat. The goal is to get the nuts just slightly brown; this releases the oils and produces an extra nutty flavor.

4. Five minutes before you're ready to serve, heat the butter in a large sauté or frying pan on medium-high heat. Add the butter, blanched beans, salt, and pepper. Once they're hot, add in the caramelized shallots and sliced almonds. Mix evenly and serve.

TIPS & TRICKS: *Blanching the beans for a short period of time and then reserving them until just before you're ready to serve them will help you get them to the table hot and perfectly cooked.*

SPECIAL DIET INFORMATION:

15-Day Detox Approved/30-Day Habit Reset Approved/Gluten-Free/ Diabetic Friendly

DR. MINDY'S NOTES

So many people are used to a starchy side dish, such as potatoes or bread. On the 45-Day Reset, we want you to start looking at lower-carb options for your side dishes. Not only will a lower-carb dish energize you, but because it has a minimal impact on your blood sugar, you can go back for seconds.

ROASTED BRUSSEL SPROUTS

YIELD: 10 SERVINGS

CARBS:
6 grams per 3-ounce serving

PREP TIME:
10 minutes

TOTAL TIME:
55 minutes

INGREDIENTS:

– 2 pounds Brussels sprouts

– 8 ounces sulfite-free bacon, cooked and chopped

– 1/4 cup balsamic vinegar

– 1/4 cup avocado oil

– 1 teaspoon sea salt

– 1 teaspoon pepper

DIRECTIONS:

1. Preheat oven to 350°F.

2. Stem and split Brussels sprouts. In a large bowl, gently toss together the Brussel sprouts, avocado oil, balsamic vinegar, salt, and pepper. Thoroughly coat all the Brussels sprouts so they're slightly shiny and a golden color from the balsamic vinegar.

3. Place in a 10-1/2" x 13" Pyrex pan or other large ovenproof baker. Bake at 350°F for approximately 45 minutes, stirring gently every 15 minutes to ensure even cooking. (Note: the leaves that fall off will cook faster; to prevent these loose leaves from burning, try to keep the Brussels sprouts compact and together, not dispersed and spread out in the pan.)

4. While the Brussels sprouts are in the oven, cook and chop the bacon and reserve. When the Brussels sprouts are finished (tender, caramelized, and smelling delicious), remove from the oven and gently toss in the chopped bacon. Serve immediately.

TIPS & TRICKS: *This sweet and salty recipe makes for great leftovers! They go great on top of a salad or even as a cold snack right out of the fridge.*

SPECIAL DIET INFORMATION:

15-Day Detox Approved/30-Day Habit Reset Approved/Gluten-Free/ Diabetic Friendly

DR. MINDY'S NOTES

Brussels sprouts are especially high in vitamin K. This vegetable promotes healthy bones, prevents calcification of tissues, serves as an antioxidant and anti-inflammatory agent, and is essential for proper brain and nerve function. It's also high in fiber, which will help lower cholesterol. Not to mention that Brussels sprouts are great for detoxification!

STEVE P'S KICKIN' CORN SALAD

YIELD: **12 CUPS**

CARBS:
12 grams per 1/2-cup serving

PREP TIME:
30 minutes

TOTAL TIME:
45 minutes

INGREDIENTS:

- 12 ears fresh organic corn
- 1-1/2 red bell peppers, diced
- 1-1/2 green bell peppers, diced
- 1 medium red onion, diced
- 2 tablespoons apple cider vinegar
- 5 tablespoons fresh lime juice
- Zest of 3 limes
- 1-1/2 teaspoons honey
- 6 tablespoons olive oil
- 3/4 teaspoon sea salt
- 3/4 teaspoon freshly ground black pepper
- 3/4 cup finely diced parsley or organic basil
- 1/8 teaspoon ground cayenne pepper

DIRECTIONS:

1. Prep: Dice the peppers and onions. Set aside.
2. Make the dressing: Zest and juice the limes and mix together with the vinegar, honey, olive oil, cayenne, sea salt, and black pepper. Set aside.
3. Shuck and boil the corn until two-thirds done (5 to 6 minutes). Drain the corn and move to a hot grill. Lightly char the corn on all sides, turning frequently (10 minutes or less). Cool slightly and cut the kernels from the cobs.
4. Mix the peppers into the corn. Stir the dressing into the vegetable mix. Add the chopped parsley. Let the salad marinate in the refrigerator for at least 2 hours so the flavors blend.
5. Serve chilled or at room temperature.

TIPS & TRICKS: *Flavor Options: For a Southwestern version, substitute cilantro for the parsley or basil. Add a healthy pinch of mild chili pepper and double the cayenne pepper in the dressing.*

Serving Suggestions: *Serve on top of organic greens along with RFK Breadcrumb-Free Crab Cakes or serve on top of an avocado and greens. Consider tossing some into your green salad or sprinkling a little on top of RFK Pizza with Herbed Cauliflower Crust. Believe me, this salad won't last long—that's exactly why I make so much of it!*

SPECIAL DIET INFORMATION:

15-Day Detox Approved/30-Day Habit Reset Approved/Gluten-Free/ Diabetic Friendly/Kid Approved

DR. MINDY'S NOTES

If you make this recipe, be sure that you get organic corn. Corn is one of those crops you can be sure is genetically modified if it's not organic. Aside from that, this recipe is one you will want to put on everything because it tastes so good.

 # GRILLED KOMBUCHA CABBAGE

YIELD: 10 CABBAGE WEDGES

CARBS:	PREP TIME:	TOTAL TIME:
17 grams per cabbage wedge	*40 minutes*	*1 hour*

INGREDIENTS:

– 2 heads cabbage

– 20 shallots, caramelized

– 3 tablespoons avocado oil

– 1/4 cup balsamic vinegar

– 2 cups kombucha (I prefer ginger flavored for this recipe)

– 1/4 cup grated ginger

– 4 cups sauerkraut (I like traditional caraway for this recipe)

– 2/3 cup sunflower seeds, toasted

– 1 teaspoon sea salt

– 1/2 teaspoon ground pepper

TIPS & TRICKS: *Believe it or not, this is a kid-approved dish!*

DIRECTIONS:

1. Preheat oven to 350°F.

2. Line 2 baking sheets or broiler pans with parchment paper. If using broiler pans, tuck the edges in between the top and the drip pan to secure.

3. Prepare the shallots by peeling, slicing thinly. In a medium frying pan, sauté them in 1 tablespoon of oil until they caramelize and are golden brown (this may take 30 minutes—add more oil if necessary). Stir occasionally, but not too often; the shallots need time to cook. If you stir too often, the caramelization won't have time to happen. But at the same time, keep a watchful eye on them so they won't burn. Once caramelized, reserve the shallots in a bowl.

4. Purée the sauerkraut in a blender. Transfer to a medium frying pan or saucepan and reduce by half (this could take 20 minutes or so). Add the grated ginger, salt, and pepper.

5. While the shallots are caramelizing and the sauerkraut is reducing, toast the sunflower seeds either on the stovetop in a frying pan or on a baking sheet in the oven. (I like to toast the sunflower seeds in the oven for this recipe so my hands are free to make the sauerkraut purée at the same time.) The goal is to get them just slightly brown; this brings out the oils and more nutty flavor.

6. Core the cabbage. Trim the bottom and the top off each. Slice each head into 5 circular slices, starting at the top. Place the cabbage on the lined baking sheets.

7. Spread some of the sauerkraut kombucha mixture on top of each cabbage slice.

8. Place in the oven and roast for 30 minutes. At the 10- and 20-minute marks, take a spoon and massage the sauerkraut kombucha mixture in between the layers of the cabbage; as the cabbage continues to roast, you'll be able to get more of the mixture between the leaves.

9. After 30 minutes, the top of the sauerkraut should be golden brown; if not, roast for another 5 to 10 minutes.

10. When done, remove from the oven and evenly distribute the caramelized shallots, sunflower seeds, and a small drizzle of balsamic vinegar on top of each—and serve.

DR. MINDY'S NOTES

Brilliant recipe! Cabbage, kombucha, and ginger make this side dish a culinary delight for your tastebuds and your gut. Add some sea salt to nourish your thyroid and you've got the perfect dish.

CARROT FRIES

YIELD: 8 1-CUP SERVINGS

CARBS:	**PREP TIME:**	**TOTAL TIME:**
12 grams per 1-cup serving	30 minutes	1 to 1-1/4 hours

INGREDIENTS:

– 8 cups carrot sticks (start with 6 pounds large organic carrots)

– 2 tablespoons avocado oil

– 3 teaspoons ground Herbes de Provence

– 1-1/2 teaspoons chili powder

– 1/16 teaspoon cayenne pepper

– 1-1/2 teaspoon salt

– 1/4 teaspoon pepper

DIRECTIONS:

1. Preheat oven to 375°F.

2. Peel the carrots and start to prepare "fries" by cutting the carrots into even lengths. Then "square off" the carrots, eliminating the round edges. Once you have square columns of carrots, slice the carrots into the thickness of your desired fries. Cut these slices into fries.

3. In a large bowl, toss the carrot fries with the avocado oil to coat evenly. Then add the salt, pepper, and herbs and toss again to incorporate evenly.

4. On large baking sheets lined with parchment paper or nonstick baking liners, arrange the fries so they're not touching each other. You'll have best results if each fry has space around it so all can brown evenly.

5. Bake for 30 to 45 minutes, checking every 10 minutes or so to make sure they are cooking evenly.

TIPS & TRICKS: *If you want to maintain the traditional fries shape, you'll need to start with a lot of carrots as eliminating the round parts reduces the number of finished "fries". You can have more fries if you're OK with a nontraditional shape. I like these carrot fries so much that I make four times the herb-salt-and-pepper mixture and store it in a spice jar to save a little time the next time I make these!*

SPECIAL DIET INFORMATION:

15-Day Detox Approved/30-Day Habit Reset Approved/Gluten-Free/Diabetic Friendly/Kid Approved

DR. MINDY'S NOTES

Everyone loves a side order of fries—but your body doesn't. Traditional fries are packed with bad oils while potatoes are high on the glycemic index. But carrot fries will build your health. Great oils, great taste, low carbs—what a winning combo!

ORANGE WILD RICE

YIELD: 7 CUPS (14 1/2-CUP SERVINGS)

CARBS:
20 grams per 1/2-cup serving

PREP TIME:
15 minutes

TOTAL TIME:
60 minutes

INGREDIENTS:

- 2 cups wild rice
  (or wild rice blend)
- 1-3/4 cups bone broth
- 4 tablespoons butter
- 1 cup scallions, thinly sliced (white
  and light green sections only)
- 1 cup sliced raw almonds
- Zest from 2 medium oranges
- 6 tablespoons freshly squeezed
  orange juice
- 1 teaspoon finely ground pepper
- Sea salt to taste

DIRECTIONS:

1. Cook the wild rice according to instructions on the package. (This is typically with 1 cup wild rice to 1-3/4 cups liquid, along with the butter, for approximately 45 minutes on simmer after you bring the mixture to a fast boil.) Check on the rice occasionally to make sure the broth is being absorbed evenly.

2. While the rice is cooking, prepare and measure the other ingredients (zest, juice, sliced scallions, and almonds) and set aside.

3. When the rice is ready, mix in all the other ingredients and serve.

TIPS & TRICKS: *Although most recipes say "don't disturb the rice," I'm a culinary rule breaker and I do interrupt rice and stir occasionally—if I feel it's necessary to make sure the liquid is being absorbed evenly and to make sure it's not sticking or burning on the bottom. Wild rice is too expensive to let burn!*

Serving suggestions: *This rice is great served with wild game (duck, venison, etc.), as well as chicken, salmon, or steak! With the leftovers, you can also fill a hollowed-out bell pepper with some goat cheese and a tomato, then bake for 35 to 45 minutes in a 350°F oven.*

SPECIAL DIET INFORMATION:

30-Day Habit Reset Approved/
Gluten-Free/Diabetic Friendly

DR. MINDY'S NOTES

Wild rice is a better option than brown or white rice because it's lower on the glycemic index. The bone broth in this recipe adds a gut repair benefit while giving this rice a complex taste that will delight your taste buds. If you're looking for more ways to get good fats into your diet, add more butter to this delicious recipe.

QUINOA TABOULI

YIELD: 6 CUPS (12 1/2-CUP SERVINGS)

CARBS:	**PREP TIME:**	**TOTAL TIME:**
5 grams per 1/2-cup serving	20	40 minutes

INGREDIENTS:

- 1/2 cup quinoa
- 1 cup frozen organic spinach, chopped
- 1 cup cherry tomatoes, quartered
- 1 cup red bell pepper, diced
- 1 cup crumbled feta cheese
- 3 tablespoons lemon juice
- 2 tablespoons apple cider vinegar
- 1 tablespoon olive oil
- 1 teaspoon ground Herbes de Provence
- 1/2 teaspoon sea salt
- 1/2 teaspoon ground pepper

DIRECTIONS:

1. Cook the quinoa per the instructions on the package. Fluff and set aside to cool in a large bowl.

2. While the quinoa is cooking is a perfect time to make the salad dressing with the lemon juice, apple cider vinegar, olive oil, sea salt, pepper, and herbs. Blend evenly and set aside.

3. Prepare the other ingredients for the salad: chop the spinach, cut the tomatoes, crumble the feta, and dice the bell peppers.

4. Once the quinoa has cooled, fluff it again with a fork. Add all the other ingredients, mix to incorporate, and then gently mix in the salad dressing.

5. Serve at room temperature or refrigerate for a few hours or overnight.

TIPS & TRICKS: *Make sure not to skip the step of rinsing the quinoa before cooking it; this keeps the grains separate and prevents clumps. If you can plan ahead, start thawing the spinach the night before in the fridge. This recipe tastes even better the next day, so if you're planning a gathering and need to prepare a few things in advance, this salad is a great candidate!*

SPECIAL DIET INFORMATION:

15-Day Detox Approved/30-Day Habit Reset Approved/Gluten-Free/ Diabetic Friendly

DR. MINDY'S NOTES

If you miss having rice in your diet, quinoa is a healthier option. Low in carbs but high in protein, quinoa makes a great addition to any meal.

SEQUOIA'S SWEET POTATO HASH BROWNS

YIELD: 3 CUPS (12 1/4-CUP SERVINGS)

CARBS:
7 grams per 1/4-cup serving

PREP TIME:
10 minutes

TOTAL TIME:
20 minutes

INGREDIENTS:

– 3 cups shredded sweet potato

– Grass-fed butter

– Salt and pepper to taste

DIRECTIONS:

1. Shred the sweet potato with a grater or food processor. (To save time, you can shred the sweet potato in advance; it saves nicely for a few days in the fridge.)

2. In a medium-size bowl, mix in the salt and pepper until evenly combined.

3. On medium heat, melt the butter in a frying pan. Place several 1/4-cup circular mounds of shredded sweet potato in the pan. Cook 4 to 5 minutes on each side, until done. The goal is tender on the inside, slightly crispy on the outside.

***

TIPS & TRICKS: *These hash browns have a magical way of adding color and flavor to any meal. Mindy's husband, Sequoia, makes a "breakfast of champions" this way: On a bed of mixed greens, place one sweet potato hash brown and serve alongside 2 fried eggs, bacon, RFK Caramelized Onions, RFK Sauerkraut—and if you're into the 30-Day Habit Reset portion of the program, you can add a chevre goat cheese medallion after Day 20. Feel free to eat this nourishing "breakfast" at any time of day! When I eat this meal, I'm not hungry for the rest of the day!*

SPECIAL DIET INFORMATION:

15-Day Detox Approved/30-Day Habit Reset Approved/Gluten-Free/ Diabetic Friendly

DR. MINDY'S NOTES

Not only does my husband love this dish, but the kids love it too! This is a great addition to eggs, and you will be amazed at how you can have restaurant-style hash browns with very little effort.

CARAMELIZED RED ONIONS

YIELD: 4 CUPS (32 2-OUNCE SERVINGS)

CARBS:	**PREP TIME:**	**TOTAL TIME:**
7 grams per 2-ounce serving	*10 minutes*	*55 minutes*

INGREDIENTS:

– 6 large red onions

– 1/3 cup avocado oil

– 1/4 cup balsamic vinegar

– 1 tablespoon salt

– 2 teaspoons ground pepper

DIRECTIONS:

1. Peel and slice onions. Toss them with oil, balsamic vinegar, salt, and pepper.

2. Caramelize the onions on a baking sheet with a nonstick liner until done — dark and sweet (approximately 35 to 45 minutes). Make sure to toss the onions every 15-20 minutes, so they don't burn.

SPECIAL DIET INFORMATION:

15-Day Detox Approved/30-Day Habit Reset Approved/Gluten-Free/ Diabetic Friendly/Kid Approved

DR. MINDY'S NOTES

Take a trip to Bonnie's kitchen and you'll notice that she has a jar of caramelized onions ready to go at all times. These are great additions to just about any meal. I like to put these yummy onions on top of a grass-fed burger wrapped in lettuce.

CHAPTER 15

SOUPS

Roasted Butternut Squash

Carrot Chestnut Ginger

Cashew Cream of Broccoli

Carrot Chestnut Ginger Soup, *page 151*

ROASTED BUTTERNUT SQUASH SOUP

YIELD: 6 1-CUP SERVINGS

CARBS:	**PREP TIME:**	**TOTAL TIME:**
17 grams per 1-cup serving	20 minutes	1-1/4 hours

INGREDIENTS:

- 4 cups butternut squash, cubed and roasted
- 1/2 cup chestnuts, peeled and split in half
- 1/2 onion, quartered and roasted
- 2 cloves garlic, smashed
- 3 tablespoons hazelnut oil
- 2-1/2 cups bone broth
- 1 tablespoon raw apple cider vinegar
- 1/4 teaspoon ground ginger
- 1/4 teaspoon ground Herbes de Provence
- 1/8 teaspoon cinnamon
- 1/4 teaspoon salt
- 1/8 teaspoon pepper
- Dash cayenne pepper

OPTIONAL GARNISH:

- 1 tablespoon fresh thyme, finely minced and sprinkled on each serving
- 1/2 cup RF Cashew Cream—add 1 tablespoon to top each serving

DIRECTIONS:

1. Preheat oven to 350°F.

2. Seed, peel, and cube the butternut squash. Cut the onion half into four wedges and add to the butternut squash. Stir in the chestnut halves and smashed garlic cloves. Toss the mixture with hazelnut oil and sprinkle with a little salt and pepper. Roast in a roasting pan or glass baking dish for 45 minutes or until tender and slightly brown.

3. While vegetables are roasting, measure out other ingredients.

4. When the vegetables are ready, cool slightly so they're a little easier to handle.

5. Once the vegetables are cool, transfer to a Vitamix, food processor, or powerful blender. Add the bone broth 1/2 cup at a time and blend. Continue adding bone broth until the soup is the desired consistency.

6. Transfer to a large saucepan, bring to a boil, and serve with optional garnishes as desired.

TIPS & TRICKS: *Don't use a roasting pan or baking dish that is too large; keep the vegetables close together so they cook evenly and the smaller pieces don't overcook or burn. Be careful when blending hot foods in a blender or food processor; open lids slowly to avoid an explosion.*

DR. MINDY'S NOTES

Wow—this soup has so many healing nutrients! Apple cider vinegar kills bad bacteria in your gut, garlic improves immunity, ginger aids in digestion, cinnamon speeds up metabolism, bone broth kills bad bacteria in the gut and repairs leaky gut, hazelnut oil gives key nutrients to your brain, and cayenne pepper will pull mucous out of your body. A powerful soup for healing.

CARROT CHESTNUT GINGER SOUP

YIELD: 4 1-CUP SERVINGS

CARBS:
10 grams per 1-cup serving

PREP TIME:
25 minutes

TOTAL TIME:
1 hour

INGREDIENTS:

- 4 cups carrots, peeled and roughly chopped
- 2 tablespoons pumpkin oil
- 2 tablespoons avocado oil
- 1/2 yellow onion, sliced and caramelized
- 1 tablespoon fresh ginger, grated
- 2 garlic cloves (chopped)
- 2 cups bone broth
- Sea salt and pepper to taste

OPTIONAL INGREDIENTS:

- 1 tablespoon RFK Cashew Cream, per serving (adds 1/2 carb to each serving)

DIRECTIONS:

1. In a sauté pan, over medium heat, add 1 tablespoon of avocado oil and sauté the yellow onion until it is caramelized, for about 20 minutes. Lower the heat if necessary to prevent the onion from burning.

2. Coat the bottom of a large stock pot with a little of the pumpkin oil, then sweat the garlic and ginger for 4 to 5 minutes on medium heat.

3. Add the carrots and stir, cooking another 4 to 5 minutes. Add the broth and cover. Reduce the heat to low and simmer on lowest heat for 30 minutes, until the carrots are very soft.

4. Transfer the vegetables and the caramelized onions to a blender and puree on high until the soup is very smooth. Season with sea salt and pepper to taste.

5. Serve as is, topped with finely chopped parsley, or add 1 tablespoon of RFK Cashew Cream (1/2 extra carb) per serving.

6. Enjoy!

TIPS & TRICKS: *This soup can be made into a warm smoothie during the cold winter months by adding the appropriate protein powders and other supplements. Use caution when blending hot food—open lids slowly! I like to use an immersion blender in soups directly on the stovetop.*

SPECIAL DIET INFORMATION:

15-Day Detox Approved/30-Day Habit Reset Approved/Gluten-Free/ Diabetic Friendly

DR. MINDY'S NOTES

Another healing soup packed with foods that will reset your gut, nourish your brain, and help your body detoxify. Carrots are a little higher in sugar, so use them in moderation when you're on the 15-Day Detox.

CASHEW CREAM OF BROCCOLI SOUP

YIELD: 4 1-CUP SERVINGS

CARBS:
Approximately 6 grams per 8-ounce serving

PREP TIME:
30 minutes

TOTAL TIME:
40 minutes

INGREDIENTS:

- 2 cups broccoli florets
- 3 inches broccoli stem
- 1/2 cup cauliflower florets
- 1/2 onion, sliced thinly, sautéed
- 3 tablespoons coconut oil
- 1/2 cup kale greens
- 1/2 cup RFK Cashew Cream
- 2 cups bone broth
- 1/4 teaspoon ground Herbes de Provence
- 1 tablespoon apple cider vinegar
- Salt and pepper to taste
- Dash cayenne pepper

OPTIONAL INGREDIENTS:

- 1/2 avocado, pureed

DIRECTIONS:

1. Sauté the sliced onions in a little coconut oil to caramelize (about 15 to 20 minutes).

2. At the same time, in a separate 10–12" frying pan, sauté broccoli florets and stems in the remaining coconut oil, along with the cauliflower. Add a little of the bone broth (1/4 cup) to the pan, cover and steam gently for about 8 minutes or until slightly tender. When the onions are done, add them to the other vegetables.

3. While the vegetables are cooking, measure other ingredients.

4. When the vegetables are ready, place them in a Vitamix or powerful blender, add all the other ingredients, and pulse until blended to the desired consistency.

5. Return these to the stove in a saucepan, bring to a boil, reduce heat, and serve.

TIPS & TRICKS: *If you're making this soup ahead of time and you plan to add the optional avocado, do this on the day you serve it to keep your soup green (because avocado has a tendency to turn brown as it oxidizes).*

SPECIAL DIET INFORMATION:

15-Day Detox Approved/30-Day Habit Reset Approved/Gluten-Free/ Diabetic Friendly

DR. MINDY'S NOTES

One comment we got from the Reset Community was that they wanted warm food. If you do the detox in the winter, it's helpful to have warm food to balance out the cold smoothies. Bonnie worked hard to find soups that incorporate many of the necessary elements of the 45-Day Reset: more fat, clean sources of protein, and low carbohydrates. This soup has all of that. Not to mention that the broccoli, cauliflower, onion, and kale help your body produce more glutathione for detoxification. You could use this soup as a substitution for a smoothie on one of your detox days.

CHAPTER 16

SALAD DRESSINGS, SAUCES, AND SPICE MIXES

Citrus Burst Salad Dressing

Mel's Spicy "Soy" Dressing

Tahini Salad Dressing

Ranch Spice Mix (for Dressing and Dip)

All-Purpose Dry Rub Mix

Sweet-and-Hot Habanero Sauce

Chimichurri Sauce

Roasted Tomato Chipotle Salsa

No-Sugar Marinara Sauce

Green-Apple Applesauce

Just Raspberry Syrup

CITRUS BURST SALAD DRESSING

YIELD: 14 OUNCES (7 2-OUNCE SERVINGS)

CARBS:	PREP TIME:	TOTAL TIME:
2 grams per 2-ounce serving	20 minutes	20 minutes

INGREDIENTS:

- 1/4 cup red wine vinegar
- 2/3 cup fresh lime juice
- Zest of 6 limes
- 1 tablesoon raw honey
- 3/4 cup olive oil
- 1-1/2 teaspoon sea salt
- 1-1/2 teaspoon ground pepper
- 1/4 teaspoon cayenne pepper

DIRECTIONS:

1. Blend all ingredients together.
2. Store in the refrigerator.
3. Shake before serving.

TIPS & TRICKS: This salad dressing tastes like summer all year long! Add some finely chopped parsley or basil on top of the salad before dressing it. If on the 15-Day Detox, consider using stevia as a substitute for the honey.

SPECIAL DIET INFORMATION:

15-Day Detox Approved (without the honey)/30-Day Habit Reset Approved/Gluten- Free/Diabetic Friendly

DR. MINDY'S NOTES

Salad dressings at the market are filled with many harmful chemicals. I have searched and searched for healthy salad dressings with the right oils, and I haven't found a single one—so making your own is definitely the best option! This dressing is not only easy to make, but it tastes light and flavorful on your salad. A great dressing to put on a bed of greens.

MEL'S SPICY "SOY" DRESSING

YIELD: APPROXIMATELY 2 CUPS (8 2-OUNCE SERVINGS)

CARBS:
3 grams per serving

PREP TIME:
10 minutes

TOTAL TIME:
10 minutes

INGREDIENTS:

- 2 lemons, zest and juice
- 2 teaspoon minced garlic
- 1/2 cup sesame oil
- 1/4 cup coconut aminos (soy substitute)
- 1/2 teaspoon sea salt
- 1/2 teaspoon pepper
- 1 teaspoon ground oregano
- 2 tablespoons chopped cilantro

DIRECTIONS:

1. Blend all ingredients together except the cilantro. Reserve the cilantro for when you plan to serve the salad dressing.

TIPS & TRICKS: I like this dressing best on crisp romaine lettuce leaves. Keep this dressing in an airtight container in the fridge.

SPECIAL DIET INFORMATION:

15-Day Detox Approved/30-Day Habit Reset/Gluten-Free/Diabetic Friendly

DR. MINDY'S NOTES

Coconut aminos can act as a great substitute for soy sauce. Soy sauce has wheat in it, so while you're on the 45-Day Reset, you'll want to find a good substitute—and coconut aminos are a great one. This salad dressing is perfect for your favorite Chinese chicken salad.

TAHINI SALAD DRESSING

YIELD: APPROXIMATELY 1-1/2 CUPS (6 2-OUNCE SERVINGS)

CARBS:	**PREP TIME:**	**TOTAL TIME:**
5 grams per 2-ounce serving	*10 minutes*	*10 minutes*

INGREDIENTS:

– 2 lemons, zest and juice

– 1/4 cup coconut aminos

– 1/4 cup sesame oil

– 1/4 cup olive oil

– 3 tablespoons sesame tahini

– 1/2 teaspoon cayenne pepper

– 1/2 teaspoon sea salt

– 1/2 teaspoon ground pepper

DIRECTIONS:

1. Blend all ingredients together with a whisk until tahini is completely incorporated.

2. Serve.

_____

TIPS & TRICKS: Keep this dressing in an airtight container in the fridge.

SPECIAL DIET INFORMATION:

15-Day Detox Approved/30-Day Habit Reset Approved/Gluten-Free/ Diabetic Friendly

DR. MINDY'S NOTES

Most store-bought salad dressings are packed with sugar and bad oils. Being able to make some of your favorite dressings with no sugar and the right oils is key to lowering inflammation in your body and losing weight. This is a great dressing to dip cut carrots or jicama into.

RANCH SPICE MIX

FOR DRESSING AND DIP

YIELD: 4 TABLESPOONS (ENOUGH FOR 4 BATCHES OF DRESSING OR DIP)

CARBS:
0 grams per serving (see directions)

PREP TIME:
5 minutes

TOTAL TIME:
5 minutes

INGREDIENTS:

- 2 tablespoons dried parsley
- 1 teaspoon dried dill
- 1 teaspoon garlic powder
- 1 teaspoon onion powder
- 1/2 teaspoon dried basil
- 1/2 teaspoon salt
- 1/2 teaspoon ground pepper

DIRECTIONS:

1. To make Ranch Dressing (1 carb per ounce or 2 tablespoons): Combine 1 tablespoon ranch mix with 2/3 cup RFK Avocado Garlic Aioli, 1/4 cup RFK almond milk, 1/3 cup raw yogurt or goat yogurt, and salt and pepper to taste.

2. To make Ranch Dip (less than 1 carb per ounce or 2 tablespoons): Combine 1 tablespoon ranch mix with 1/3 cup RFK Avocado Garlic Aioli, 1/3 cup raw yogurt or goat yogurt, 1/8 teaspoon xanthan gum, and salt and pepper to taste.

TIPS & TRICKS: *This is kid approved and a much better solution to adding flavor to your dipping veggies than store-bought dips!*

SPECIAL DIET INFORMATION:

30-Day Habit Reset Approved/ Gluten-Free/Diabetic Friendly/Kid Approved

DR. MINDY'S NOTES

Kids love ranch dressing, and Bonnie and I talked about it for months: How could we get a recipe that tastes as good as the chemical-filled ranch dressings in the market? Could we get a healthy version of ranch dressing that kids would love? Well, Bonnie did just that! Tested on our kids, this one is a winner! Great for dipping veggies into.

ALL-PURPOSE DRY RUB MIX

YIELD: ENOUGH FOR 2 LARGE PIECES OF MEAT

CARBS:	PREP TIME:	TOTAL TIME:
0 grams per serving	5 minutes	5 minutes + marinating time

INGREDIENTS:

- 1 tablespoon sea salt
- 2 tablespoons paprika
- 1 tablespoon garlic powder
- 1/2 teaspoon chili powder
- 1/2 teaspoon ground cumin
- 1/8 teaspoon cayenne

DIRECTIONS:

1. Mix all ingredients together. Let sit at room temperature for at least 2 hours and then up to 24 hours in the fridge.

2. Rub this on your steaks or roasts before cooking.

_____

TIPS & TRICKS: *This is a fast and easy way to add some extra flavor to your meats!*

SPECIAL DIET INFORMATION:

15-Day Detox Approved/30-Day Habit Reset Approved/Gluten-Free/ Diabetic Friendly

DR. MINDY'S NOTES

The secret to any yummy kitchen is having great staples such as rubs. Pre-make this rub and have it ready to put on your grass-fed meat or organic chicken.

SWEET-AND-SPICY HABANERO SAUCE

YIELD: 8 CUPS (LOTS TO SAVE FOR LATER!)

CARBS:
5 grams per 1-ounce serving

PREP TIME:
30 minutes

TOTAL TIME:
30 minutes

INGREDIENTS:

- 1-½ cups avocado oil
- 4 red bell peppers, cored, seeded, and quartered
- 1 to 4 habanero chilies, halved (seeds removed for less heat)
- 1 red onion, peeled and cut into 8 pieces
- ¾ cup fresh-squeezed orange juice
- 5 limes, zest and juice
- 1-½ tablespoons ground cumin
- ¼ cup fresh oregano leaves, packed
- 1 teaspoon sea salt
- 1 teaspoon finely ground pepper
- 2 teaspoons Dijon mustard
- 1-½ teaspoons ground cardamom

DIRECTIONS:

1. In a Vitamix or large blender, blend all ingredients until smooth (approximately 4 minutes).

2. Warm the amount of sauce you're ready to use in a saucepan and save the rest for later in the refrigerator or freezer.

3. Enjoy with steak, chicken, salmon, shrimp—almost anything!

TIPS & TRICKS: *This recipe is so delicious, you'll want to make the whole recipe and save some for later! It freezes very well; use ice cube trays or other freezer-safe containers. The integrity and fresh flavors are not lost in the freezing process.*

SPECIAL DIET INFORMATION:

30-Day Habit Reset Approved/15-Day Detox Approved (without the maple syrup)

DR. MINDY'S NOTES

Just like salad dressings, sauces are filled with the wrong oils, sugars, and chemicals. The habaneros in this sauce will speed up your metabolism, while the sea salt will stimulate your thyroid. Make sure all your spices are organic, as spices can be heavily sprayed with pesticides.

CHIMICHURRI SAUCE

YIELD: 2 CUPS (8 2-OUNCE SERVINGS)

CARBS:
0 grams per serving

PREP TIME:
15 minutes

TOTAL TIME:
15 minutes

INGREDIENTS:

- 1 cup fresh cilantro, firmly packed
- 1 cup fresh parsley, firmly packed
- 10 cloves garlic, mashed
- 1/4 cup apple cider vinegar
- 1/4 cup lemon juice
- 1/4 cup olive oil
- 1/2 teaspoon sea salt
- 1/2 teaspoon ground cumin
- 1/2 teaspoon ground pepper
- 1/2 teaspoon crushed red pepper
- 1/2 teaspoon cayenne pepper

DIRECTIONS:

1. In a Vitamix, food processor, or blender, combine all ingredients. Mix well using a few pulses, but do not purée.

TIPS & TRICKS: This sauce can be enjoyed on your choice of steak, chicken, or fish. It can even be used as a dip. It's best if used immediately due to the delicate fresh herbs, but it can withstand a couple of days in the refrigerator.

SPECIAL DIET INFORMATION:

15-Day Detox Approved/30-Day Habit Reset Approved/Gluten-Free/ Diabetic Friendly

DR. MINDY'S NOTES

Cilantro is great for pulling heavy metals out of your body. Apple cider vinegar will kill bad bacteria in your gut. Cayenne pepper pulls mucus out of your gut. Garlic kills cancer cells. Parsley alkalizes your body and builds your immune system. And sea salt nourishes your thyroid. With all those ingredients in one sauce, I recommend putting this on any and everything you can find!

ROASTED TOMATO CHIPOTLE SALSA

YIELD: APPROXIMATELY 4 CUPS (10 3-OUNCE SERVINGS)

CARBS:
7 grams per 3-ounce serving

PREP TIME:
30 minutes

TOTAL TIME:
1 hour

INGREDIENTS:

- 3 pounds tomatoes
- 4 jalapeño peppers
- 3 chipotle peppers in adobo sauce
- 3 tablespoons avocado oil
- 1 head garlic
- 2 red onions, finely chopped
- 1/2 cup cilantro, finely chopped
- 1/4 cup raw apple cider vinegar
- 1 teaspoon sea salt
- 1/2 teaspoon ground black pepper
- 1/2 teaspoon cayenne pepper

DIRECTIONS:

1. Preheat oven to 400°F.

2. Prepare roasted garlic: Remove the top of the garlic head to expose individual cloves. Place in a small baking dish or garlic baker. Drizzle with 1 tablespoon of avocado oil. Bake for 35 to 45 minutes or until lightly golden brown and soft. Cool. When cool enough to handle, remove the garlic from each clove with a small spoon or by squeezing. Set aside.

3. While the garlic is roasting, prepare the other ingredients. Core the tomatoes and slice them in half, lengthwise. Place them cut side down in a large baking dish. Brush the tomatoes with the remaining avocado oil. Halve the peppers and remove the seeds and stems. Place them cut side down in the baking dish. Roast, uncovered, until the pepper skins are charred and the tomatoes are tender (25 to 30 minutes). Cool. Once cool, remove the tomato skins. Set aside.

4. Place the garlic, peppers, and chipotle peppers in a Vitamix, food processor, or blender. Cover and blend with a few pulses until finely chopped. Add half of the tomatoes, cover, and blend with a few pulses until coarsely chopped. Transfer to a large mixing bowl.

5. Coarsely chop the remaining tomatoes and combine with other chopped tomatoes.

6. Add the chopped red onions, cilantro, salt, pepper, and cayenne into the tomato mixture; stir to combine.

7. Cover, chill, and serve after a few hours of letting the flavors blend.

TIPS & TRICKS: This recipe tastes better when made ahead of time, so the flavors have time to meld!

SPECIAL DIET INFORMATION:

15-Day Detox Approved/30-Day Habit Reset/Gluten-Free/Diabetic Friendly

DR. MINDY'S NOTES

Another nutrient-packed recipe. I love how Bonnie uses apple cider vinegar in this recipe. Apple cider vinegar is incredibly powerful for the gut, as it kills bad bacteria fast. With garlic, sea salt, and cayenne pepper added to this recipe, you'll have a plate full of foods that support your thyroid and immune system.

NO-SUGAR MARINARA SAUCE

YIELD: APPROXIMATELY 6 CUPS (12 4-OUNCE SERVINGS)

CARBS:
6 grams per 4-ounce serving

PREP TIME:
20 minutes

TOTAL TIME:
40 to 50 minutes

INGREDIENTS:

– 6 large red tomatoes
– 2 red bell peppers
– 1 teaspoon balsamic vinegar
– 2 tablespoons tomato paste
– 2 tablespoons avocado oil
– 2 cloves garlic
– 3/4 teaspoon Herbes de Provence
– 1/2 teaspoon sea salt
– 1/2 teaspoon ground pepper

DIRECTIONS:

1. Core the tomatoes, cut them into chunks, and reserve half. Remove the stem and deseed the bell peppers, then cut them into chunks.

2. Put one-half of the tomato chunks, all of the bell peppers, and all the other ingredients into a Vitamix, food processor, or powerful blender. Pulse a few times, just to create a consistent texture. Don't purée, as you want some texture.

3. Transfer to a medium saucepan and add the remaining tomato chunks. Bring to a boil and then reduce to a simmer until the sauce thickens to your desired consistency (about 20 to 30 minutes).

4. Serve or cool and store in an airtight container in your fridge for up to one week.

_____

TIPS & TRICKS: *Did you know that most store-bought marinara sauces contain sugar? If you're trying to avoid sugar, as I am, here's an easy recipe that's even more delicious than even the best store-bought brand!*

SPECIAL DIET INFORMATION:

15-Day Detox Approved/30-Day Habit Reset Approved/Gluten-Free/ Diabetic Friendly

DR. MINDY'S NOTES

Start reading the labels on your marinara sauce—you'll see that the sugar content is high. A plate of spaghetti and sauce can spike your blood sugar dramatically. Bonnie has solved the marinara problem for you with this sauce. With only 4g carbs, this sauce will have a minimal effect on your blood sugar.

GREEN-APPLE APPLESAUCE

YIELD: APPROXIMATELY 5 CUPS (10-1/2 CUP SERVINGS)

CARBS:
12 grams per 1/2 cup serving

PREP TIME:
10 minutes

TOTAL TIME:
30 minutes

INGREDIENTS:

- 6 large green Granny Smith apples, sliced, skin on
- 1 cup water
- 1 tablespoon lemon juice
- 1 teaspoon cinnamon
- 1/2 teaspoon ground ginger
- 1/4 teaspoon cloves

DIRECTIONS:

1. Place all ingredients in a 4-quart saucepan on medium heat; toss to make sure that the spices have been fully integrated.

2. Bring to a rolling boil, then reduce heat to a simmer. Let simmer for 15 to 20 minutes or until the apple is soft and pliable.

3. Serve warm or cold.

TIPS & TRICKS: *Serve this tangy and tart applesauce with the RFK Roasted Pork Loin or add a little bit to your breakfast cereal. Whether accompanying savory or sweet, this applesauce is the perfect date!*

SPECIAL DIET INFORMATION:

15-Day Detox Approved/30-Day Habit Reset Approved/Gluten-Free/Diabetic Friendly/Kid Approved

DR. MINDY'S NOTES

You'll see green apples throughout many of my recommendations. Green apples are the lowest in sugar of all apples. This is a great recipe to serve your kids or put next to your favorite pork dish, including the RFK Roasted Pork Loin recipe in this book!

JUST RASPBERRY SYRUP

YIELD: APPROXIMATELY 2 CUPS (8 2-OUNCE SERVINGS)

CARBS:
10 grams per 2-ounce serving

PREP TIME:
10 minutes

COOK TIME:
10 minutes

INGREDIENTS:

– 3 cups frozen raspberries

– 1/4 cup water

DIRECTIONS:

1. In a medium saucepan on medium heat, add the raspberries and water.

2. Melt the raspberries about 7 to 10 minutes, until they become a sauce. Remove from heat. Let cool to very warm. When the temperature is manageable, blend in a Vitamix or powerful blender for 2 to 3 minutes until the mixture becomes a purée. The end result is best when the seeds practically disappear in the blending process.

3. Pour into a glass container and store in the refrigerator for up to one week.

─────────────

TIPS & TRICKS: *Enjoy this fresh raspberry sauce on waffles and ice cream, or use it to make your own RFK Raspberry Chia Jam.*

SPECIAL DIET INFORMATION:

15-Day Detox Approved/30-Day Habit Reset Approved/Gluten-Free/ Diabetic Friendly/Kid Approved

DR. MINDY'S NOTES

Raspberries are another low-sugar fruit. Eat as much of them as you want in both the 15-Day Detox and 30-Day Habit Reset. This purée will be great in any of your smoothies or on top of RFK Waffles.

CHAPTER 17

GRAIN-FREE BAKES

Gone-Nuts Loaf

Almond Coconut Bread

Savory Mini Flourless Soufflés

Biscuits – 3 Ways

Cauliflower Turmeric Tortillas

Spicy Zucchini Apple Muffins

GONE-NUTS LOAF

YIELD: 2 LOAVES (12 SLICES EACH)

CARBS:
Plain: 15 grams per slice/Spiced: 17 grams per slice /Cacao Spice: 20 grams per slice

PREP TIME:
10 minutes (+ variable rest time)

COOK TIME:
55 to 60 minutes

INGREDIENTS:

- 1 cup raw sunflower seeds
- 1 cup raw pumpkin seeds
- 1/2 cup whole flax seeds
- 1/2 cup sesame seeds
- 1/2 cup raw hazelnuts
- 1/2 cup raw macadamia nuts
- 3 cups rolled oats
- 1/4 cup chia seeds
- 1/2 cup whole psyllium husks
  2 teaspoons sea salt
- 2 tablespoons maple syrup
- 6 tablespoons coconut oil, melted
- 3 cups water

OPTIONAL INGREDIENTS:

- 1/4 cup cricket powder

Cinnamon Spice Variation
(add these ingredients):

- 2 tablespoons cinnamon
- 1 tablespoon freshly ground nutmeg
- 1 cup shredded coconut
- 2 tablespoons maple syrup

Cacao Spice Variation
(now add these ingredients, too):

- 1 cup raw cacao powder
- 3 tablespoons whole psyllium husks
- 2 tablespoons maple syrup
- 1/3 cup water

SPECIAL DIET INFORMATION:

15-Day Detox Approved (without the maple syrup)/30-Day Habit Reset Approved/Gluten-Free/Diabetic Friendly

DIRECTIONS:

1. Line the bottom of your loaf pans with parchment and then coat the inside of the pans with a thin layer of coconut oil.

2. In a small bowl, whisk the liquid ingredients (maple syrup, oil, and water) together and then set aside.

3. In a large bowl, mix all the dry ingredients, stirring well to evenly incorporate.

4. Add the wet ingredients to the dry ingredients and combine until all the moisture has been absorbed. If your dough is too thick and difficult to manage, add a little bit of water, 1 teaspoon at a time, until it's easier to work with. Don't add too much water, as the dough is supposed to be dense.

5. Divide the mixture evenly into 2 loaf pans. Press the batter down into the pans, getting rid of any bubbles.

6. Let the loaves rest at room temperature. The duration is variable and up to you—hours, overnight, or all day. This rest period is what allows the ingredients to bind together so your loaves will be easy to slice and won't crumble. You will know your loaf is ready for baking if it retains its shape when you pull the dough away from the pan.

7. When you're ready to bake your loaves, preheat the oven to 350°F.

8. Bake for 20 minutes, then remove the loaf from the pan and continue baking for another 35 to 45 minutes, this time upside down and directly on the oven rack. When the loaves make a hollow sound when tapped with a wooden spoon, they have finished baking.

9. Let the loaves cool completely before slicing.

TIPS & TRICKS: *First, of course the cricket powder is optional! But I bet you won't even be able to tell that it's in there! Cricket powder is a sustainable protein that's rich in iron, calcium, and B12, to name just a few of its benefits. This loaf will store for up to a week in the fridge (it gets eaten long before that in my house). It can also be sliced and then frozen for storage. I pull a few slices out and broil them for 4 minutes on each side in the oven for a toasted, nutty flavor. There are many spreads in this cookbook that are delicious on this loaf, but the Pumpkin Seed Spread is a real crowd pleaser, and spreading it on the RFK Gone-Nuts Loaf makes for a kid-approved combo! You might want to choose a silicon baking pan for easier handling.*

DR. MINDY'S NOTES

I absolutely LOVE this bread! If you think you have to go without bread for your 45-Day Reset, think again. Not only is this bread packed with more nutrients and health than I have space to write about, but it tastes amazing. But beware: This bread acts like a broom to sweep your colon because of the psyllium husk. I personally love this bread with the RFK Pumpkin Spread on top.

ALMOND COCONUT BREAD

YIELD: 2 LOAVES (15 SLICES EACH)

CARBS:
9 grams per slice

PREP TIME:
10 minutes

BAKE TIME:
55 minutes

INGREDIENTS:

– 2 cups almond flour

– 1-1/2 cups coconut flour

– 2/3 cup hemp seeds

– 1/2 cup ground flaxseed

– 1/2 cup whole psyllium husk

– 2 tablespoons baking powder

– 2 teaspoons ground anise seed (optional, or spice of choice)

– 2 teaspoons salt

– 12 eggs, room temperature

– 1 cup raw cheddar cheese, grated

– 2/3 cup coconut oil, melted

– 1-1/2 cups raw-milk kefir

TIPS & TRICKS: *Enjoy these slices toasted with grass-fed butter and RFK Raspberry Chia Jam.*

DIRECTIONS:

1. Preheat oven to 350°F.

2. In a large bowl, combine all the dry ingredients. Stir well to incorporate the seeds evenly.

3. In a separate large bowl, beat the eggs, then incorporate the other wet ingredients until a smooth batter is formed.

4. Slowly incorporate the dry ingredients into the wet ingredients. (The coconut oil might clump a bit here, but don't worry, this will work itself out during baking.) Mix thoroughly. Pour into greased bread pans lined with parchment.

5. Bake for 45 to 50 minutes or until done. You'll know the bread is done when a toothpick comes out clean.

6. Remove from the oven, then remove loaves from the pans and cool directly on a cooling rack so the crust dries; otherwise, it will get soggy, cooling in the pan.

7. Let cool completely before slicing. Slice and toast right away, or slice and store in the freezer. This makes it easy to enjoy one slice at a time and not worry if it's going to go bad because it has no preservatives in it.

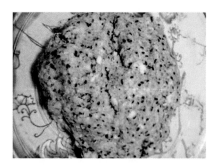

SPECIAL DIET INFORMATION:

15- Day Detox Approved/30-Day Habit Reset Approved/Gluten-Free/ Diabetic Friendly

DR. MINDY'S NOTES

Another great recipe if you are missing bread. The great things about the flours that Bonnie uses in this recipe is that they are packed with protein and fiber. Traditional wheat flour has nowhere near the protein that almond flour does. You can even have this on your 15-Day Detox. Enjoy!

SAVORY MINI FLOURLESS SOUFFLÉS

YIELD: 16 SOUFFLES

CARBS:
8 grams per souffle

PREP TIME:
15 minutes

COOK TIME:
40 to 45 minutes

INGREDIENTS:

- 2 cups blanched almond flour
- 1/2 cup arrowroot flour
- 1 teaspoon baking powder
- 1/2 teaspoon baking soda
- 1 teaspoon sea salt
- 6 large eggs
- 1/4 cup raw-milk kefir
- 1 tablespoon raw apple cider vinegar
- 1 cup green onions, finely minced
- 2 cups raw sharp cheddar cheese (or goat cheddar cheese), grated and firmly packed

DIRECTIONS:

1. Preheat oven to 350°F.

2. In a medium-size bowl, mix together the dry ingredients (almond flour, arrowroot flour, baking powder, baking soda, and salt).

3. In a small bowl, beat the eggs with the apple cider vinegar and raw-milk kefir. Blend with the green onions and grated cheese.

4. Silicon muffin cups are recommended because they do not require any additional oil. If you don't have silicon, simply put paper liners in the muffin pans. Add about 1/4 cup of batter to each cup.

5. Bake at 350°F for 25 to 30 minutes and enjoy!

TIPS & TRICKS: *Silicon muffin pans are preferred because it's much easier to get your muffins out of them to cool, and no muffin is wasted or peeled off, as happens with muffin liners.*

SPECIAL DIET INFORMATION:

30-Day Habit Reset Approved/ Gluten-Free/Diabetic Friendly

DR. MINDY'S NOTES

The best thing about goat cheese is that it's easier for your gut to digest. Apple cider vinegar is also great for the gut, as it kills the bad bacteria often associated with SIBO and leaky gut. Sea salt nourishes your thyroid, and almond flour is packed with protein. All of that makes this not only a tasty treat, but one that builds your health.

BISCUITS
3 WAYS: HERB, ORANGE, AND LAVENDER

YIELD: 15 3-INCH BISCUITS

CARBS:	PREP TIME:	BAKE TIME:
20 grams per 3-inch biscuit	*15 minutes (followed by a 2-hour refrigerator rest)*	*20 minutes*

INGREDIENTS:

- 3-1/2 cups blanched almond flour (+ some for dusting)
- 1-1/2 cups arrowroot flour
- 1 teaspoon sea salt
- 1 teaspoon baking powder
- 1/2 teaspoon baking soda
- 5 large eggs (reserve 1 for coating the tops before baking)
- 1/2 cup avocado oil
- 2 tablespoons raw honey

TIPS & TRICKS: *Delicious and won't make your blood sugar spike!*

DIRECTIONS:

1. In a large bowl, combine the dry ingredients (almond flour, arrowroot flour, salt, baking soda, baking powder, and any dry herbs from a flavored variation mentioned below).

2. In a medium-size bowl, whisk together the wet ingredients (4 of the eggs, avocado oil, honey, and any wet ingredients from a flavor variation mentioned below).

3. Mix the wet ingredients into the dry ingredients. Blend until thoroughly incorporated and then make a round disk-like shape with the dough. Cover the dough and place in the refrigerator for at least 2 hours, or overnight.

4. When ready to bake, preheat the oven to 350°F. Line the baking sheet with parchment paper. On a flat surface, place one piece of parchment under the dough disk and one piece on top. Using a rolling pin, roll the dough out to a 1-inch thickness between the 2 pieces of parchment paper. (You might want to use a little extra almond flour between the dough and the parchment to keep the dough from sticking.) Cut out 3-inch circles and place on a baking sheet lined with parchment paper. Gather up the extra dough left over and roll it out again to get a few more biscuits.

5. Whisk the remaining egg in a small bowl and brush on top of the biscuits. This will give the biscuits a golden brown color during the baking process.

6. Bake at 350°F for 15 to 20 minutes or until golden brown.

SPECIAL DIET INFORMATION:

15-Day Detox Approved (without the honey)/30-Day Habit Reset Approved/Gluten-Free/Diabetic Friendly

DR. MINDY'S NOTES

Grain-free biscuits? Who would have thought that a biscuit without flour could taste so good! Almond flour is a fabulous flour substitute, and unlike conventional flour, it's packed with magnesium, potassium, calcium, and vitamin E—not to mention it's much higher in protein than regular bread. That is great news for your blood sugar level.

VARIATIONS:

<u>**Herb Variation:**</u> Add 1 tablespoon of Herbes de Provence or rosemary to the dry ingredients in Step 1.

<u>**Orange Variation:**</u> Add 1 tablespoon of orange oil and 2 teaspoons of orange zest to the wet ingredients in Step 2.

<u>Lavender Variation:</u> Add 1 tablespoon of dried lavender to the dry ingredients in step 1 and 1 teaspoon of lavender extract to the wet ingredients.

CAULIFLOWER TURMERIC TORTILLAS

YIELD: 12 TORTILLAS

CARBS:	**PREP TIME:**	**TOTAL TIME:**
3 grams per tortilla	*25 minutes*	*50 minutes*

INGREDIENTS:

- 2 heads cauliflower (approximately 8 cups, chopped), steamed
- 1 cup chopped green onions (approximately 2 bunches)
- 5 large eggs, beaten
- 1/2 teaspoon sea salt
- 1/2 teaspoon finely ground pepper
- 1/2 teaspoon ground turmeric
- 3/4 teaspoon xanthan gum

DIRECTIONS:

1. Preheat oven to 350°F.

2. Steam the cauliflower heads until tender. Use a food processor or Vitamix (recommended) to blend the cauliflower and green onions until smooth (they will have a slightly green color because of the onions; don't worry, once you add the turmeric, they'll turn yellow). This mixture should make about 32 fluid ounces.

3. Strain this mixture through cheesecloth or a nut milk bag to get rid of excess liquid.

4. In a medium-size bowl, mix the cauliflower mixture with the spices, eggs, and xanthan gum.

5. On a baking sheet with parchment paper or a nonstick silicon baking liner, create "tortillas" using 1/4 cup of the batter for each.

6. Bake at 350°F for 25 minutes on one side only.

7. Let cool before removing from the baking liner.

TIPS & TRICKS: *Timesaving tip: These tortillas can be made in advance and stored in the fridge for a few days; make sure you layer them in between parchment paper so they don't stick together. They're great as a breakfast burrito or served with RFK Pulled Pork.*

SPECIAL DIET INFORMATION:

15-Day Detox Approved/30-Day Habit Reset Approved/Gluten-Free/ Diabetic Friendly

DR. MINDY'S NOTES

Who wants to give up tortillas during your 45-Day Reset? Well, thanks to this amazing recipe, you don't have to. If you read my earlier chapters, you know that I am a huge fan of turmeric. Not only does it have anticarcinogenic qualities, but it lowers inflammation throughout your body. The cauliflower will boost your glutathione levels. Best of all, low in carbohydrates, this dish won't spike your blood sugar very high.

SPICY ZUCCHINI APPLE MUFFINS

YIELD: 24 MUFFINS

CARBS:
6 grams per muffin

PREP TIME:
20 minutes

TOTAL TIME:
40 minutes

INGREDIENTS:

- 2 cups grated zucchini
- 2 cups grated green apple
- 1 cup almond flour
- 1/4 cup coconut oil, melted
- 1 cup RFK Nut Butter of the Gods
- 6 smashed Medjool dates
- 4 eggs
- 3 teaspoons vanilla extract
- 1 teaspoon baking powder
- 1/2 teaspoon baking soda
- 4 teaspoons ground cinnamon
- 1 teaspoon ground ginger
- 1-1/2 teaspoons freshly ground nutmeg
- 3/4 teaspoon ground cloves
- 1/2 teaspoon salt

DIRECTIONS:

1. Preheat oven to 350°F.

2. Grate the zucchini and apple with the peel on. Squeeze out the excess liquid from the zucchini.

3. Smash the dates by either using a mortar and pestle or mincing the dates until they resemble a paste.

4. In a large bowl, mix together the wet ingredients, starting with blending the nut butter with the eggs and smashed dates. Then add the zucchini, apple, coconut oil, and vanilla. Blend thoroughly.

5. In a separate bowl, mix together the dry ingredients: almond flour, baking powder, baking soda, and spices (cinnamon, ginger, nutmeg, ground cloves, and sea salt).

6. Blend the dry mixture evenly into the wet mixture.

7. Lightly oil a silicon muffin pan or silicon muffin cups. If you don't have silicon, simply put paper liners in the muffin pan. Add about 1/4 cup of batter to each cup.

8. Bake at 350°F for 15 to 20 minutes or until a toothpick comes out clean from the center.

SPECIAL DIET INFORMATION:

30-Day Habit Reset Approved/
Gluten-Free/Diabetic Friendly

DR. MINDY'S NOTES

Anytime you can find a recipe that tastes like grains but acts like fat in your bloodstream, you've got a winner. Using a green apple lowers the carb count, and adding in the RFK Nut Butter of the Gods increases your fat count for the day. This recipe is not only a brilliant combination of key nutrients needed to reset your health, but it tastes so good you'll want to cry with joy!

Kale Chips, *page 180*

KALE CHIPS

YIELD: 6 SERVINGS

CARBS:
3 grams per serving

PREP TIME:
10 minutes

TOTAL TIME:
22 minutes

INGREDIENTS:

– 1/2 pound curly kale leaves

– 2 tablespoons avocado oil

– Sea salt, to taste

DIRECTIONS:

1. Preheat the oven to 425°F.

2. Remove the tough stems from the kale. Wash and dry the leaves. Tear the leaves into bite-size pieces and put them in a large bowl.

3. Drizzle the kale with the avocado oil and massage into the leaves.

4. Spread the kale leaves evenly on a lined baking sheet and put in the oven. At the 5-minute mark, use a spatula to separate any leaves of kale that are sticking together.

5. Continue cooking the kale for about 12 minutes, until the leaves are crisp.

6. Remove from the oven and sprinkle with salt.

TIPS & TRICKS: *Get creative with your salts. There are many great flavored salts out there that can add a kick to your chips, like truffle salt or spicy salt. Kale chips do not have to be boring!*

SPECIAL DIET INFORMATION:

15-Day Detox Approved/30-Day Habit Reset Approved/Gluten-Free/Diabetic Friendly

DR. MINDY'S NOTES

If you like crunch, this recipe is for you. It may not be a potato chip, but it's a close second. Kale is packed with antioxidants to support your immune system and fight cancer, while the avocado oil nourishes your brain and lowers your inflammation levels.

PIZZA CHIA SEED CRACKERS

YIELD: 12 SERVINGS

CARBS:
7 grams per serving

PREP TIME:
15 minutes

TOTAL TIME:
1-1/4 hours

INGREDIENTS:

- 1/2 cup chia seeds
- 1-1/2 to 2 cups water (used in 2 places in recipe)
- 1/2 cup flaxseed
- 1/2 cup sesame seeds
- 1/2 cup sunflower seeds
- 3/4 cup pumpkin seeds
- 1 teaspoon salt
- 1 teaspoon garlic powder
- 4 tablespoons tomato powder

DIRECTIONS:

1. Preheat oven to 350° F.

2. In a small bowl, mix chia seeds with 1 cup of water. Soak for 10 to 15 minutes to activate natural gel properties of the chia seeds.

3. While the chia seeds are activating, measure out all the other seeds and blend together with the salt, garlic powder, and tomato powder.

4. Combine the chia seed gel with the dry seed mixture and blend well. Add 1/2 to 1 cup of water.

5. Prepare 2 sheets of parchment paper the size of your baking sheet. On a flat surface, place the seed mixture between the 2 sheets of parchment paper and spread evenly with a rolling pin.

6. Transfer the parchment paper to your baking sheet. Peel off the top layer of parchment paper.

7. Use a pizza cutter or knife to score 12 or 24 crackers.

8. Bake in the oven for 60 minutes.

9. Cool completely before cutting along the scores to break into crackers.

TIPS & TRICKS: *Store the crackers in an airtight container. These crackers will freeze, but you'll want to toast them when you take them out of the freezer so they don't get soggy from the defrosting process.*

SPECIAL DIET INFORMATION:

15-Day Detox Approved/30-Day Habit Reset Approved/Gluten-Free/ Diabetic Friendly

DR. MINDY'S NOTES

You don't have to give up on snacking altogether while on the 45-Day Reset. Although you may be getting used to not munching on your Doritos chips, these crackers are great with raw cheese or dipped in hummus. Chia seeds are a powerful cleanser and an antioxidant as well.

LOUISE'S CHICKPEA CRACKERS

YIELD: 24 CRACKERS (12 2-CRACKER SERVINGS)

CARBS:
9 grams per 2-cracker serving

PREP TIME:
10 minutes

TOTAL TIME:
1 hour

INGREDIENTS:

– 1 cup chickpea flour
– 1/2 cup almond flour
– 1 cup sesame seeds
– 1/2 cup flax seeds
– 1 teaspoon salt
– 1 egg
– 1/4 to 1/2 cup avocado oil

DIRECTIONS:

1. Preheat oven to 350° F.

2. In a large bowl, mix all dry ingredients together and set aside.

3. Beat the egg and 1/4 cup of the avocado oil. Blend into the dry-ingredients mixture. Add more oil, 1 teaspoon at a time, to get a nice consistency that sticks together.

4. Prepare 2 sheets of parchment paper the size of your baking sheet. On a flat surface, place the seed mixture between the 2 sheets of parchment paper and spread it thinly but evenly with a rolling pin.

5. Transfer the parchment paper to your baking sheet. Peel off the top layer of parchment paper.

6. Use a pizza cutter or knife to score 24 crackers.

7. Bake in the oven for 45 minutes; while still warm, cut along the scores to separate crackers. Cool completely (approximately 20 to 30 minutes).

8. Bake for a second time in the oven for 10 to 15 minutes or until crunchy.

────────

TIPS & TRICKS: *These crackers pair well with the RFK vegetable spreads, as well as hummus.*

SPECIAL DIET INFORMATION:

15-Day Detox Approved/30-Day Habit Reset Approved/Gluten-Free/ Diabetic Friendly

DR. MINDY'S NOTES

Flaxseeds are known to lower inflammation and prevent colon and breast cancer. They also help detoxify your cells and balance hormones. You want to include flaxseeds in as many of your meals as possible. Eating these crackers is a great way to increase your flaxseed consumption while satisfying your taste buds.

FRESH MINT AND PEA SPREAD

YIELD: 3 CUPS (24 2-TABLESPOON SERVINGS)

CARBS:
3 grams per serving

PREP TIME:
10 minutes

TOTAL TIME:
10 minutes

INGREDIENTS:

- 3 cups fresh peas
- 1/2 cup almond, ground to consistency of flour
- Zest of 1 lemon
- 2 cups fresh mint, well packed
- 3 tablespoons lemon juice
- 1 shishito pepper
- 2 ounces goat cheese
- 1/2 cup avocado oil

DIRECTIONS:

1. In a Vitamix or powerful blender, place all ingredients into the carafe and blend on medium speed until the spread is the desired consistency.

2. Store in the refrigerator in a glass container. Spread will last in the fridge 5 to 7 days.

SPECIAL DIET INFORMATION:

15-Day Detox Approved (without the goat cheese)/30-Day Habit Reset Approved/Gluten-Free/Diabetes Friendly

DR. MINDY'S NOTES

Mint can help with digestion, promote weight loss, help with irritable bowel syndrome, relieve respiratory conditions, improve memory, and even alleviate pain from shingles. This spread will benefit your health, and it's a great complement to the cracker recipes in this book.

RAW BROCCOLI AND BASIL SPREAD

YIELD: 3 CUPS (24 2-TABLESPOON SERVINGS)

CARBS:
2 grams per 2-tablespoon serving

PREP TIME:
10 minutes

TOTAL TIME:
10 minutes

INGREDIENTS:

- 1/2 large head of broccoli (approximately 3 cups), chopped
- 1 cup hazelnuts
- 2 cloves garlic
- 1 cup basil leaves, densely packed
- 3/4 cup walnut oil
- 2 tablespoons lemon juice
- 1 teaspoon salt
- 1/2 teaspoon pepper
- Zest from 1 lemon
- 1 cup raw shredded Parmesan cheese

DIRECTIONS:

1. In a Vitamix blender, pulse the hazelnuts until they reach a flourlike consistency.
2. Add all other ingredients and continue to purée until the desired consistency is reached.

SPECIAL DIET INFORMATION:

15-Day Detox Approved (without the cheese)/30-Day Habit Reset Approved (dairy should be raw)/Gluten-Free/Diabetic Friendly

DR. MINDY'S NOTES

Remember glutathione—what a powerful detoxifier it is? Well, eating broccoli will stimulate your body's own natural glutathione production. The healthiest way to eat broccoli is raw. And although I don't like the taste of raw broccoli, I could eat this spread all day long. Be sure to get the Parmesan raw for all the extra digestive enzymes.

WALNUT AND SUN-DRIED TOMATO PÂTÉ

YIELD: 2 CUPS (16 2-TABLESPOON SERVINGS)

CARBS:
3 grams per 2-tablespoon serving

PREP TIME:
10 minutes (+ overnight soak)

TOTAL TIME:
10 minutes (+ overnight soak)

INGREDIENTS:

- 2 cups walnuts, soaked overnight
- 1/2 cup sundried tomatoes, rehydrated then drained
- 30 sage leaves
- 1/2 cup walnut oil
- 2 ounces goat cheese
- 1 Medjool date
- 1/2 teaspoon sea salt
- 1/4 teaspoon ground pepper

DIRECTIONS:

1. Soak walnuts overnight, drain, and set aside.
2. Soak the sundried tomatoes in olive oil overnight, then drain and set aside. When ready to make the paté, place all ingredients into a carafe and blend to the desired consistency.

_____

TIPS & TRICKS: *Add a little more sweetness by adding another half or whole date. If the paté is too thick, add a little more oil.*

SPECIAL DIET INFORMATION:

15-Day Detox Approved (without the dates)/30-Day Habit Reset Approved/Gluten-Free/Diabetic Friendly/Kid Approved

DR. MINDY'S NOTES

Spreads are such a good way to get key nutrients and healthy fats into your cells in an easy and convenient way. Walnuts are packed with magnesium, omega-3 fatty acids, and melatonin. This delicious recipe was inspired by Louise, one of our Reset community members in Denmark!

PUMPKIN SPICE SPREAD

YIELD: 2-1/2 CUPS (20 2-TABLESPOON SERVINGS)

CARBS:
5 grams per 2-tablespoon serving

PREP TIME:
10 minutes

TOTAL TIME:
10 minutes

INGREDIENTS:

– 1 cup raw pumpkin seeds

– 1 cup almond flour

– 3/4 cup pumpkin purée

– Up to 1/2 cup pumpkin oil

– 1 tablespoon lemon juice

– 2 teaspoons cinnamon

– 2 tablespoons + 1 teaspoon honey

– 1/2 teaspoon cloves

– Nutmeg, freshly ground

– 1 cup green apple, grated

DIRECTIONS:

1. In a Vitamix or powerful blender, place the pumpkin seeds and pulse until the seeds are finely ground.

2. Add all other ingredients (except for the green apples). Blend until the desired consistency.

3. Remove spread to a glass storage container. Spread will last in the fridge for 5 to 7 days.

TIPS & TRICKS: *If the spread is too thick, add a small amount of almond milk. If the spread is too thin, add more almond flour. This spread is delicious served on top of the RF Gone Nuts Loaf, and I could eat it all day long! The good news is that you can't because a single serving is so filling! Real food is real fuel; there's a reason you can't eat too much!*

SPECIAL DIET INFORMATION:

15-Day Detox Approved/30-Day Habit Reset Approved/Gluten-Free/ Diabetes Friendly/Kid Approved

DR. MINDY'S NOTES

My kids love this spread—they can't stop eating it! It's the perfect amount of sweetness, and I like it on top of a slice of Gone-Nuts Loaf. Pumpkin is a great source of vitamin A, zinc, and potassium. Pumpkin has also been known to boost your mood and help you sleep.

SPICY COCONUT CURRY HUMMUS

YIELD: 3-1/2 CUPS (28 2-TABLESPOON SERVINGS)

CARBS:
10 grams per 2-tablespoon serving

PREP TIME:
15 minutes

TOTAL TIME:
15 minutes

INGREDIENTS:

- 6 cups chickpeas, drained
- 2 cloves garlic
- 2 tablespoons Coconut Manna
- 2 tablespoons tahini
- 1/4 cup lime juice
- 4 tablespoons water
- 1 teaspoon garlic powder
- 8 teaspoons yellow curry powder
- 1/2 teaspoon ground turmeric
- 4 teaspoons honey
- 1/3 cup olive oil
- Sea salt and pepper to taste
- 4 teaspoons water
- 2 tablespoons shredded coconut, unsweetened
- 1/2 cup jalapeño, finely diced

DIRECTIONS:

1. In a Vitamix or powerful blender, combine everything except the shredded coconut and the diced jalapeño. If the mixture is too thick, add water and/or olive oil.

2. Once the desired consistency is achieved, spoon in the shredded coconut and diced jalapeño.

TIPS & TRICKS: *This hummus is sweet and spicy, with a big kick. It serves well as a dip with seeded crackers and raw vegetables (jicama, bell pepper, and carrots).*

SPECIAL DIET INFORMATION:

30-Day Habit Reset Approved/
Gluten-Free/Diabetic Friendly

DR. MINDY'S NOTES

I have a favorite coconut curry hummus spread I like to buy at my local natural food market. I asked Bonnie to see if she could re-create it, because it had a few ingredients that were not optimal. And bam! She came up with this amazing hummus! You will want to scoop this directly into your mouth, it is so good. Coconuts are great for boosting your immune system, reducing your sugar cravings, increasing your metabolism, and rehydrating. Curry is known to help with arthritis, lower inflammation, control blood sugar levels, and aid digestion.

GENERAL GUIDELINES FOR FAT-BURNING SMOOTHIES

Liquids

- Organic unsweetened almond milk
- Organic coconut milk (canned)
- Organic raw kefir
- Acai juice
- Water

Good Fats

- Organic coconut oil
- Organic MCT oil
- Avocado
- Raw nut butters

Fruits (organic when possible)

- Green apples
- Cherries
- Blueberries
- Raspberries
- Strawberries
- Pomegranates
- Lemon
- Lime

Vegetables (organic when possible)

- Carrots (in moderation)
- Cucumbers
- Celery
- Romaine lettuce
- Ginger
- Turmeric
- Mint

Protein Powders (organic preferred)

- Grass-fed whey
- Hemp
- Pea protein

Other Acceptable Powders

- Raw cacao powder
- GI revive or L-glutamine
- Maca powder
- Supergreens powder

BELLYBIOTIC SMOOTHIE

YIELD: APPROXIMATELY 4 CUPS

CARBS:
41 grams total

PREP TIME:
1 minute

TOTAL TIME:
1 minute

INGREDIENTS:

- 2 cups raw kombucha tea (with less than 5 grams sugar per serving)
- 2 cups spinach, chopped
- 1 small green apple, chopped
- 1 scoop protein powder
- 1 cup ice
- 1 tablespoon coconut oil

DIRECTIONS:

1. Put all ingredients in a blender.
2. Blend on a low to medium speed.
3. Put in a glass and enjoy.

───────────

TIPS & TRICKS: *I like to do this one with a ginger-flavored kombucha. Also, I find it helpful to use a protein powder that has a very neutral flavor. If you use a ginger kombucha, try adding a few slices of ginger to give it a tangier taste.*

SPECIAL DIET INFORMATION:

15-Day Detox Approved/30-Day Habit Reset Approved/Gluten-Free

DR. MINDY'S NOTES

I like to put kombucha in everything! If you're looking for diversity with your smoothies, add this one into your weekly routine. Great for the gut, fun for your taste buds!

SWEET KEFIR DREAMS SMOOTHIE

YIELD: APPROXIMATELY 2 CUPS

CARBS:	**PREP TIME:**	**TOTAL TIME:**
30 grams total	5 minutes	5 minutes

INGREDIENTS:

- 1 cup raw kefir
- 1/2 cup cherries
- 1/4 cup raw organic cacao powder
- 1 scoop protein powder
- 1 tablespoon coconut oil
- 1 cup ice

DIRECTIONS:

1. Pour kefir into a blender.
2. Add in cherries, cacao powder, coconut oil, ice, and powder.
3. Pour into a glass and enjoy.

_____

TIPS & TRICKS: *Always put the liquid into the blender first and then add the other ingredients. I like to add the ice and powder last, to avoid having the powder stick to the sides of the blender.*

SPECIAL DIET INFORMATION:

15-Day Detox Approved/30-Day Habit Reset Approved/Gluten-Free

DR. MINDY'S NOTES

This is my go-to smoothie—most mornings I run out the door with this smoothie in hand because it's quick and easy to make. Sometimes I add shredded coconut. Sometimes I leave out the cacao powder. The key to this smoothie is making sure you get raw kefir. Just because it says kefir, doesn't mean it's raw. Most health food markets don't carry raw kefir, so most of the time I have to find this at my local farmer's market.

CARROT ZINGER SMOOTHIE

YIELD: APPROXIMATELY 4 CUPS

CARBS:
Approximately 44 grams total

PREP TIME:
5 minutes

TOTAL TIME:
5 minutes

INGREDIENTS:

- 1 cup almond or coconut milk
- 2 whole medium carrots, chopped
- 1 tablespoon grated ginger
- 1 teaspoon powdered turmeric
- 1 small green apple, chopped
- 1 scoop plant-based protein
- 1 scoop collagen or L-glutamine powder
- 1 cup ice

DIRECTIONS:

1. Pour the milk into a blender.
2. Add in the chopped carrots and apple.
3. Add in the turmeric and grated ginger.
4. Scoop in the protein powder and collagen powder.
5. Add ice.
6. Blend until fully mixed.
7. Serve cold in a glass.

TIPS & TRICKS: *If the smoothie gets too thick when blending, don't be afraid to add some water into the mixture. Add more apple if you want it sweeter. A plant-based vanilla-flavor powder works wells with this smoothie.*

SPECIAL DIET INFORMATION:

15-Day Detox Approved/30-Day Habit Reset Approved/Gluten-Free

DR. MINDY'S NOTES

Sometimes you need a break from the sweeter fruit smoothies. This smoothie is perfect for that. The ginger will help aid digestion. The turmeric will lower inflammation in your body. And the carrot is packed with antioxidants.

THE ALKALINATOR SMOOTHIE

YIELD: APPROXIMATELY 4 CUPS

CARBS:
35 grams total

PREP TIME:
5 minutes

TOTAL TIME:
5 minutes

INGREDIENTS:

- 1 cup coconut milk
- 1 large peeled and cubed cucumber
- 1 cup ice cubes
- 1 sprig fresh mint, chopped
- 1 small green apple, chopped
- Juice from 1 lime
- 1 scoop protein powder
- 1 scoop collagen

DIRECTIONS:

1. Put liquid at bottom of blender.
2. Add in cucumber, mint, apple, and ice.
3. Add in lime juice and ice.
4. Add powders.
5. Blend on high speed.
6. Serve cold in a glass.

———————

TIPS & TRICKS: *Serve this one cold. It's refreshing and won't be as tasty at room temperature.*

SPECIAL DIET INFORMATION:

15-Day Detox Approved/30-Day Habit Reset Approved/Gluten-Free

DR. MINDY'S NOTES

There is nothing more refreshing than cucumber, mint, and lime. Personally, I like a vanilla grass-fed whey protein powder in this smoothie. Many times, patients tell me that smoothies make them feel full—this one won't do that. Add water to make it even lighter.

BLACK AND BLUE SMOOTHIE

YIELD: APPROXIMATELY 4 CUPS

CARBS:
35 grams total

PREP TIME:
5 minutes

TOTAL TIME:
5 minutes

INGREDIENTS:

- 1 13.5-ounce can unsweetened full-fat coconut milk
- 1 cup frozen blackberries
- 1/4 cup raw cacao powder
- 2 teaspoons vanilla extract
- 1 cup ice
- 1 scoop protein powder
- Pinch of sea salt

DIRECTIONS:

1. Put the coconut milk in a blender.
2. Add in the blackberries and vanilla.
3. Add in the ice.
4. Add in the powders and salt.
5. Blend on high.
6. Pour in a glass and enjoy!

TIPS & TRICKS: *Put liquid in first and powders last. Smoothies are always best served chilled.*

SPECIAL DIET INFORMATION:

15-Day Detox Approved/30-Day Habit Reset Approved/Gluten-Free

DR. MINDY'S NOTES:

Blackberries and chocolate are one of my favorite combinations. I like to add a creamier coconut milk to this one. You can find the creamier one in a can, or you can use the one that comes in a carton at the store. Just look out for chemical fillers, like carrageenan, in your coconut milk.

GARDEN IN A GLASS SMOOTHIE

YIELD: APPROXIMATELY 5 CUPS

CARBS:
35 grams total

PREP TIME:
5 minutes

TOTAL TIME:
5 minutes

INGREDIENTS:

- 4 leaves romaine lettuce, chopped
- 2 cups kale
- 2 stalks celery, chopped
- 1 small green apple, chopped
- 1 tablespoon chopped ginger (optional)
- 2 tablespoons coconut or MCT oil
- 2 tablespoons fresh-squeezed lemon
- 2 tablespoons fresh-squeezed lime
- 1 scoop protein powder
- 1 can full-fat coconut milk
- 1 cup ice
- Pinch of sea salt

DIRECTIONS:

1. Put coconut cream first into a blender.
2. Squeeze in lemon and lime.
3. Put in chopped romaine, kale, celery, apple, and ginger.
4. Add protein powder.
5. Blend on high.
6. Pour into a glass and drink immediately.

TIPS & TRICKS: *This smoothie can get quite thick, so don't be shy to add more water to thin it out. You can also add other greens to this smoothie, such as watercress or cucumber. Works best with an unsweetened plant-based protein.*

SPECIAL DIET INFORMATION:

15-Day Detox Approved/30-Day Habit Reset Approved/Gluten-Free

DR. MINDY'S NOTES

Many of my patients have asked for a smoothie that was not sweet. This one is great for that. When you're doing the 15-Day Detox, a veggie-based smoothie can be a great break from fruit smoothies. This smoothie is also packed with so many greens it will help put your body on the alkaline side. The more alkaline your body is, the stronger your immune system will be.

GREEN GODDESS SMOOTHIE

YIELD: APPROXIMATELY 3-1/2 CUPS

CARBS:
30 grams total

PREP TIME:
5 minutes

TOTAL TIME:
5 minutes

INGREDIENTS:

- 1 green apple
- 1/2 avocado
- 1 cup chopped mint
- 1 tablespoon squeezed lime
- 1 cup coconut milk or almond milk
- 1 scoop protein powder
- 1 cup ice

DIRECTIONS:

1. Pour the liquid in a blender first.
2. Add in the apple and mint.
3. Scoop the avocado out of its skin and put it in the blender.
4. Add in the protein powder and ice.
5. Pour into a glass and serve chilled.

TIPS & TRICKS: *If this smoothie gets too thick, be sure to add water. Also, this smoothie is best served chilled. Best made with a vanilla plant protein that is not sweet.*

SPECIAL DIET INFORMATION:

15-Day Detox Approved/30-Day Habit Reset Approved/Gluten-Free

DR. MINDY'S NOTES

The first time I put an avocado in a smoothie, I was a bit apprehensive. But what I found was that it gave a creaminess to the smoothie that no other ingredient did. I now put avocados in many of my smoothies. It's a great way to get more good fat into your diet as well. This is another unsweetened smoothie that will be a welcome addition to your 15-Day Detox.

CLASSIC BERRY SMOOTHIE

YIELD: APPROXIMATELY 3 CUPS

CARBS:
45 grams total

PREP TIME:
5 minutes

TOTAL TIME:
5 minutes

INGREDIENTS:

- 2 cups frozen blueberries or berry blend

- 1 cup almond milk, coconut milk, or raw kefir

- 1 tablespoon coconut oil

- 1 scoop vanilla protein

- 1 cup ice

DIRECTIONS:

1. Pour the liquid of your choice into the blender.

2. Put in the berries, coconut oil, protein powder, and ice.

3. Blend on high.

4. Serve chilled in a glass.

TIPS & TRICKS: *Put the liquid in first and the powders last. Smoothies are always best served chilled.*

SPECIAL DIET INFORMATION:

15-Day Detox Approved/30-Day Habit Reset Approved/Gluten-Free

DR. MINDY'S NOTES

This is one of my go-to shakes. When I am rushing out the door to get to the office and want to make a quick smoothie, this is the easiest one to make. Very little prep time, tastes great, and lower on the carb count than some of the other smoothies.

CHOCOLATE CHERRY HEAVEN SMOOTHIE

YIELD: 1 TO 2 GLASSES

CARBS:	PREP TIME:	TOTAL TIME:
31 grams total	*5 minutes*	*5 minutes*

INGREDIENTS:

- 1 cup almond milk or coconut milk
- 1/2 cup acai juice
- 1/2 cup frozen cherries
- 1 scoop chocolate protein powder
- 1 tablespoon coconut oil
- 1 cup ice

DIRECTIONS:

1. Put milk and acai juice in blender.
2. Add cherries and coconut oil.
3. Put ice in blender.
4. Blend on high.
5. Put in a glass and serve chilled.

TIPS & TRICKS: *Put liquid in first and powders last. Smoothies are always best served chilled.*

SPECIAL DIET INFORMATION:

15-Day Detox Approved/30-Day Habit Reset Approved/Gluten-Free

DR. MINDY'S NOTES

Missing your favorite chocolate treat? Here's a great smoothie that will help satisfy your chocolate sweet tooth. Cherries and chocolate are one of my favorite combinations. Add water and less juice to make it not so sweet. This smoothie is higher on the carb count, so if you are trying to lose weight, you might want to do take it in moderation or avoid it altogether.

RASPBERRY GUT ZINGER SMOOTHIE

YIELD: APPROXIMATELY 3 CUPS

CARBS:
25 grams total

PREP TIME:
5 minutes

TOTAL TIME:
5 minutes

INGREDIENTS:

– 1 cup coconut milk or raw kefir (adds 4g carbs)
– 1 cup raspberries
– 1/2 avocado
– 1 tablespoon coconut oil
– 1/4 cup chopped ginger
– 1 scoop protein powder
– 1 cup water

DIRECTIONS:

1. Place the milk in a blender.
2. Add the raspberries, ginger, and coconut oil.
3. Scoop the avocado out of its skin and put it in a blender.
4. Put in the protein powder and ice.
5. Blend on high until thoroughly mixed.
6. Serve chilled in a glass.

TIPS & TRICKS: *The avocado can make this smoothie thick, so add more water if needed.*

SPECIAL DIET INFORMATION:

15-Day Detox Approved/30-Day Habit Reset Approved/Gluten-Free

DR. MINDY'S NOTES

If you have digestive issues, you'll love this smoothie. The added fat of the avocado will fill you up, while the ginger will help your digestion. Raspberries are low in sugar, so add more if desired.

SMOOTHIE ICE CREAM

YIELD: 3 CUPS (6 1/2-CUP SERVING)

CARBS:	PREP TIME:	FREEZE TIME:
11 grams per 1/2-cup serving	*10 minutes*	*2 hours*

INGREDIENTS:

1/2 cup RFK Almond Milk (or approved almond milk from store)

1 scoop protein powder

1 tablespoon L-glutamine powder

3 tablespoons RFK Nut Butter of the Gods (or substitute raw almond butter)

1/2 cup raw cashews

2 cups frozen mixed berries

DIRECTIONS:

1. In a blender (Vitamix recommended), add the ingredients in the order they're listed.

2. Start blending at low speed and then increase speed to develop a smooth, creamy texture. You'll need to periodically stop and push down the ingredients (do this instead of adding more liquid because more liquid will change the texture and make it difficult for it to become "ice cream"). Blend less if you like the nuts to be larger and want to create a crunchier end product.

3. When the texture is to your liking (I like firm and creamy with some small chunks of nuts), transfer to a freezer-proof container and freeze for a minimum of 2 hours. I recommend stirring the mixture every 30 minutes to make sure the firmness is consistent.

4. Scoop and enjoy!

TIPS & TRICKS: *Add the ingredients to the Vitamix in the order they're listed (liquid on the bottom, then powders, then heavier items). This causes the heavier ingredients on top to push the other ingredients down toward the blades during blending, thus preventing the dry ingredients from flying around.*

DR. MINDY'S NOTES

This recipe was a huge hit in our Reset Community. People wanted an option other than smoothies to get in their protein powder and L-glutamine. Bonnie came up with this delicious treat—a great substitute for a smoothie during your 15-Day Detox. It's also a great way to get more fats into your daily diet. My kids loved it too when we tested it—they even went back for a second helping!

SOUR CHERRY AND LIME ELIXIR

YIELD: 24 OUNCES (12 2-OUNCE SERVINGS)

CARBS:	PREP TIME:	TOTAL TIME:
5 grams per 2-ounce serving	10 minutes, 2 to 4 days prior to consuming	10 minutes, 2 to 4 days prior to consuming

INGREDIENTS:

2 cups organic frozen sour cherries

1 cup sparkling water or RFK Water Kefir

1 cup raw apple cider vinegar

1/4 cup raw honey

1 tablespoon fresh ginger, grated

1 lime, zest and juice

DIRECTIONS:

2-Day Version:

1. Using a Vitamix or powerful blender, add ingredients and begin pulsing, gradually increasing the speed. Continue until all ingredients are thoroughly blended.

2. Pour into a glass jar and either ferment on your countertop for 1 to 2 days to generate some good probiotics or place directly in the fridge for 1 to 2 days before serving. During this time, the flavors will meld together and the vinegar flavor will lessen.

3. When ready to serve, use about 2 tablespoons of the Sour Cherry and Lime Elixir with one cup of sparkling water; use as much or as little syrup as you like to suit your taste.

4-Day Version:

1. If using water kefir to add some effervescence to your elixir, make sure your RFK Kefir Water is already made, as this takes a few days.

2. After the syrup has rested on the counter or in the fridge for 1 to 2 days, prepare for a secondary fermentation (to create the effervescence) by combining the Water Kefir and fruit syrup in a bottle with a tightly fitting cap. (I like to reuse French lemonade bottles that have a cap that locks down.) Allow this mixture to rest on the countertop for another 1 to 2 days. Carefully open the cap to check your carbonation level and release some pressure. Chill and enjoy!

TIPS & TRICKS: *Covering your fermentation bottles with a dish towel helps reduce the amount of direct light and encourages the natural process. The ideal temperature for fermentation is approximately 68° to 72°F. Colder weather will slow down the process and warmer weather will speed up the process. Refrigeration slows the process.*

SPECIAL DIET INFORMATION:

30-Day Habit Reset Approved/ Gluten-Free/Diabetic Friendly

DR. MINDY'S NOTES

Getting good bacteria into your body from a variety of sources is key to the healing process. Bonnie discovered this yummy and thirst-quenching drink. Not only is it tasty, but it's also easy to make and less expensive than buying probiotic-rich drinks at your local natural foods store. Great substitute for kombucha if you are not a kombucha fan. You can also substitute this for detox water in the morning.

SUNSHINE ELIXIR

YIELD: 2 CUPS (4 1/2-CUP SERVINGS)

CARBS:
8 grams per 1/2-cup serving

PREP TIME:
5 minutes

TOTAL TIME:
5 minutes

INGREDIENTS:

- 2 cups sparkling water
- 1 lime, quartered
- 1 lemon, quartered
- 4 inches fresh turmeric, peeled and cut into 4 pieces
- 4 inches fresh ginger, grated
- 1 large green apple, cored and quartered

DIRECTIONS:

1. In a Vitamix or powerful blender or food processor, blend all ingredients together. Pour a little sunshine for yourself and a friend—and enjoy!

———————

TIPS & TRICKS: *Add more apple and/or fresh ginger if the citrus peel (great fiber) makes it a little bitter. The final drink should be sweet and tart!*

SPECIAL DIET INFORMATION:

15-Day Detox Approved/30-Day Habit Reset Approved/Gluten-Free/Diabetic Friendly

DR. MINDY'S NOTES

We discovered that many people had to give up a soda habit when they started their 45-Day Reset. This drink is a good way to satisfy your taste buds with some sweet and sparkly liquid but not destroy your body with large amounts of sugar, chemicals, or caffeine. The ginger will aid digestion and the turmeric will lower any inflammation in your body.

HEALTHY HOT AND COLD CACAO

YIELD: 16 OUNCES (2 8-OUNCE SERVINGS)

CARBS:	PREP TIME:	TOTAL TIME:
8 grams per 8-ounce serving	5 minutes	10 minutes + cooling time for cold version

INGREDIENTS:

- 16 ounces RFK Almond Milk (or store-bought organic almond milk)
- 1 tablespoon raw cacao powder
- 1 teaspoon ground cinnamon
- 1 teaspoon coconut sugar
- 1 teaspoon raw honey

DIRECTIONS:

1. Warm all ingredients over low-medium heat, whisking gently to break up any clumps, melting the sugar, and blending the flavors.

2. This recipe can be enjoyed warm or cold. If you choose to enjoy it cold, chill in the refrigerator in a glass container.

3. Enjoy!

TIPS & TRICKS: *This is a healthy alternative to traditional hot cacao, which is full of sugar and chemicals.*

SPECIAL DIET INFORMATION:

30-Day Habit Reset Approved (in moderation)/Gluten-Free/Diabetic Friendly/Kid Approved

DR. MINDY'S NOTES

As Bonnie mentioned above, most hot cacaos are packed with sugar and chemicals. Yet if your kids are anything like ours, on a cold winter night, there's nothing better than a cup of warm cacao. So try this yummy alternative. Warning: This one is higher in approved sugars than many of the other drinks in this chapter. If you're trying to lose weight, I would wait until you finish your 45-Day Reset to enjoy this treat.

VIRGIN KIWI APPLE MOJITO

YIELD: 2 CUPS (4 1/2-CUP SERVINGS)

CARBS:
12 grams per 1/2-cup serving (6 grams per 1/2-cup serving of the cucumber alternate version)

PREP TIME:
5 minutes

TOTAL TIME:
10 minutes

INGREDIENTS:

- 2 large kiwis, peeled
- 1 medium green apple, cored and quartered, skin on
- 1-1/2 limes, quartered
- 10 stems fresh mint leaves
- 4 cups sparkling water

ALTERNATIVE INGREDIENTS:

- 3/4 large cucumber (in place of kiwis or apple)

DIRECTIONS:

1. Prepare the individual glasses by placing 1/4 lime wedge and 2 stems of mint leaves in the bottom of each glass. Vigorously smash the lime and mint together to release and meld their flavors.

2. In a Vitamix or powerful blender, puree the kiwis, green apple, 1/2 of a lime, 2 stems of mint leaves, and 2 cups of sparkling water. Blend until thick and smooth.

3. Place a few ice cubes in each glass and pour 1/2 cup sparkling water (or kefir water, but consider additional carbs) over the ice.

4. Pour 1/2 cup of the mojito blend into each glass.

5. Enjoy!

TIPS & TRICKS: *A lower-carb alternative of this drink would be to substitute the kiwis (11g carbs each) or the apple (approximately 25g carbs) with 3/4 of a cucumber (0g carbs). An alternative version of this using RFK Water Kefir for the water poured over ice in the individual glasses would deliver a nice dose of probiotics in this refreshing summer drink.*

SPECIAL DIET INFORMATION:

15-Day Detox Approved (without the kiwi)/30-Day Habit Reset Approved/ Gluten-Free/Diabetic Friendly

DR. MINDY'S NOTES

Another brilliant drink by Bonnie. I like the idea of adding in the kefir water to make it a probiotic-rich drink. If you are on the 15-Day Detox, just take the kiwi out and you have an approved drink (kiwis are higher in sugar). Once you're on the 30-Day Habit Reset, you can add the kiwi back in.

TURMERIC GOLDEN MILK

YIELD: APPROXIMATELY 1-1/3 CUPS PASTE (20+ TABLESPOONS, WHICH WILL MAKE 20+ CUPS OF GOLDEN MILK)

CARBS:	PREP TIME:	TOTAL TIME:
9 grams per 1-cup serving of golden milk	*15 minutes for the paste, 2 to 5 minutes for the golden milk*	*20 minutes*

INGREDIENTS (FOR THE PASTE):

- 6 tablespoons turmeric powder
- 2 tablespoons ginger powder
- 3/4 teaspoon ground black pepper
- 1/8 teaspoon cayenne
- 1/8 teaspoon ground cardamom
- 1 teaspoon ground cinnamon
- 1/16 teaspoon ground cloves
- 1 cup filtered water

INGREDIENTS (FOR THE GOLDEN MILK):

- 2 tablespoons turmeric golden milk paste (above)
- 2 cups coconut milk
- 2 teaspoons raw honey
- A few drops of Udo's oil

DIRECTIONS (FOR THE PASTE):

1. In a small saucepan, thoroughly combine all ingredients.

2. On low heat, make a paste, stirring continuously for about 8 minutes.

3. Remove from heat and cool. Store in a glass container in the fridge. Paste will last in the   fridge for 2 to 3 weeks.

DIRECTIONS (FOR THE GOLDEN MILK):

1. In a small saucepan, combine the turmeric golden milk paste with the coconut milk and honey. Whisk to incorporate ingredients and eliminate lumps. Warm to desired temperature on medium-low heat; do not boil.

2. Pour 8 ounces into 2 mugs. Top with a few drops of Udo's oil.

TIPS & TRICKS: *This recipe is a triple threat: (1) It's good for you (the healing properties of the turmeric and Udo's Oil in combination with the pepper make for easy absorption); (2) it's easy (making the paste in advance makes the making of the golden milk a snap); and (3) it's versatile (it's delicious both hot and cold, although when cold, the coconut milk can get clumpy—but I don't mind that)! I'm in love with this recipe! It has become a staple in my fridge! Sometimes if I want to lighten it up, I mix 1 part golden milk with 1 part RFK Almond Milk. I enjoy this hot or cold.*

SPECIAL DIET INFORMATION:

15-Day Detox Approved (without the honey)/30-Day Habit Reset Approved/Gluten-Free/Diabetic Friendly/Kid Approved

DR. MINDY'S NOTES

One of Bonnie's special gifts is finding a food product in a store and reconstructing it at home. That is exactly what she did with this turmeric milk—only I think it tastes better than the one in the store! Not only will you love the taste of this drink, but the turmeric will benefit your body in many ways. You can find Udo's oil at your local health food store. It is a high-potency omega-3 oil that will lower inflammation. Brilliant recipe!

BUTTERED COFFEE

YIELD: APPROXIMATELY 1 CUP

CARBS:	PREP TIME:	TOTAL TIME:
0 grams per 1-cup serving	*Depends on how you brew coffee*	*Once coffee is made, 2 to 3 minutes*

INGREDIENTS:

- 1 cup organic coffee
- 1 tablespoon grass-fed butter
- 1 tablespoon coconut oil or MCT oil
- 1 teaspoon cinnamon

DIRECTIONS:

1. Brew coffee any way you choose.
2. Once coffee is brewed, pour one cup in a blender.
3. Add in the butter, coconut oil, and cinnamon.
4. Blend on high for 5 seconds.
5. Pour into a mug and drink.

TIPS & TRICKS: *I like French-press coffee because it gives it a richer taste. You don't need to blend it for long to get a frothy cup of coffee.*

SPECIAL DIET INFORMATION:

15-Day Detox Approved/30-Day Habit Reset Approved/Gluten-Free/ Diabetic Approved

DR. MINDY'S NOTES

This is my favorite way to make coffee. The good fat delivers the caffeine right to your brain and makes your brain alert and clear. If you find that you get jittery from coffee, try this technique. It gives you a nice sustained lift of energy. Great for those of you who are new to intermittent fasting and want something to fill you up and give you energy in the morning.

DETOX WATER

YIELD: 1 CUP

CARBS:	**PREP TIME:**	**TOTAL TIME:**
0 grams per 1-cup serving	1 minute	1 minute

INGREDIENTS:

– 1 cup filtered water

– 1 tablespoon Bragg's Apple
  Cider Vinegar

– 1/2 fresh lemon

– Dash cayenne pepper

– Dash cinnamon

DIRECTIONS:

1. Pour water into a pint-size glass.

2. Add in cider vinegar, cayenne, and cinnamon.

3. Squeeze in lemon.

4. Stir until all ingredients are mixed together.

TIPS & TRICKS: *You can make a pitcher of this drink ahead of time if you want to have it ready in the morning. If the taste is too sour for you, add a dash of stevia. Also, adding ginger to this drink gives it a more complex taste.*

SPECIAL DIET INFORMATION:

15-Day Detox Approved/30-Day
Habit Reset Approved/Gluten-Free/
Diabetic Friendly

One of the beauties of the fermentation process is that the chemical interactions actually lower the carbohydrate count of the food you are fermenting. During fermentation, sugars and starches are eaten by the bacteria cultures, converting them to lactic acid, carbon dioxide, and more bacteria. So, by definition, fermentation is a process one could use to lower the dietary carbohydrate levels found in various foods. The challenge is that it is difficult to know the exact carbohydrate count of a fermented food. If you are monitoring your carbohydrate intake, there is one principle to keep in mind: the longer the fermentation time, the more carbohydrates are eaten up by the organisms, the more sour the ferment, the lower the dietary carbohydrate count. With this in mind, the carbohydrate counts provided in the following recipes are educated estimates.

CHAPTER 20

FERMENTATION FOR BEGINNERS

Ginger Beet Sauerkraut

SunnyKraut

Ginger Apple Spice Kraut

Fermented Salsa

Fermented Pesto

Fermented Pickles

Water Kefir

Coconut Probiotic Topping

Milk Kefir

Goat Cream Cheese and Whey

Stacey's Kombucha SCOBY

Stacey's Kontinuous Kombucha

GINGER BEET SAUERKRAUT

YIELD: APPROXIMATELY 14 CUPS (112 2-TABLESPOON SERVINGS)

CARBS:	PREP TIME:	FERMENTATION TIME:
1 grams per 1-ounce serving (2 tablespoons)	30 minutes	5 to 14 days

INGREDIENTS:

– 1-1/2 heads red cabbage

– 6 medium to large red beets

– 1/3 cup fresh ginger, finely grated

– 2 tablespoons sea salt

– 2 tablespoons apple cider vinegar

ADDITIONAL BRINE:

– 4 cups purified water

– 1 tablespoon sea salt

– 1 tablespoon apple cider vinegar

TIPS & TRICKS: *Wear gloves and clothes that can't get stained when making this recipe; the beet juice will stain your hands and could permanently stain your clothes. Lots of ginger is what gives this sauerkraut great flavor. After 5 to 6 days, the sauerkraut is crunchy and deliciously fresh. After about 10 days, the flavor gets a little tarter and the texture is softer.*

DIRECTIONS:

1. Pull 5 large leaves off one of the heads of cabbage and set aside. Shred the remaining cabbage. When shredding cabbage, I prefer the control that a sharp chef's knife gives me, but you can also use a food processor or mandolin. When grating the beets, I prefer to use a food processor to contain all the bright red beet juice. Grate the ginger using a fine rasp grater.

2. Mix the shredded cabbage, beets, and ginger in a big bowl (I prefer a stainless bowl) with the apple cider vinegar and sea salt. Massage the cabbage mixture with your hands until it breaks down and starts to soften (5 to 10 minutes). Then let it sit for 20 to 30 minutes to give it time to continue to break down and release more juices.

3. Massage the mixture for another 5 to10 minutes.

4. With a large long-handled spoon, pack the cabbage mixture into two 36-ounce Mason jars. Pack the mixture in tightly, all the way down to the bottom. You want the mixture to be submerged in brine (the natural juices created through the maceration process). Leave about 1-1/2 inches of space from the top of the jar.

5. Typically, I need to make additional brine. This is done by combining 1 teaspoon of sea salt with 1 cup of water and 1 tablespoon of apple cider vinegar. Continue to add brine until the cabbage mixture is submerged.

6. Roll up the cabbage leaves you set aside and place them in the jar to push the cabbage under the brine. Screw on the jar loosely so gas can escape as fermentation takes place. Set on the counter for 5 to 14 days in a cool, shaded place. During fermentation, the sauerkraut will bubble a little and become cloudy. If scum or mold appears at the top or on the whole cabbage leaves, remove and discard; replace these with new cabbage leaves to keep the cabbage submerged.

7. Taste the sauerkraut every day, and when you like the flavor, remove the rolled-up cabbage leaves and place the sauerkraut in the refrigerator, which slows down the fermentation process.

SPECIAL DIET INFORMATION:

15-Day Detox Approved/30-Day Habit Reset Approved/Gluten-Free/ Diabetic Friendly

DR. MINDY'S NOTES

One of the greatest strategies you can apply to improve your gut health is eating fermented foods. A probiotic supplement you buy at the store will have 50 to 100 billion good bacteria in it at best. Sauerkraut has trillions of good bacteria. This recipe also has ginger in it to aid in digestion, and beets are packed with antioxidants.

Ginger Beet Sauerkraut (red) and SunnyKraut (yellow)

SUNNYKRAUT

YIELD: APPROXIMATELY 14 CUPS (112 2-TABLESPOON SERVINGS)

CARBS:	**PREP TIME:**	**FERMENTATION TIME:**
1 grams per 1-ounce serving (2 tablespoons)	30 minutes	2 to 3 days

INGREDIENTS:

- 2 heads green cabbage, shredded
- 1 whole fresh pineapple, chopped
- 1/3 cup fresh turmeric, finely grated
- 1/3 cup fresh ginger, finely grated
- 2 tablespoons sea salt
- 2 tablespoons apple cider vinegar

ADDITIONAL BRINE:

- 4 cups purified water
- 1 tablespoon sea salt
- 1 tablespoon apple cider vinegar

TIPS & TRICKS: *Wear gloves and clothes that can get stained when making this recipe; the turmeric juice will stain your hands and could permanently stain your clothes. The pineapple gives this sauerkraut a refreshingly different flavor. Fruit such as pineapple can accelerate the fermentation process and might take less time to achieve a flavor of your liking. After 5 to 6 days, the sauerkraut is crunchy and deliciously fresh. After about 10 days, the flavor gets a little tarter and the texture is softer. This sauerkraut is the perfect accompaniment for a breakfast dish.*

SPECIAL DIET INFORMATION:

30-Day Habit Reset Approved/ Gluten-Free/Diabetic Friendly

DIRECTIONS:

1. Pull 4 to 5 large leaves off one of the heads of cabbage and set aside. Shred the remaining cabbage. When shredding cabbage, I prefer the control that a sharp chef's knife gives me, but you can also use a food processor or mandolin. I like using a fine rasp grater for the ginger and turmeric.

2. Mix the shredded cabbage, turmeric, ginger, salt, and vinegar in a large bowl (I prefer a stainless steel bowl because the turmeric won't stain it bright yellow, as it will my hands). Wear gloves and massage the cabbage mixture with your hands until it breaks down and starts to soften (5 to 10 minutes). Then let it sit for 20 to 30 minutes to give it time to continue to macerate and release more juices.

3. Massage the mixture for another 5 to 10 minutes.

4. With a large long-handled spoon, pack the cabbage mixture into two 36-ounce Mason jars. Pack the mixture in tightly, all the way down to the bottom. You want the mixture to be submerged in brine (the natural juices created through the maceration process). Leave about 1-1/2 inches of space from the top of the jar.

5. Typically, I need to make additional brine. This is done by combining 1 teaspoon of sea salt with 1 cup of water and 1 tablespoon of apple cider vinegar. Continue to add brine until the cabbage mixture is submerged.

6. Roll up the cabbage leaves you set aside and place them in the jar to push the cabbage under the brine. Screw on the jar loosely so gas can escape as fermentation takes place. Set on the counter for 2-3 days in a cool, shaded place. During fermentation, the sauerkraut will bubble a little and become cloudy. If scum or mold appears at the top or on the whole cabbage leaves, remove and discard; replace these with new cabbage leaves to keep the cabbage submerged.

7. Taste the sauerkraut every day and, when you like the flavor, remove the rolled-up cabbage leaves and place the sauerkraut in the refrigerator, which slows down the fermentation process. I like this kraut best after only 2 days because I like the fresh flavor.

DR. MINDY'S NOTES

This is my favorite of Bonnie's sauerkraut recipes. It has a sweet-and-sour taste to it. Pineapple has an enzyme called bromelin that is anti-inflammatory and helps with injury repair to muscles and ligaments. Turmeric is also one of the best anti-inflammatory foods I know. Sea salt stimulates the thyroid. Ginger helps break down food for digestion. Apple cider vinegar kills any bad bacteria in your gut. Put that all in a sauerkraut that's packed with trillions of good bacteria and you've got yourself a delicious body-repairing treat.

GINGER APPLE SPICE KRAUT

YIELD: 10 CUPS (80 2-TABLESPOONS SERVINGS)

CARBS:	**PREP TIME:**	**FERMENTATION TIME:**
Approximately 5 grams per serving	*30 minutes*	*5 to 7 days*

INGREDIENTS:

- 1-1/2 heads cabbage, thinly sliced
- 3 tablespoons sea salt
- 6 medium apples, grated, skin on
- 3 tablespoons fresh ginger, grated
- 2 teaspoons cinnamon
- 1/2 teaspoon ground cloves
- 1/4 freshly ground nutmeg
- 1/4 cup lemon juice
- 1 tablespoon apple cider vinegar

ADDITIONAL BRINE:

- 4 cups purified water
- 1 tablespoon sea salt
- 1 tablespoon apple cider vinegar

DIRECTIONS:

1. Pull 4 to 5 large leaves off one of the heads of cabbage and set aside. Shred the remaining cabbage. When shredding cabbage, I prefer the control that a sharp chef's knife gives me, but you can also use a food processor or mandolin. I like using a fine rasp grater for the ginger and turmeric.

2. Grate the green apple by hand or in a food processor. Mix the shredded cabbage, ginger, and cinnamon in a large bowl (I prefer a stainless steel bowl because the turmeric won't stain it bright yellow, as it will my hands). Wear gloves and massage the cabbage mixture with your hands until it breaks down and starts to soften (5 to 10 minutes); then let it sit for 20 to 30 minutes to give it time to continue to macerate and release more juices.

3. Massage the mixture for another 5 to 10 minutes.

4. With a large long-handled spoon, pack the cabbage mixture into two 36-ounce Mason jars. Pack the mixture in tightly all the way down to the bottom. You want the mixture to be submerged in brine (the natural juices created through the maceration process). Leave about 1-1/2 inches of space from the top of the jar.

5. Typically, I need to make additional brine. This is done by combining 1 teaspoon of sea salt with 1 cup of water and 1 tablespoon of apple cider vinegar. Continue to add brine until the cabbage mixture is submerged.

6. Roll up the cabbage leaves you set aside and place them in the jar to push the cabbage under the brine. Screw the lid on the jar loosely so gas can escape as fermentation takes place. Set on the counter for 5 to 14 days in a cool, shaded place. During fermentation, the sauerkraut will bubble a little and become cloudy. If scum or mold appears at the top or on the whole cabbage leaves, remove and discard; replace these with new cabbage leaves to keep the cabbage submerged.

7. Taste the sauerkraut every day and, when you like the flavor, remove the rolled-up cabbage leaves and place the sauerkraut in the refrigerator, which slows down the fermentation process.

SPECIAL DIET INFORMATION:

15-Day Detox Approved (if made with green apples)/30-Day Habit Reset Approved/Gluten-Free/Diabetic Friendly

DR. MINDY'S NOTES

The more I study the microbiome of the human gut, the more convinced I am that eating good bacteria in your foods is the most beneficial way to get good bacteria into your gut. I put sauerkraut on as many things as I can. This recipe makes it easy to have sauerkraut as a dessert. Bonnie and I even talked about this recipe going with your Thanksgiving meal.

FERMENTED SALSA

YIELD: APPROXIMATELY 12 CUPS (96 2-TABLESPOON SERVINGS)

CARBS:
Less than 1 gram per 2-tablespoon serving

PREP TIME:
60 minutes

TOTAL TIME:
60 minutes + 2 days to ferment

INGREDIENTS:

- 3 pounds tomatoes
- 3 yellow onions, finely diced
- 2 red bell peppers, finely diced
- 7 jalapeño peppers, seeded and finely diced
- 1/2 cup fresh cilantro, no stems, finely chopped (approximately 1 large bunch)
- 2 tablespoons minced garlic
- 1 lemon, zest and juice
- 2 limes, zest and juice
- 1/2 teaspoon cayenne pepper
- 1/4 teaspoon cumin
- 2 tablespoons sea salt
- 1/2 teaspoon ground pepper
- 1/2 cup goat milk whey (see RFK Goat Cream Cheese and Whey)

DIRECTIONS:

1. Chop the tomatoes, onions, peppers, and cilantro; mince the garlic and place in a large bowl. Add the citrus zest and juices and toss all ingredients to evenly incorporate.

2. Add salt and spices to taste.

3. Add the whey and stir well to incorporate.

4. Pour into 3-quart, 1-quart, or half-gallon Mason jars and cap tightly.

5. Leave on the counter for approximately 2 days, covered with a kitchen towel. Burp jars once daily to release the pressure from gases created during the fermentation process; this is simply done by opening the lids and then replacing them loosely.

6. Transfer to the fridge.

———————

TIPS & TRICKS: *Your fermented salsa will last in the fridge for several months.*

SPECIAL DIET INFORMATION:

15-Day Detox Approved/30-Day Habit Reset Approved/Gluten-Free/ Diabetic Friendly

DR. MINDY'S NOTES

Once you get the general idea for fermentation, you'll see that there is great benefit in fermenting as many things as possible. When Bonnie made this fermented salsa for us, my family loved it! Sweet, a little tangy, and delicious. My family loves breakfast burritos. We do organic corn tortillas, Paleo Wraps, or cauliflower tortillas combined with eggs, organic bacon, avocado, and this salsa. The family loves it, and I'm happy because my kids are getting clean proteins, good fats, and a plate full of good probiotics.

FERMENTED PESTO

YIELD: APPROXIMATELY 4 CUPS (16 2-TABLESPOONS SERVINGS)

CARBS:
3 grams per 2-tablespoons serving

PREP TIME:
20 minutes

TOTAL TIME:
20 minutes + 2 days to ferment

INGREDIENTS:

- 1 cup pine nuts
- 5 cups fresh basil leaves
- 2 cups olive oil
- 8 cloves garlic
- 1 lemon, zest and juice
- 1 teaspoon salt
- 1/2 teaspoon ground pepper
- 4 tablespoons vegetable starter culture liquid, goat milk whey (see RFK Goat Cream Cheese and Whey), or liquid from a previously lacto-fermented batch (like homemade sauerkraut)

OPTIONAL INGREDIENT:

- 1 cup finely grated raw Parmesan cheese

DIRECTIONS:

1. In a Vitamix, food processor, or powerful blender, add the pine nuts, basil, garlic, lemon zest, and juice. Pulse until finely chopped.
2. Add the olive oil slowly and blend until combined.
3. Add the Parmesan cheese and blend.
4. Add salt and pepper to taste and blend once more.
5. Remove from the processor and place the pesto in a canning jar.
6. Add your choice of starter (do one of the following):
7. In a measuring cup, mix the goat milk whey with the 1/4 teaspoon of extra salt until dissolved. Add the whey mixture to the pesto, stirring in by hand.
8. Or dissolve the starter culture packet in water, then stir into the pesto by hand.
9. Or stir in 4 tablespoons of brine from another previously lacto-fermented food.
10. Firmly press down the pesto to remove any trapped air bubbles. Pour a small amount of olive oil on the top to cover the pesto (1/4-inch).
11. Ferment at room temperature (60° to 70°F is preferred) for 24 to 48 hours. If using a tight lid, burp daily to release excess pressure. After 48 hours, place the jar in the refrigerator. Lacto-fermented pesto will keep for more than 6 months—if it's in a jar with an airtight lid and placed on the countertop for 48 hours. That is, if it doesn't disappear before then!

TIPS & TRICKS: *Depending on how thick or thin you like your pesto, you can add more or less olive oil. Looking for vegetable starter culture? It can be purchased on Amazon.com.*

DR. MINDY'S NOTES

Another fantastic idea of Bonnie's: Take a favorite recipe and ferment it. Once you get the hang of fermenting, you'll see how easy it is to get good bacteria into your gut. There are thousands of different strains of good bacteria in your gut, so when you eat a wide variety of fermented foods, you're not only adding to the amount of bacteria, but also to the diversity of bacteria as well.

FERMENTED PICKLES

YIELD: 1/2-GALLON JAR OF PICKLES

CARBS:
1-1/2 grams per medium pickle

PREP TIME:
20 minutes

TOTAL TIME:
20 minutes + 2 days to ferment

INGREDIENTS:

Enough pickling cucumbers to fill a half-gallon jar

2 quarts distilled water (chlorine free)

12 cloves garlic, peeled

3 large heads dill

5 tablespoons sea salt

1 tablespoon black peppercorns

2 teaspoons red pepper flakes

1 tablespoon mustard seeds

9 grape leaves

DIRECTIONS:

1. Prepare the pickling brine by dissolving 5 tablespoons sea salt in 2 quarts of chlorine-free water.

2. Mix the spices in a separate bowl.

3. In a half-gallon Mason jar, place 3 grape leaves, 4 cloves of garlic, 2 heads of dill, and a third of the spices.

4. Pack the cucumbers tightly on top of the spices. Place the tallest cucumbers on the bottom of the jar.

5. Repeat a layer of leaves, garlic, and spices. Add another tightly packed layer of cucumbers. Top them off with more garlic and spices.

6. Using a wide-mouth funnel, pour the brine over the pickles, leaving 1 to 2 inches of space at the top. Place the remaining grape leaves on top of the pickles as a cover between the pickles and the surface of the brine. (If necessary, use a fermentation weight to keep the pickles under the liquid. A fermentation weight is a food-safe glass disc that can be placed on top of the food being fermented, to keep it submerged in the salt brine so it ferments and does not spoil).

7. Cover the jar with a tight lid, an airlock, a Mason-top lid (available on Amazon. com), or a coffee filter secured with a rubber band.

8. Ferment at room temperature (60° to 70°F is preferred) until desired flavor and texture are achieved. If using a tight lid, burp daily to release excess pressure. The brine should turn cloudy and bubbly, and the pickles should taste sour when done.

9. Eat some right away and store the rest in the refrigerator.

_____

TIPS & TRICKS: *Fermented pickles will last several months in the refrigerator.*

SPECIAL DIET INFORMATION:

15-Day Detox Approved/30-Day Habit Reset Approved/Gluten-Free/ Diabetic Friendly

DR. MINDY'S NOTES

Who doesn't love pickles? But do you know that when you buy a pickle in the jar at your local grocery store, it has been pasteurized? That means that they've killed all the good bacteria in those pickles. But not with these pickles! When you make your own pickles, you get the benefit of great taste along with a large dose of good bacteria.

WATER KEFIR

YIELD: 8 CUPS (8 1-CUP SERVINGS)

CARBS:
Approximately 10g per 8-ounce serving

PREP TIME:
5 minutes

TOTAL TIME:
5 minutes + fermentation time

INGREDIENTS:

– 1/2 cup hydrated water kefir grains (available on Amazon.com)

– 8 cups nonchlorinated filtered water

– 1/2 cup organic unprocessed rapadura sugar

DIRECTIONS:

1. Dissolve the sugar in a small amount of hot water in a half-gallon Mason jar.

2. When the sugar is dissolved, fill the rest of the jar with cool filtered water. It's very important that the water be room temperature as kefir grains don't like warm or hot water.

3. Add the hydrated water kefir grains.

4. Cover with cheesecloth or a coffee filter, with a rubber band to keep out insects, then cover loosely with a kitchen towel to keep out direct sunlight.

5. Leave on the counter (preferably at 70° to 75°F) for 24 to 48 hours. The longer you leave it, the more sugar ferments out, so if you're limiting carbs, 48 hours is recommended. (But don't leave longer than this as it can starve the kefir grains!)

6. After 48 hours, you have water kefir!

7. Strain the water through a bamboo or mesh strainer (avoid metal), capturing the kefir grains in the strainer (so they can be reused) and gathering the water kefir into two quart-size jars. (Quart-size containers are a bit more convenient to store in the fridge.)

8. Kefir grains are alive and want to keep working for you, so restart the process in your half-gallon Mason jar by dissolving more sugar in water, adding cool water, and adding water kefir grains. In 48 hours, you'll have more water kefir.

9. To carbonate your water kefir, combine a few ounces of fruit juice in a 4:1 ratio (grape, apple, pomegranate, or cherry work well but avoid citrus) with some of the strained water kefir in an old-fashioned Grolsch-type bottle with a locking top (available on Amazon.com). Lock the lid and leave on the counter for secondary fermentation for an additional 1 to 3 days (burping 1 to 2 times a day to release built-up pressure).

10. When ready, refrigerate and enjoy—and then start again with a new batch!

SPECIAL DIET INFORMATION:

30-Day Habit Reset Approved/ Gluten-Free/Diabetic Friendly (Count your carbs when adding juice for a secondary fermentation!)

DR. MINDY'S NOTES

Rapadura sugar is sugar cane juice that is very lightly processed. It's really as raw as solid sugar gets. The result is that it's much closer to a natural plant product, and it therefore comes with all sorts of health benefits. The benefits of this sugar are that it's low on the glycemic index and high in nutrients like iron, magnesium, and potassium.

TIPS & TRICKS: *Do not substitute honey for the sugar! Chemically, it just doesn't work. Making water kefir is a continuous effort if you want to keep your grains alive; if this is too much water kefir to keep up with, consider making a smaller batch. Kefir grains are alive, and making water kefir is a continuous process. Here are a few tips for putting your water kefir grains on pause.*

Taking a short break (up to 3 weeks) from your water kefir grains: Add water kefir grains to 1 quart fresh sugar water (1/4 cup sugar dissolved in 1 quart water). Put a tight lid on the container and place in the refrigerator, as the cold temperature slows down the process. The water kefir grains should be safe and healthy for up to 3 weeks. When you're ready to make water kefir again, separate the grains from the storage liquid, place in fresh sugar water, and culture as usual. It may take a couple of batches for the grains to wake up and get back to work. The storage liquid should be fine to consume, as long as it has a pleasing aroma and flavor.

Taking a long break (up to 6 months) from your water kefir grains: If a longer break is required, drying your water kefir grains is recommended. Rinse the grains thoroughly with filtered water. Lay them on a piece of unbleached parchment paper in a safe location. Dry at room temperature for 3 to 5 days, depending on humidity and room temperature. Or use a dehydrator, as long as the grains do not get heated above 85°F. Once the kefir grains are fully dry, store in a Ziploc bag in the refrigerator for up to 6 months. When you're ready to make water kefir again, rehydrate the grains according to the instructions that came with the culture originally.

If you use reverse-osmosis water, consider adding a few drops of trace minerals back into the water or sticking a rinsed pastured egg shell in for minerals. If you just have tap water, boil it to remove chlorine and cool before using.

COCONUT PROBIOTIC TOPPING

YIELD: 4-1/2 CUPS (18 2-OUNCE SERVINGS)

CARBS:
4 grams per 2-ounce serving

PREP TIME:
10 minutes

TOTAL TIME:
10 minute + 4 days

INGREDIENTS:

4-1/2 cups full-fat unsweetened coconut cream (the hard part only)

5 grams (1/6 of an ounce) yogurt culture

2 tablespoons coconut nectar

5 teaspoons coconut extract

DIRECTIONS:

1. In a medium bowl, combine all ingredients.

2. Pour into a one-liter Mason jar and close loosely so that air can escape.

3. Place the Mason jar in the oven with the light on for 12 to 24 hours; stir twice daily.

4. Then place the Mason jar on your countertop, covered with a kitchen towel, for another 12 to 24 hours.

5. The probiotic topping is ready when the mixture starts to thicken and you can start to see air pockets form along the glass. The mixture should have a bit of a sour smell to it, but it should smell good, not bad.

6. Add any additional coconut nectar or lemon juice to perfect the flavor you're looking for (just make sure you add carbs for these items.)

7. Move the Mason jar to the fridge and enjoy on top of fresh berries, RFK chocolate quinoa cake, or your favorite healthy dessert.

***

TIPS & TRICKS: *This is a delicious nondairy substitute that makes you feel as if you're splurging! It's a great way to get in some good-for-you coconut oil and probiotics.*

SPECIAL DIET INFORMATION:

15-Day Detox Approved/30-Day Habit Reset Approved/Gluten-Free/ Diabetic Friendly

DR. MINDY'S NOTES

I love a food that gives you the combination of good fats and good bacteria. And this recipe does exactly that! Coconuts are one of the earth's most healing foods. They're rich in good saturated fats to nourish your brain, lower inflammation of your cells, and train your body to burn energy from fat. Add in good bacteria to heal your gut, and this healing food will delight your taste buds and move your health in a positive direction.

MILK KEFIR

YIELD: 1 QUART (8 4-OUNCE SERVINGS)

CARBS:	**PREP TIME:**	**TOTAL TIME:**
2 grams per 4-ounce serving	5 minutes	5 minutes + fermentation time

INGREDIENTS:

– 1 heaping tablespoon hydrated milk kefir grains (available on Amazon.com)

– 1 quart raw whole milk

DIRECTIONS:

1. Place the hydrated milk kefir grains in the bottom of a clean Mason jar. Cover with 1 quart fresh milk.

2. Very loosely, place the lid and band on the Mason jar. You do not want to tighten it because, as with all fermentation, carbon dioxide is created and needs to escape. Culture for 24 to 48 hours at room temperature.

3. Once culturing is complete, strain the milk kefir into a new Mason jar, cap, and refrigerate.

4. Begin reculturing a new batch of kefir with your milk kefir grains.

TIPS & TRICKS: *Milk kefir grains are alive, and making milk kefir is a continuous process. Here are a few tips on putting your milk kefir grains on pause.*

Taking a short break (up to 3 weeks) *from your milk kefir grains: Add milk kefir grains to 2 to 4 cups fresh milk. More milk for longer breaks is best, to keep the grains well-fed. Put a tight lid on the container and place in the refrigerator. The milk kefir grains should be safe and healthy for up to 3 weeks. When ready to make milk kefir again, separate the grains from the storage milk, place in fresh milk, and culture as usual. Keep in mind that it may take a couple of batches for the grains to wake up and get back to work. The storage liquid should be fine to consume, as long as it has a pleasing aroma and flavor.*

Taking a short break (up to 6 months) *from your milk kefir grains: Drying your milk kefir grains is recommended if you plan to take an extended break from making milk kefir. To do this, rinse the grains thoroughly with filtered water. Lay them on a piece of unbleached parchment paper in a safe location. Dry at room temperature for 3 to 5 days, depending on humidity and room temperature, or use a dehydrator as long as the grains do not get heated above 85 degrees. Place dried milk kefir grains in a Ziploc bag; add a small amount of powdered milk. Store in the refrigerator for up to 6 months.*

SPECIAL DIET INFORMATION:

30-Day Habit Reset/Gluten-Free/ Diabetic Friendly

DR. MINDY'S NOTES

I love raw kefir in my smoothie. It adds a nice tart taste plus a surge of good bacteria. Be sure to make this recipe with raw milk, as pasteurized milk has a higher sugar content. If you look for raw kefir at your local natural health food store, you'll see that it has lots of added sugar and that they pasteurize it, killing all the good bacteria.

GOAT CREAM CHEESE AND WHEY

YIELD: APPROXIMATELY 20 OUNCES CREAM CHEESE (20 2-TABLESPOON SERVINGS)

CARBS:
1 gram per 2-tablespoon serving of cream cheese

PREP TIME:
5 minutes

TOTAL TIME:
5 minutes + 12-hour wait

INGREDIENTS:

- 32 ounces full-fat organic plain goat yogurt
- Cheesecloth or very thin dish towel
- Medium-size bowl
- String or rubber bands

DIRECTIONS:

1. Pour the yogurt into cheesecloth or a thin towel (if the towel is too thick, it will absorb too much whey).

2. Gather the ends of the towel up and secure them with string or a rubber band.

3. Tie the towel with the yogurt in it to a cabinet. Place a bowl underneath to capture the whey as it drips out overnight.

4. In the morning, if the dripping has stopped, pour the liquid into a glass jar and store in the fridge for up to six months.

5. The "yogurt" left in the towel is now actually cream cheese. Put it in its own container and use as you would store-bought cream cheese.

6. The clear liquid that drained from the yogurt is the whey, which can be used as one method for making lacto-fermented fruits, vegetables, and beverages.

TIPS & TRICKS: *Whey can be kept in the refrigerator for up to 6 months.*

SPECIAL DIET INFORMATION:

30-Day Habit Reset Approved/ Gluten-Free/Diabetic Friendly

DR. MINDY'S NOTES

Lacto-fermentation is the art of preserving food by adding good lactobacillus bacteria—it's been done for centuries. The good bacteria produce lactic acid that stops bad bacteria from growing in and rotting food. It also increases the vitamin and enzyme level in foods and eases digestion. Here in the Reset Factor Kitchen, we use organic goat yogurt for this recipe because it's easier for the body to digest than cow's milk yogurt.

STACEY'S KOMBUCHA SCOBY

You need a SCOBY to make kombucha! SCOBY stands for Symbiotic Colony of Bacteria and Yeast.
Following are the instructions to make a SCOBY for kombucha:

YIELD: 1 SCOBY

CARBS:	PREP TIME:	TOTAL TIME:
0 grams	15 minutes	1 to 2 hours prep and cooling time. Allow 6 to 8 days for SCOBY to form.

INGREDIENTS:

- 4 teabags (black tea works best)
- 4 cups boiling water
- 1/4 cup organic cane sugar

DIRECTIONS:

1. Add 4 teabags to 4 cups boiling water in a heatproof glass container such as one made by Pyrex.

2. Add 1/4 cup of sugar and stir. Steep tea for 20 to 30 minutes and remove teabags.

3. Allow tea to cool to room temperature.

4. In a large glass bowl, add the tea and 2 cups of unfermented kombucha (or one bottle of commercial kombucha).

5. Cover securely with a dishcloth and rubber band.

6. Place in a dark, warm place for 6 to 8 days. A SCOBY will form!

Note: The remaining tea is probably too strong to drink, but you can use it as you would vinegar or discard it.

TIPS & TRICKS: *The unfermented kombucha used in this recipe can be purchased commercially or obtained from a friend. The final product will have a slightly fermented smell—this is perfectly normal. Don't allow metal to touch the kombucha as it can harm the culture. Use a linen dishtowel or other tight-weave cloth to cover the SCOBY. It needs some air; however, you will want to keep bugs out. DO NOT use cheesecloth, or bugs can get in.*

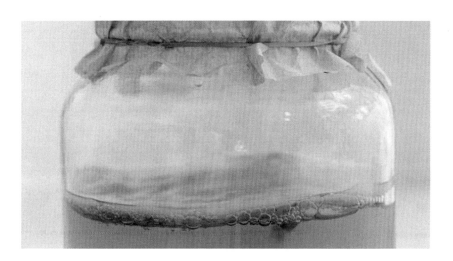

STACEY'S KONTINUOUS KOMBUCHA

YIELD: APPROXIMATELY 1 GALLON

CARBS:
Carbs vary based on your own recipe and ingredients. (If you're diabetic, it's best to drink store-bought kombucha, which has an exact carb count. See note below.)

PREP TIME:
20 minutes

TOTAL TIME:
1 to 2 hours prep and cooling time. Allow 6 to 8 days to ferment.

STANDARD METHOD:

INGREDIENTS:

– 16 teabags, black tea, green tea, or other tea containing caffeine

– 16 cups water

– 1 cup sugar

Note: Carbohydrates vary based on your own recipe and ingredients. I usually guesstimate 7g-8g carbs for an 8 oz. serving, and add additional carbs for additional fruit or flavorings added during a second fermentation. (If you are diabetic, you may want to consider store-bought kombucha, which has an exact carb count on the label.)

DIRECTIONS:

1. Add 16 teabags to 16 cups boiling water in a heatproof glass container such as one made by Pyrex.

2. Add 1 cup sugar and stir.

3. Steep tea for 20 to 30 minutes and remove teabags.

4. Allow tea to cool to room temperature.

5. Pour tea into a large glass container and add SCOBY.

6. Cover securely with a dishcloth and rubber band and place in a dark, warm place for 6 to 8 days to ferment.

7. Pour off 2 to 4 cups of the kombucha at a time if you're using the continuous method. If you wish to drink the tea right away, cool in the refrigerator for a few hours for the best taste.

VARIATION: Second fermentation with fruit. After the tea has fermented for 6 to 8 days, pour off 2 to 4 cups into a separate bottle or jar and add chopped fruit or whole or chopped berries. Cover the bottle or jar securely with a dishcloth and rubber band and place in a dark place for 24 hours to 3 or 4 days. The longer the tea sits, the stronger it will become. You'll find that the flavor peaks and then changes to more of a vinegary taste, so check every day or so until you find what works best for you.

Note: For best taste, pour liquid off into another container and chill before drinking. The fruit gives off a stale taste if you leave it in the tea in the refrigerator.

TIPS & TRICKS: *A few chunks of pineapple, a handful of berries, or a few slices of ginger or turmeric will work for your second fermentation with fruit. You can experiment with different combinations of fruits, like melon and pear. The berries do not have to be chopped, but they may add a stronger flavor if they are. Whole blueberries can be used multiple times. Chill kombucha before drinking, as warm kombucha doesn't taste very good.*

It can be hard to tell if kombucha has fermented long enough at first, so pour a small amount off and smell it. Put it in the fridge for a while and then taste it. After a while, you can get a sense of what it will taste like by the smell. It's helpful to brew in a container with a spigot—just make sure it's nonmetallic. Don't allow metal to touch the SCOBY.

CONTINUOUS-BREW METHOD:

You may use the entire batch of kombucha to start over using the same SCOBY and let ferment another 6 to 8 days. If you want a continuous supply, just pour off 2 to 4 cups at a time and replace with the same amount of fresh tea. Allow to sit for 1 to 2 days before pouring more off.

INGREDIENTS:

– 4 teabags

– 4 cups boiling water

– 1/4 cup organic cane sugar

DIRECTIONS:

1. Add 4 teabags to 4 cups boiling water in a heatproof glass container such as one made by Pyrex.

2. Add 1/4 cup of sugar and stir.

3. Steep the tea for 20 to 30 minutes and remove teabags.

4. Allow the tea to cool to room temperature and pour back into kombucha container.

5. Let it sit for 1 to 2 days before pouring more off.

6. After a while, a new SCOBY will form and your original SCOBY will get bigger. At this time, you can remove some of the SCOBY and discard it or share it with a friend. If you're using a container with a spigot, a SCOBY may form and clog the spigot. This is a good time to wash out the container, make sure the spigot is clear, and start over with fresh tea mixture. Handle your SCOBY as little as possible to avoid getting it dirty. If you ever want to make a new SCOBY, reserve 2 cups of kombucha and follow the directions for making a SCOBY above.

A NOTE ABOUT SUGAR: Most any type of organic sugar can be used in the continuous-brew method. Feel free to experiment with coconut sugar or other types of sugar you may have on hand. Some kombucha recipes state only regular white sugar works, but I've found this isn't true. What doesn't work is skimping on the sugar—you need enough to feed the culture and to ferment properly. However, the final product has minimal caffeine and sugar as it is converted into the culture.

SPECIAL DIET INFORMATION:

30-Day Habit Reset Approved/
Gluten-Free/Kid Approved

DR. MINDY'S NOTES

I love kombucha! It has become a family-favorite drink. No sodas in our house, only kombucha. And the kids love it! A kombucha habit can be expensive, so making your own is a great option. This is a great homemade recipe that will taste as good as the kombucha you buy in the store. Enjoy!

CHAPTER 21

SWEET-BUT-NOT-SO-SINFUL DESSERTS

STRAWBERRY RHUBARB TART

YIELD: 1 8-INCH TART (12 SLICES)

CARBS:
22 grams per slice

PREP TIME:
20 minutes + 10 to 12 minutes prep baking for crust

TOTAL TIME:
1-1/4 hours

INGREDIENTS:

CRUST:

- 2 cups almond flour
- 1/2 cup butter, melted
- 1/4 cup coconut sugar
- 2 teaspoons almond extract
- 1/4 teaspoon cinnamon

FILLING:

- 3 cups rhubarb, diced
- 2 tablespoons grass-fed butter
- 2 cups strawberries, diced
- 1/4 cup arrowroot flour
- 1/2 cup coconut sugar
- 1/4 teaspoon ground cinnamon
- 1/4 teaspoon ground nutmeg
- Dash ground cardamom

DIRECTIONS:

1. To prepare the filling, sauté rhubarb in butter until tender (about 20 minutes). If your rhubarb is particularly fibrous, this may take longer and you may want to cover it and simmer for some extra time.

2. While the rhubarb is cooking, cut the strawberries and measure all other ingredients.

3. Prepare the crust: Preheat oven to 350°F. Mix almond flour butter, coconut sugar, almond extract, and cinnamon well. Press into an 8-inch tart pan. Bake 10 to 12 minutes at 350°F.

4. While the crust is baking, check the rhubarb. When the rhubarb is tender, place the rhubarb and strawberries in a large bowl and set aside. In a small bowl, mix the arrowroot flour, coconut sugar, and spices. Gently mix the spices into the strawberry mixture. Set the filling mixture aside.

5. When the crust is finished, fill the crust with the filling mixture.

6. Bake for approximately 35 to 40 minutes at 350°F. Check periodically; you'll know it's done when the fruit is bubbling and the crust is toasted and starting to brown.

TIPS & TRICKS: *Strawberries and rhubarb are a classic flavor combination that doesn't require a lot of sweetness (carbs) to satisfy the taste buds.*

SPECIAL DIET INFORMATION:

30-Day Habit Reset Approved (in moderation)/Gluten-Free/Diabetic Friendly/Kid Approved

DR. MINDY'S NOTES

Want to lose weight, improve your digestion, prevent Alzheimer's, stimulate bone growth, prevent cancer, improve your circulation, and protect yourself against cardiovascular conditions? Then eat more rhubarb! This yummy, low-glycemic treat tastes great, gives you all the health benefits of rhubarb, and doesn't leave you feeling guilty after you eat it.

VANILLA CASHEW ICE CREAM

YIELD: APPROXIMATELY 5 CUPS (10 1/2-CUP SERVINGS)

CARBS:
Approximately 19 grams per 1/2-cup serving

PREP TIME:
15 minutes + overnight soaking of nuts

TOTAL TIME:
15 minutes + overnight soaking of nuts + overnight freezing of ice cream

INGREDIENTS:

- 2 cups raw organic cashews (soaked overnight)
- 1-1/2 cups RFK Almond Milk
- 1/4 cup raw organic honey
- 1 vanilla bean, split and seeded (might require soaking overnight)
- 1 teaspoon vanilla extract

DIRECTIONS:

1. Soak cashews and vanilla bean overnight.

2. The next day, split the vanilla bean and extract the seeds. Set aside.

3. In a Vitamix or powerful blender, begin by pulsing the cashews and almond milk, then blend until thick and creamy.

4. Add the remaining ingredients and blend until combined.

5. Use an ice cream maker and follow the manufacturer's instructions.

TIPS & TRICKS: *If you do not have an ice cream maker, you can freeze this recipe in a BPA-free freezer-proof plastic container. But there will be more crystals in the mixture, so to minimize this, stir every hour or so. Without an ice cream maker, it may take up to 6 to 8 hours to freeze to a firm, scoopable thickness. If left to freeze overnight or longer, this method may also require some time at room temperature to defrost a bit before scooping and serving.*

SPECIAL DIET INFORMATION:

30-Day Habit Reset Approved (in moderation)/Gluten-Free/Diabetic Friendly/Kid Approved

DR. MINDY'S NOTES

Think resetting your health means you have to give up ice cream? Well, it doesn't! This great recipe will satisfy your ice cream cravings while giving you lots of good fats and protein. Be sure that the cashews are raw. Cashews will help you prevent cancer and heart disease. They're packed with magnesium to help support healthy bones and muscles and ligaments, and they're high in copper—which gives your hair a healthy glow. They've also been known to lower blood pressure.

Quinoa Cacao Cake, Vanilla Ice Cream (page 233), *Just Raspberry Syrup* (page 166)

QUINOA CACAO CAKE

YIELD: 12 SERVINGS

CARBS:	**PREP TIME:**	**TOTAL TIME:**
26 grams per serving	30 minutes	2 hours

INGREDIENTS:

- 2/3 cup quinoa
- 1/3 cup RFK Almond Milk
- 1-1/3 cups apple sauce
- 3/4 cup coconut oil
- 2 teaspoons vanilla extract
- 1/4 cup honey
- 2 eggs
- 1/3 cup coconut sugar
- 1 cup raw cacao powder
- 1-1/2 teaspoons baking powder
- 1/2 teaspoon baking soda
- 1/2 teaspoon sea salt

DIRECTIONS:

1. Cook quinoa per package instructions. (Typically, instructions are to rinse quinoa grains, boil grains with 1-1/3 cup water, reduce heat, simmer for 10 minutes, let stand for 10 minutes, and let cool for 15 minutes.)

2. While the quinoa is cooking, measure all other ingredients and prepare an 8" x 8"–square glass baking pan with coconut oil and oiled parchment paper at the bottom. Set aside.

3. Once the quinoa is cool enough to handle, preheat the oven to 350°F.

4. In a Vitamix, food processor, or powerful blender, pulse to blend in 3 stages: First combine the almond milk, apple sauce, coconut oil, vanilla extract, and honey. Then add the cooked quinoa, eggs, and coconut sugar. Finally, pulse in the cacao powder, baking powder, baking soda, and salt.

5. Transfer to the baking dish and bake for 1 hour and 25 minutes, or until a toothpick comes out clean in the center.

TIPS & TRICKS: *This is the moistest gluten-free cake you will ever eat! The final product makes you think there's pudding in the cake. Don't pulse the batter too much; the texture of the quinoa in the final baked cake adds to its unique, slightly crunchy texture and helps the cake remain moist.*

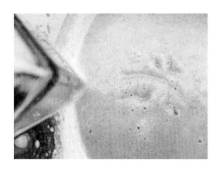 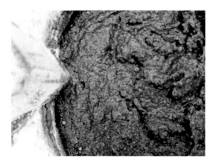 

DR. MINDY'S NOTES

I love using quinoa in as many places as possible. It's high in protein, packed with vitamins, and low on the glycemic index so it won't spike your blood sugar. The benefits of cacao are truly fantastic as well. Cacao can improve your memory, increase your serotonin levels, reduce heart disease, help you shed fat, boost your immunity, and create loads of energy for you. Put that in a dessert that tastes great and you have a win-win recipe! Your sweet tooth is satisfied, and your body loves all the healthy nutrients.

COCONUT CACAO CHIA PUDDING

YIELD: APPROXIMATELY 4-1/2 CUPS (13 1/3-CUP SERVINGS)

CARBS:
Approximately 11 grams per 1/3-cup serving

PREP TIME:
15 minutes

TOTAL TIME:
15 minutes + variable wait time

INGREDIENTS:

- 3 cups coconut milk
- 2/3 cup chia seeds
- 1/2 cup raw cacao powder1 teaspoon vanilla extract
- 1 teaspoon ground cinnamon (optional)
- 1/2 teaspoon sea salt

OPTIONAL INGREDIENT:

- 1/3 cup maple syrup (this adds approximately 5g carbs to each serving)

DIRECTIONS:

1. In a large mixing bowl, combine all ingredients and blend vigorously.

2. Chill in the fridge between 3 hours and overnight. The goal is for the mixture to have a pudding-like consistency and to be chilled through.

3. Leftovers keep covered in the fridge for 2 to 3 days, though this pudding is best when it's fresh.

4. Serve chilled.

5. Serving suggestions: Top with RFK Coconut Probiotic Topping, raw almonds, raspberries, blueberries, shaved coconut flakes, and finely sliced mint leaves.

TIPS & TRICKS: *If you're serving this for a party, you might want to consider putting the pudding in individual ramekins, pudding cups, or glasses before refrigerating. Then add toppings before serving. This healthy dessert can also substitute as a breakfast treat—you'll start your day fueled with nutrients and antioxidants! Zero-carb sweeteners like stevia can be substituted for the maple syrup, reducing the carb count by 8g per serving.*

SPECIAL DIET INFORMATION:

15-Day Detox Approved (without the maple syrup)/30-Day Habit Reset Approved (in moderation)/ Gluten-Free/Diabetic Friendly/Kid Approved

DR. MINDY'S NOTES

Chia seeds are one of my favorite health treats. They are gelatinous, which helps them bind to toxins in your body. They're also high in antioxidants, which helps protect you against free-radical damage. Cinnamon will speed up your metabolism. Cacao will give you a blissful feeling. Sea salt will nourish your thyroid. Who doesn't want all of that?

QUINOA PUDDING

YIELD: APPROXIMATELY 5 CUPS (10 1/2-CUP SERVINGS)

CARBS:
Approximately 19 grams per 1/2-cup serving

PREP TIME:
10 minutes

TOTAL TIME:
40 minutes

INGREDIENTS:

- 1 cup quinoa
- 4 cups RFK Almond Milk or coconut milk
- 1 vanilla bean
- 1/4 cup coconut sugar
- 1 teaspoon cinnamon
- Pinch of freshly ground nutmeg
- 1/2 teaspoon sea salt

OPTIONAL INGREDIENT:

- 1 teaspoon vanilla extract

DIRECTIONS:

1. Rinse quinoa in cold water in a fine-mesh strainer.

2. In a medium-size saucepan, combine the almond or coconut milk, coconut sugar, and seeds from the inside of the vanilla bean.

3. Bring the liquid to a rapid simmer at medium-high heat. Add the spices and rinsed quinoa and then reduce the heat to low. Stir every few minutes for 30 minutes, until the quinoa blooms and the milk reduces to your desired pudding consistency.

4. If you want additional sweetness, add the vanilla extract at the end. If you prefer a less sweet end result, omit the vanilla extract.

5. Serve warm or chilled.

TIPS & TRICKS: *Make sure the coconut milk you purchase comes in BPA-free cans. This pudding will last up to 5 days in the fridge—if it doesn't get eaten before then! Zero-carb sweeteners like stevia can be substituted for the coconut sugar, reducing the carb count by 4g per serving.*

SPECIAL DIET INFORMATION:

30-Day Habit Reset Approved/ Gluten-Free/Diabetic Friendly/Kid Approved

DR. MINDY'S NOTES

Another great treat to satisfy your sweet tooth without destroying your health. What I like about this sweet treat is the vanilla. Vanilla has been used for centuries as an antioxidant and cognitive enhancing agent. Vanilla contains chemicals called vanilloids, which activate receptors that reduce inflammation and improve mental performance. Vanilla has also been used to calm stomach pains, reduce hunger pangs, and help digestion. Vanilla has been used around the world as a medicinal food that can help many ailments. For years, Europeans have believed in vanilla's abilities to reduce joint pain, and South Pacific islanders have been known to use vanilla to reduce nausea in pregnant women with morning sickness.

ALMOND MACAROONS
3 WAYS: LEMON, CACAO, AND MAPLE VANILLA

YIELD: 20 COOKIES

CARBS:
5 grams lemon / 7 grams cacao / 6 grams maple vanilla

PREP TIME:
10 minutes (4-hour refrigerator rest)

BAKE TIME:
15 minutes a batch

BASE INGREDIENTS:

- 1 cup blanched almond flour
- 1 cup unsweetened shredded coconut
- 2 teaspoons vanilla extract
- 6 large egg whites
- 2 tablespoons coconut oil, melted
- 1/4 teaspoon sea salt

CHOOSE YOUR FLAVOR:

FOR LEMON, ADD:

- 1/4 cup honey
- 1 teaspoon lemon oil
- Zest from 2 lemons
- 3 tablespoons lemon juice

FOR CACAO, ADD:

- 1/4 cup honey
- 1/2 cup raw cacao powder

FOR MAPLE VANILLA, ADD:

- 1/4 cup maple syrup
- 1 extra teaspoon vanilla extract

DIRECTIONS:

1. Melt the coconut oil.

2. Measure the ingredients for the particular flavor you want to make and set aside. Keep the wet ingredients separate from the dry ingredients.

3. In a medium-size bowl, combine the almond flour, shredded coconut, and salt. (If you're making the chocolate flavor, add the cacao powder here.)

4. In a separate medium-size bowl, whisk the egg whites, sweetener from the flavor you're making (honey or maple syrup), and vanilla, until fluffy. If you're making the lemon flavor, add the zest, juice, and lemon oil here.

5. Fold the dry ingredients into the wet ingredients. Fold in the coconut oil last.

6. Refrigerate the batter for at least 4 to 5 hours. (You want the batter firm so you can scoop it with a mini ice cream scoop.)

7. When the batter is ready (firm enough to scoop with a mini ice cream scoop), preheat the oven to 350°F. Make mounds of dough with a mini ice cream scoop and place on a lined baking sheet.

8. Bake at 350ºF for 15 minutes. Let cool on the baking sheet.

TIPS & TRICKS: *These cookies do not rise or expand, so they can be closer together than normal cookies. Allow them to cool on the baking sheet; as they cool, they set and become firmer. If you try to move them while they're still warm, they tend to fall apart.*

SPECIAL DIET INFORMATION:

30-Day Habit Reset Approved (in moderation)/Gluten-Free/Diabetic Friendly/Kid Approved

DR. MINDY'S NOTES

This recipe is the perfect combination of sweet and protein. Anytime you combine something sweet with a protein or fat, you slow down the absorption of the sweetness in your blood. This causes your body to need less insulin to process that food. This recipe is also rich in good fats, so eating just a few will fill you up and keep you full for hours.

CHOCOLATE CHIP COOKIES

YIELD: 24 COOKIES

CARBS:	**PREP TIME:**	**BAKE TIME:**
Approximately 14 grams per cookie	35 minutes + 2-hour refrigerator rest	12 to 15 minutes per batch

INGREDIENTS:

Dry Ingredients

- 1-1/4 cups blanched almond flour, finely ground
- 1-1/4 cups tiger nut flour
- 1 teaspoon baking soda
- 3 teaspoons xanthan gum
- 1 teaspoon sea salt
- 1-1/2 cups (9-ounce bag) Lily's Dark Chocolate Chips (stevia sweetened)
- 1-1/2 to 2 cups walnuts, chopped

Wet Ingredients

- 1 cup grass-fed butter, melted (warm, not hot)
- 1 cup coconut sugar
- 2 teaspoons vanilla extract
- 2 eggs, beaten

DIRECTIONS:

1. In a small saucepan, gently melt the butter; remove from heat once melted. Mix in the coconut sugar and set aside to melt (about 10 minutes).

2. While the butter and coconut sugar mixture is cooling, measure out all other ingredients.

3. In a small bowl, beat the eggs with the vanilla and put aside.

4. In a medium-size bowl, combine all dry ingredients.

5. After the butter and coconut sugar mixture has cooled, quickly blend with the egg (and vanilla) mixture.

6. Blend the dry ingredients into the wet ingredients.

7. Refrigerate the dough at least 2 hours. Then take it out and make 24 dough balls.

8. Preheat oven to 350°F.

9. Place the dough balls on a cookie sheet. Before placing in the oven, smash them with the palm of your hand to make the dough look like hockey pucks.

TIPS & TRICKS: *When the dough balls are formed into hockey puck shapes, they cook more evenly.*

DR. MINDY'S NOTES

Who wants to give up chocolate chip cookies while you're resetting your health? Not me. That is why I was so happy when Bonnie made this amazing treat. If you're not familiar with tiger nut flour, let me introduce you. The first thing to know about tiger nut is that it's actually not a nut—it's a tuber. Tiger nut flour is rich in magnesium, which helps with chronic pain and insomnia. It can control your blood pressure, prevent cancer, and give you a potassium boost. It's also lower on the glycemic index, which makes it ideal to cook with during your 45-Day Reset.

NOT-YOUR-AVERAGE SPICE COOKIES

YIELD: 36 COOKIES

CARBS:	PREP TIME:	BAKE TIME:
14 grams per cookie	10 minutes + 4 to 5 hours chill time	10 to 12 minutes per batch

INGREDIENTS:

- 1-1/2 cups grass-fed butter
- 2 cups coconut sugar
- 2 large eggs
- 1/2 cup RFK Coconut Sugar Simple Syrup
- 2 cups almond flour
- 2 cups tiger nut flour
- 1 teaspoon xanthan gum
- 1 teaspoon baking soda
- 1 teaspoon sea salt
- 2 teaspoons ground cloves
- 2 teaspoons ground ginger
- 4 teaspoons ground cinnamon

DIRECTIONS:

1. Mix wet ingredients (butter, sugar, and eggs), adding the RFK Coconut Sugar Simple Syrup last. Set aside.

2. Mix together all dry ingredients: almond flour, tiger nut flour, xanthan gum, salt, baking soda, and spices. Add this mixture to the creamed mixture one-third at a time until blended.

3. Chill dough 4 to 5 hours.

4. Roll 1-1/2 inch dough balls. Place chilled dough balls, evenly distributed, on a nonstick baking sheet (the silicon Silpat-type sheets are best). The cookies will get fairly flat during the baking process, so make sure you space them far enough apart.

5. Bake at 350°F for 10 to 12 minutes.

TIPS & TRICKS: *Refrigerating the dough helps prevent the cookies from melting too much in the fridge and coming out too flat. Cold dough balls will melt slower and create a thicker cookie.*

SPECIAL DIET INFORMATION:

30-Day Habit Reset Approved (in moderation)/Gluten-Free/Diabetic Friendly (in moderation)/Kid Approved

DR. MINDY'S NOTES

When Bonnie gave me these cookies to sample, I almost cried—they tasted amazing! She has included several high-protein sugared flours in this recipe, which will stabilize your blood sugar. The cloves, nutmeg, and cinnamon give this cookie a nice depth of taste while giving you several health benefits. Nutmeg is known to be a good antifungal, antidepressant, and aphrodisiac, and it's packed with copper, potassium, manganese, and magnesium. Cloves have been used for centuries for their antibacterial and antiviral qualities. Cinnamon has been known to help stabilize your blood sugar and lower bad LDL levels, and it also has antifungal, antiviral, and antibacterial qualities.

HEAVENLY FREEZER FUDGE

YIELD: 36 1-TEASPOON-SIZE FREEZER FUDGE BITES

CARBS:
Approximately 3-1/3 grams per
1-teaspoon serving

PREP TIME:
5 minutes

TOTAL TIME:
5 minutes + 2 to 3 hours freezer time

INGREDIENTS:

– 1 cup RFK Nut Butter of the Gods

– 3 tablespoons raw cacao powder

– 1 teaspoon vanilla extract

– 1/8 teaspoon sea salt

OPTIONAL INGREDIENT:

– 1/2 teaspoon raw honey

DIRECTIONS:

1. Mix all ingredients together until a thick uniform paste is formed.

2. Spoon into silicon ice cube trays. The one I use has heart shapes that take 1 teaspoon of the fudge paste to fill.

3. Cover with parchment paper (then plastic wrap to keep it secure) and place on a flat surface in the freezer. Freeze for at least 2 to 3 hours or until frozen (depending on size).

TIPS & TRICKS: *These sweet treats taste REALLY good and are REALLY good for you! How many chocolates out there can you say are serving your health? Well, you can say it about these! They're packed with protein and good fat from the RFK Nut Butter of the Gods, PLUS the raw cacao powder delivers a powerful punch of potassium, zinc, iron, magnesium, phosphorus, copper, and manganese.*

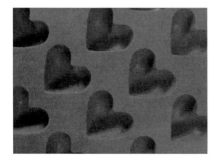

SPECIAL DIET INFORMATION:

15-Day Detox Approved (without the honey)/30-Day Habit Reset Approved (in moderation)/ Gluten-Free/Diabetic Friendly/Kid Approved

DR. MINDY'S NOTES

Fudge? What? Yes, you read the title of this recipe right. You can have fudge on your 45-Day Reset. You just need to follow the guidelines Bonnie has created in this recipe. One thing I will point out here is that she has you using raw honey. Raw honey has many medicinal qualities: it's a great source of antioxidants, and it's also an antifungal and antibacterial. It's filled with phytonutrients, it helps with digestive issues, and it can improve your allergies.

CASHEW NUT BUTTER COOKIES

YIELD: 24 COOKIES

CARBS:
18 grams per cookie

PREP TIME:
15 minutes

TOTAL TIME:
30 minutes

INGREDIENTS:

– 1 cup grass-fed butter, softened

– 1 cup smooth RFK Raw Cashew Nut Butter

– 1 cup coconut sugar

– 2 eggs, beaten

– 1 teaspoon vanilla extract

– 2 cups coconut flour

– 1 teaspoon sea salt

– 1 teaspoon baking soda

– 1-1/2 teaspoons xanthan gum

DIRECTIONS:

1. Pre-heat oven to 350°F.

2. In a medium-size bowl, cream together the nut butter and butter. Stir in the coconut sugar.

3. In a small bowl, beat the eggs and add the vanilla. Add this to the butter and nut butter mixture. Let sit about 10 minutes so the coconut sugar granules have time to dissolve.

4. In a second medium-size bowl, combine the remaining dry ingredients (coconut flour, salt, baking soda, and xanthan gum).

5. When 10 minutes has passed, combine the wet and dry ingredients.

6. Form round balls. Place on a nonstick baking sheet.

7. Cook balls for 6 minutes. Remove from oven and mark them with a dinner fork. Return them to the oven for 4 more minutes. This recipe yields 24 cookies.

8. Let cool on the cookie sheet.

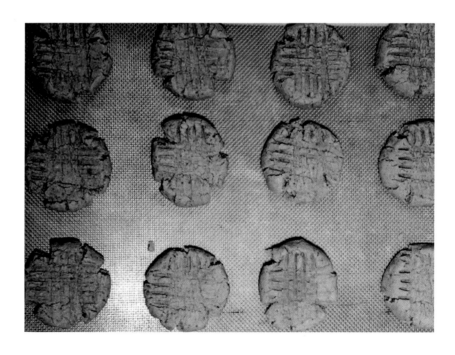

CHAPTER 22

45-DAY MENU PLAN
ALL RECIPES ARE RFK

HEALTH TIPS

1. To minimize hunger, eat more fat

2. Great snack ideas:

- Vegetables with one of the spreads in Chapter 18
- Raw almonds, pecans, walnuts, and macadamia nuts
- Hummus with good oils
- Green apples with nut butters

3. If you're too full for a second smoothie, you don't have to drink a second one.

4. Drink lots of water to flush toxins out (6 to 8 glasses a day).

5. If you feel light-headed for the first few days, eat more of the approved foods. Feeling light-headed or fluish can be normal if this is your first detox.

	DAY 1	DAY 2	DAY 3
	Detox Water	Detox Water	Detox Water
Breakfast	Sweet Kefir Smoothie	Carrot Zinger Smoothie	Black and Blue Smoothie
Lunch	The Best Roasted Chicken Roasted Turmeric Cauliflower	Lemon Ginger Salmon Roasted Brussels Sprouts	Braised Beef in Bone Broth Grilled Kombucha Cabbage
Dinner	The Alkalinator Smoothie	Classic Berry Smoothie	Raspberry Gut Zinger Smoothie
Snacks	Cut vegetables Any food from Chapter 18 Green apple and nut butter	Cut vegetables Any food from Chapter 18 Green apple and nut butter	Cut vegetables Any food from Chapter 18 Green apple and nut butter

HEALTH TIPS

1. By the fourth day, you should be feeling better. If your hunger is down and energy is starting to increase, you're beginning to feel the effects of having stable blood sugar.

2. If there's a particular smoothie you love, feel free to keep having that one over and over again.

3. If you need more variety, use several different protein powders (chocolate and vanilla).

4. Make lunches the night before so that you're ready to go the next day.

	DAY 4	DAY 5	DAY 6
	Detox Water	Detox Water	Detox Water
Breakfast	Classic Berry Smoothie	Sweet Kefir Smoothie	Classic Berry Smoothie
Lunch	Raspberry Gut Zinger Smoothie	The Best Roasted Chicken Carrot Fries	The Alkalinator Smoothie
Dinner	Roasted Pork Loin with Green-Apple Applesauce Roasted Brussels Sprouts	Green Goddess Smoothie	Pizza with Herbed Cauliflower Crust Mixed green salad with Mel's Spicy "Soy" Dressing
Snacks	Cut vegetables Any food from Chapter 18 Green apple and nut butter	Cut vegetables Any food from Chapter 18 Green apple and nut butter	Cut vegetables Any food from Chapter 18 Green apple and nut butter

HEALTH TIPS

1. If the detox water is hard to drink, try just having a glass of lemon water first thing when you get up.
2. Room-temperature water is best on your digestive system.

	DAY 7	**DAY 8**	**DAY 9**
	Detox Water	Detox Water	Detox Water
Breakfast	Black and Blue Smoothie	Classic Berry Smoothie	Raspberry Gut Zinger Smoothie
Lunch	Bellybiotic Smoothie	The Best Roasted Chicken Grilled Kombucha Cabbage	The Best Roasted Chicken Roasted Turmeric Cauliflower
Dinner	Roasted Leg of Lamb Green Beans with Caramelized Shallots	Green Goddess Smoothie	The Alkalinator Smoothie
Snacks	Cut vegetables Any food from Chapter 18 Green apple and nut butter	Cut vegetables Any food from Chapter 18 Green apple and nut butter	Cut vegetables Any food from Chapter 18 Green apple and nut butter

HEALTH TIPS

1. By this point, your hunger should be minimal. If it isn't, try getting about 60% of your diet over the next few days from good fat.
2. You many also be noticing that you're sleeping more deeply and waking up more easily.
3. If you're not noticing favorable results, hang in there. The longer you stay on the detox, the better the results you'll get.
4. If you haven't lost much weight at this point, start tracking your carbohydrates.
5. Download the Carb Manager app on your phone and track your daily carbs. Keep carb count under 50 grams/day.

	DAY 10	**DAY 11**	**DAY 12**
	Detox Water	Detox Water	Detox Water
Breakfast	Classic Berry Smoothie	Raspberry Gut Zinger Smoothie	Black and Blue Smoothie

Lunch	Carrot Zinger Smoothie	Lemon Ginger Salmon Mixed green salad with Citrus Burst Salad Dressing	Pizza with Herbed Cauliflower Crust | 1/2 avocado
Dinner	The Best Roasted Chicken Steve P's Kickin' Corn Salad	Garden In A Glass Smoothie	Green Goddess Smoothie
Snacks	Cut vegetables Any food from Chapter 18 Green apple and nut butter	Cut vegetables Any food from Chapter 18 Green apple and nut butter	Cut vegetables Any food from Chapter 18 Green apple and nut butter

HEALTH TIPS

1. If you're loving the detox and want to stay on it longer than 15 days, that's OK. Many of my patients do that.

2. Add in some of the soups for variety and warmth.

3. Smoothie Ice Cream is added to dinner this week to give you some variety and a break from your typical smoothie.

	DAY 13	**DAY 14**	**DAY 15**
	Detox Water	Detox Water	Detox Water
Breakfast	Classic Berry Smoothie	Raspberry Gut Zinger Smoothie	Black and Blue Smoothie
Lunch	Bellybiotic Smoothie	Roasted Pork Loin with Green Apple Applesauce Mixed green salad with Citrus Burst Salad Dressing	Carrot Zinger Smoothie
Dinner	Roasted Leg of Lamb Carrot Fries 1/2 avocado	Smoothie Ice Cream	Braised Beef in Bone Broth Roasted Brussels Sprouts
Snacks	Cut vegetables Any food from Chapter 18 Green apple and nut butter	Cut vegetables Any food from Chapter 18 Green apple and nut butter	Cut vegetables Any food from Chapter 18 Green apple and nut butter

HEALTH TIPS

1. As you transition to your 30-Day Habit Reset, this is a great time to add in daily intermittent fasting and to start tracking your carbohydrates, keeping them under 50 grams/day.

2. Keeping carbs low and adding in intermittent fasting will accelerate weight loss.

3. If you're tired of smoothies, you can stop them and eat only food.

4. Be aware that many people have a tremendous amount of energy when on the detox but lose a little of that energy once they transition to the 30-Day Habit Reset.

5. Experiment with the elixirs.

	DAY 16	DAY 17	DAY 18
Breakfast	Chocolate Cherry Heaven Smoothie	Sweet Kefir Smoothie	Classic Berry Smoothie
Lunch	Mixed green salad with Citrus Burst Salad Dressing Grilled chicken (any way you like) 1/2 avocado with SunnyKraut	Lemon Ginger Salmon Mixed green salad with Citrus Burst Salad Dressing	Pulled Pork in Bone Broth Green Beans with Caramelized Shallots
Dinner	Fish in Parchment Paper Orange Wild Rice Mixed green salad with Citrus Burst Salad Dressing	Green Beans with Caramelized Shallots The Best Roasted Chicken Steve P's Kickin' Corn Salad	Kitchen Sink Quiche Mixed green salad with Citrus Burst Salad Dressing
Snacks	Cut vegetables Any food from Chapter 18 Green apple and nut butter	Cut vegetables Any food from Chapter 18 Green apple and nut butter	Cut vegetables Any food from Chapter 18 Green apple and nut butter

HEALTH TIPS

1. For maximum weight loss:

- Keep carbohydrate intake under 50 grams/day.
- A good rule for protein intake is half your ideal body weight. If 130 pounds is your ideal weight, then eat no more than 65 grams/day of protein.
- Shoot for keeping good fat high (around 60% of your daily intake).

	DAY 19	DAY 20	DAY 21
Breakfast	Black and Blue Smoothie	RFK Granola with raw grass-fed yogurt or milk	Raspberry Gut Zinger Smoothie
Lunch	Pizza with Herbed Cauliflower Crust Mixed green salad with Citrus Burst Salad Dressing	Grass-fed beef burgers 1/2 avocado with SunnyKraut	Healthy Chicken Nuggets Grilled Kombucha Cabbage
Dinner	Roasted Pork Loin with Green Apple Applesauce Mixed green salad with Citrus Burst Salad Dressing	Lemon Ginger Salmon Roasted Brussels Sprouts	Breadcrumb-Free Crab Cakes Roasted Turmeric Cauliflower
Snacks	Cut vegetables Any food from Chapter 18 Green apple and nut butter	Cut vegetables Any food from Chapter 18 Green apple and nut butter	Cut vegetables Any food from Chapter 18 Green apple and nut butter

HEALTH TIPS

1. Stop looking at the scale and start looking at a ketone reader.
2. Optimal fat-burning zone: Ketones in the range of 0.5–5.0

	DAY 22	DAY 23	DAY 24
Breakfast	Chocolate Cherry Heaven Smoothie	Waffles 3 Ways Raspberry Chia "Jam"	Black and Blue Smoothie
Lunch	Bacon-Avo-Egg Mixed greens with Citrus Burst Salad Dressing	Grass-fed beef burgers 1/2 avocado with SunnyKraut Quinoa Tabouli	Healthy Chicken Nuggets Carrot Fries Mixed green salad with Mel's Spicy "Soy" Dressing

Dinner	Pizza with Herbed Cauliflower Crust Mixed green salad with Mel's Spicy "Soy" Dressing	Braised Beef in Bone Broth Carrot Fries 1/2 avocado with SunnyKraut	Lemon Ginger Salmon Mixed green salad with Citrus Burst Salad Dressing
Snacks	Cut vegetables Any food from Chapter 18 Green apple and nut butter	Cut vegetables Any food from Chapter 18 Green apple and nut butter	Cut vegetables Any food from Chapter 18 Green apple and nut butter

---

HEALTH TIPS

1. If you're reading your ketones and practicing intermittent fasting, take your ketone measurement when you first wake up and right before you eat your first meal. You should see your ketones rise well above 0.5 when you're in a semi-fasted state.

2. Now is a great time to add in exercise if you haven't already. Start with 3 days a week.

	DAY 25	**DAY 26**	**DAY 27**
Breakfast	Classic Berry Smoothie	Waffles 3 Ways	Bacon-Avo-Egg
Lunch	Grilled Chicken Breast Steve P's Kickin' Corn Salad	Lemon Ginger Salmon Mixed green salad with Citrus Burst Salad Dressing	Grass-fed beef burgers (made any way you like) 1/2 avocado with SunnyKraut
Dinner	Grilled chicken (made your way Grilled Kombucha Cabbage	The Best Roasted Chicken Roasted Brussels Sprouts	Pizza with Herbed Cauliflower Crust 1/2 avocado with Sunnykraut
Snacks	Cut vegetables Any food from Chapter 18 Green apple and nut butter	Cut vegetables Any food from Chapter 18 Green apple and nut butter	Cut vegetables Any food from Chapter 18 Green apple and nut butter

HEALTH TIPS

1. At this point in your reset experience, you will have discovered your favorite foods, which you may keep eating over and over. Be sure to experiment with new recipes too. Boredom can kill your motivation, so keep your meals interesting.

2. Be sure you find us on social media, as we will be posting new recipes all the time.

	DAY 28	**DAY 29**	**DAY 30**
Breakfast	Raspberry Gut Zinger Smoothie	Chocolate Cherry Heaven Smoothie	Black and Blue Smoothie
Lunch	Pulled Pork in Bone Broth Grilled Kombucha Cabbage	Pizza with Herbed Cauliflower Crust Mixed green salad with Citrus Burst Salad Dressing	Carrot Chestnut Ginger Soup 1/2 avocado with SunnyKraut
Dinner	Pizza with Herbed Cauliflower Crust	Fish in Parchment Paper Mixed green salad with Citrus Burst Salad Dressing	Breadcrumb-Free Crab Cakes Green Beans with Caramelized Shallots
Snacks	Cut vegetables Any food from Chapter 18 Green apple and nut butter	Cut vegetables Any food from Chapter 18 Green apple and nut butter	Cut vegetables Any food from Chapter 18 Green apple and nut butter

HEALTH TIPS

1. If you've followed all my recommendations exactly to this point and are still not losing weight, there's a good chance you have an abundance of toxins in your body.

2. Get yourself tested for heavy metals such as mercury, lead, and aluminum, as those metals can make you weight-loss resistant. Also check out heavy metals in Chapter 5: "Ingredients That Will Destroy Your Health"

	DAY 31	**DAY 32**	**DAY 33**
Breakfast	Classic Berry Smoothie	Skip breakfast today; try intermittent fasting	RFK Granola with raw grass-fed yogurt or milk
Lunch	Healthy Chicken Nuggets 1/2 avocado with Beet Ginger Sauerkraut	Roasted Butternut Squash Soup Mixed green salad with Citrus Burst Salad Dressing	Bacon-Avo-Egg Mixed green salad with Citrus Burst Salad Dressing

Dinner	Kitchen Sink Quiche Mixed green salad with Citrus Burst Salad Dressing	Roasted Leg of Lamb Sweet Potato Hashbrowns Mixed green salad with Citrus Burst Salad Dressing	Grass-fed burgers (made your way) Grilled Kombucha Cabbage Quinoa Tabouli
Snacks	Cut vegetables Any food from Chapter 18 Green apple and nut butter	Cut vegetables Any food from Chapter 18 Green apple and nut butter	Cut vegetables Any food from Chapter 18 Green apple and nut butter

---

HEALTH TIPS

1. Don't be afraid to try the 2-2-2 protocol I outlined in Chapter 7: "Accelerating Your Results."

2. Adding a day of bone-broth fasting into your weekly routine will help speed up weight loss.

3. Desserts can be added in as desired.

	DAY 34	**DAY 35**	**DAY 36**
Breakfast	Raspberry Gut Zinger Smoothie	Black and Blue Smoothie	Chocolate Cherry Heaven Smoothie
Lunch	Grass-fed beef burgers (made your way) 1/2 avocado with SunnyKraut	Grilled chicken (made your way) Grilled Kombucha Cabbage	The Best Roasted Chicken Carrot Fries Mixed green salad with Citrus Burst Salad Dressing
Dinner	Lemon Ginger Salmon Roasted Turmeric Cauliflower	Roasted Pork Loin with Green Apple Applesauce Roasted Brussels Sprouts	Breadcrumb-Free Crab Cakes
Snacks	Cut vegetables Any food from Chapter 18 Green apple and nut butter	Cut vegetables Any food from Chapter 18 Green apple and nut butter	Cut vegetables Any food from Chapter 18 Green apple and nut butter

HEALTH TIPS

1. If you've gotten this far into your reset experience and are getting great results, reach out to us! Find us on social media—we loving hearing about people's successes.

2. Keep checking your ketones at least twice weekly to make sure you're getting yourself into the best fat-burning zone possible.

3. Now is a great time to take a meta-oxy test. It's inexpensive and a powerful tool to measure your inflammation levels. For more information, check our website at http://familylifechiropractic.com/our-stores/

4. If you have followed the program exactly as it's laid out and score above a 5 on your meta-oxy test, there's a good chance you have neurotoxins that need to be addressed.

5. If your meta-oxy test is lower than 3, congrats! You are lowering inflammation in your body.

	DAY 37	DAY 38	DAY 39
Breakfast	Classic Berry Smoothie	RFK Granola with raw grass-fed yogurt or milk	Waffles 3 Ways
Lunch	Kitchen Sink Quiche 1/2 avocado with Ginger Beet Sauerkraut	Healthy Chicken Nuggets Grilled Kombucha Cabbage 1/2 avocado with Sunnykraut	Grilled chicken (made your way) Grilled Kombucha Cabbage
Dinner	Pulled Pork in Bone Broth Orange Wild Rice Mixed green salad with Citrus Burst Salad Dressing	Lemon Ginger Salmon Green Beans with Caramelized Shallots Mixed green salad with Citrus Burst Salad Dressing	The Best Roasted Chicken Roasted Turmeric Cauliflower
Snacks	Cut vegetables Any food from Chapter 18 Green apple and nut butter	Cut vegetables Any food from Chapter 18 Green apple and nut butter	Cut vegetables Any food from Chapter 18 Green apple and nut butter

HEALTH TIPS

1. If you've been keeping carbs under 50 grams/day, doing daily intermittent fasting, and following the 2-2-2 rule, there's a good chance at this point you feel and look fantastic. Many people tell me they have lost interest in food by this time because their blood sugar is so stable.

2. Stay the course. You've worked hard to get yourself healing at the accelerated rate you're at right now.

	DAY 40	DAY 41	DAY 42
Breakfast	The Alkalinator Smoothie	Black and Blue Smoothie	Raspberry Gut Zinger Smoothie
Lunch	Healthy Chicken Nuggets Grilled Kombucha Cabbage	Breadcrumb-Free Crab Cakes Green Beans with Caramelized Shallots	The Best Roasted Chicken Roasted Turmeric Cauliflower
Dinner	Pulled Pork in Bone Broth Mixed green salad with Citrus Burst Salad Dressing	Kitchen Sink Quiche Mixed green salad with Citrus Burst Salad Dressing	Braised Beef in Bone Broth Mixed green salad with Citrus Burst Salad Dressing
Snacks	Cut vegetables Any food from Chapter 18 Green apple and nut butter	Cut vegetables Any food from Chapter 18 Green apple and nut butter	Cut vegetables Any food from Chapter 18 Green apple and nut butter

HEALTH TIPS

1. Last 3 days. Woohoo! You did it!

2. Two new nutritional concepts to think about:
   * 80/20 Rule
   * If you've gotten the results you wanted, you can transition to eating 80% the way you have been for the past 45 days and 20% eating whatever you want (that equates to two meals a week). I usually save these up for my weekends.

3. Block Fasting

4. If you want deeper results, try a 4-day bone broth fast. This a fantastic, quick way to help your body burn more fat.

5. Need more help? Reach out. I do virtual nutritional consultations for Resetters all the time. Check out **drmindypelz.com** for more information.

	DAY 43	DAY 44	DAY 45
Breakfast	Chocolate Cherry Heaven Smoothie	Waffles 3 Ways	Black and Blue Smoothie
Lunch	Roasted Leg of Lamb Green Beans with Caramelized Shallots	Roasted Pork Loin with Green Applesauce Sweet Potato Hashbrowns	Bacon-Avo-Egg Mixed green salad with Citrus Burst Salad Dressing
Dinner	Pizza with Herbed Cauliflower Crust Mixed green salad with Citrus Burst Salad Dressing	Fish in Parchment Paper Roasted Brussels Sprouts	The Best Roasted Chicken Steve P's Kickin' Corn Salad
Snacks	Cut vegetables Any food from Chapter 18 Green apple and nut butter	Cut vegetables Any food from Chapter 18 Green apple and nut butter	Cut vegetables Any food from Chapter 18 Green apple and nut butter

ABOUT DR. MINDY PELZ

Dr. Mindy H. Pelz has been serving health to her community for over twenty years. After receiving an undergraduate degree in exercise physiology and nutrition from the University of Kansas, she went on to get her doctorate in chiropractic from Palmer West College of Chiropractic, where she graduated with clinical honors.

Dr. Mindy knows what it's like to have your health taken from you. At a young age, she was diagnosed with chronic fatigue syndrome (CFS) and told to drop out of school and wait for medication to work. Refusing to believe the prognosis the doctors gave her, she went searching for answers. Her personal journey back to health ignited a voracious passion in her to understand why the human body breaks down—and how these breakdowns can be fixed by removing toxins, adding in good nutrition, and working with the healing laws of the body.

In the 20 years she has been in practice, Dr. Mindy has helped tens of thousands of people reset their health. Her unique approach to health and her passion for nutrition has led her to work with professionals, Olympic and collegiate athletes, Academy Award winning actors, professional musicians, and Silicon Valley CEOs. Her best selling book, The Reset Factor, was released in 2015, giving people all over the world access to a clear step-by-step path to a healthier life. She lectures all over the country and has been hired by numerous corporations to help their employees reduce stress, maximize their nutrition, and remove harmful toxins from their life so they can be healthier, happier, more productive people.

Raising a family of her own, Dr. Mindy is deeply concerned about the toxic world our children are growing up in today and the breakdown many women are experiencing in their perimenopausal years. Dr. Mindy believes that healthy adults start with healthy children. In her own practice, she works closely with all members of the family to give them a tool set to steer their health in whatever direction they choose. The principles she teaches empower every family member to be the boss of their own health and give them a path to predictable health—free of disease, drugs, and surgeries.

Still maintaining an active wellness practice, Dr. Mindy lives in Silicon Valley with her husband and two teenage kids.

ABOUT BONNIE CARLSON

Bonnie Carlson is a proud mother of two who also happens to love to cook and collect industrial kitchen tools. She has spent the bulk of her professional career in sales and marketing in the software industry in California's Silicon Valley. However, in 1999, she took a two-year "foodie detour" to the California Culinary Academy in San Francisco and travel the world enjoying and studying the many diverse cultures and foods.

Many years later, Bonnie's passion for food reignited after one of her children was diagnosed with type 1 diabetes—and she wholeheartedly embraced the mantra that "food is medicine." It was a huge relief to discover that the right kind of foods, in combination with insulin, could be part of the treatment to better manage blood-sugar levels. And that's how this collection of recipes was born—destined to happen because Bonnie desperately needed these recipes for her family. A pure bonus is that she gets to share them with others who also want to reset their family's health.

When not working or cooking for her family, you can probably find Bonnie cheering for her kids on a sideline somewhere. Without them, this book would not have had such great results, as they were her toughest critics; if a recipe did not pass their tastebuds, it did not make it into this book!

ABOUT ELIZABETH VANDERLIET PATTERSON

Elizabeth Vanderliet Patterson, photographer for The Reset Factor Kitchen, has an infectious enthusiasm for life. Whether on her mountain bike, painting in her studio, or behind a camera, her passion for health is ever present.

Elizabeth graduated in 1988 from California Polytechnic State University, San Luis Obispo, with a BS in graphic design and a concentration in photography. She lives in Alamo, California, with her husband, three children, and their dog, Sage.